AFTER THE CRADLE FALLS

After the Cradle Falls

WHAT CHILD ABUSE IS, HOW WE RESPOND TO IT, AND WHAT YOU CAN DO ABOUT IT

Melissa Jonson-Reid, PhD
Brett Drake, PhD

OXFORD
UNIVERSITY PRESS

OXFORD
UNIVERSITY PRESS

Oxford University Press is a department of the University of Oxford. It furthers
the University's objective of excellence in research, scholarship, and education
by publishing worldwide. Oxford is a registered trade mark of Oxford University
Press in the UK and certain other countries.

Published in the United States of America by Oxford University Press
198 Madison Avenue, New York, NY 10016, United States of America.

© Oxford University Press 2018

Library of Congress Cataloging-in-Publication Data
Names: Jonson-Reid, Melissa, author. | Drake, Brett, author.
Title: After the cradle falls : what child abuse is, how we respond to it,
and what you can do about it / Melissa Jonson-Reid, PhD, Brett Drake, PhD.
Description: New York : Oxford University Press, 2018. |
Includes bibliographical references and index.
Identifiers: LCCN 2017022810 (print) | LCCN 2017050446 (ebook) |
ISBN 9780190653033 (updf) | ISBN 9780190653040 (epub) | ISBN 9780190653026 (hardback)
Subjects: LCSH: Child abuse—United States. | BISAC: SOCIAL SCIENCE /
Social Work. | LAW / Child Advocacy.
Classification: LCC HV6626.52 (ebook) | LCC HV6626.52 .J66 2017 (print) |
DDC 364.15/5540973—dc23
LC record available at https://lccn.loc.gov/2017022810

9 8 7 6 5 4 3 2 1

Printed by Sheridan Books, Inc., United States of America

The authors would like to express his gratitude to Hal Leonard LLC
for permission to use the complete lyrics from the following musical composition:

Hell Is For Children
Words and Music by Pat Benatar, Neil Giraldo and Roger Capps
Copyright (c) 1980 BMG Monarch, Big Tooth Music, Neil Giraldo Music and
Muscle Tone Music
All Rights Administered by BMG Rights Management (US) LLC
All Rights Reserved Used by Permission
Reprinted by Permission of Hal Leonard LLC

To our children, Harrison and Thomas, in hopes that their generation and those that follow live in a society where all children and families can thrive.

Contents

Acknowledgments

WE THANK DIANE WITTLING AND LARA GERASSI for their review of the book in its early stages and helpful suggestions about the contents, title, and many other things. Special thanks to Dr. Edward Lawlor for granting us the time to begin work on this project and for his astute comments about not leaving the work without some suggested next steps for the reader. Also special thanks to Allison Dunnigan and Ellie Wideman who read through a later draft, looking for errors and adding thoughtful comments that were invaluable. Finally, thanks to our editor, Dana Bliss, who was willing to take a chance on the concept and provided invaluable guidance.

Introduction

THIS BOOK IS designed to be a conversation with you, the reader, about child abuse and neglect. Child abuse and neglect (often simply termed "child maltreatment") is a common concern, and it is quite likely that you have heard about it, know someone who has experienced it, or may have even experienced it yourself. There are many good reasons for us (as a society) to be deeply concerned about this issue, and yet it is not a common part of public discourse. Few of us have the knowledge needed to avoid misinformation and engage in effective debate about how to address the safety and well-being of our children. Thomas Jefferson (1789) famously said, "Whenever the people are well-informed, they can be trusted with their own government; . . . whenever things get so far wrong as to attract their notice, they may be relied on to set them to rights."[1] It is our hope that this book encourages awareness and inspires change.

WHY THIS BOOK AND WHY NOW?

While too many children still face threats to their safety and well-being, children are clearly held in more esteem now than they have been in the past. Evidence of this can be found many places in American culture (e.g., songs, stories, media coverage, substantial recent advances in legal protections and access to services, etc.). Perhaps the clearest international expression of this can be found in the United Nations Convention on the Rights of the Child. This document not only brings to the forefront the physical conditions children live in and how they're treated but also frames children as having their own rights as human beings—rights separate from those of families or community.[2] By describing children as having "rights" we don't mean that the UN is encouraging children to sue their parents for not providing for their every desire, we are talking about far more basic rights, such as the right to an education and freedom from harm. While the assertion of such basic rights may seem minimal, this is a distinct departure from the past, when many cultures didn't view children as having even basic human rights; they were treated as the disposable property of their parents. This makes us hopeful that we are ready to have this conversation.

Why a whole book? Child abuse and neglect has been called a "wicked problem"[3] with an array of related factors, confusion about its definition, and many missing pieces of needed information. There are also myths and controversies that further complicate our ability to find or implement solutions. We can take heart from the fact that many other complex issues in our society were at one time or another thought impossible to solve. It was not simple to go to the moon, put a robot on Mars, procure voting rights in the Jim Crow South, cure polio, or develop effective HIV drugs. These were enormously complex problems with multiple issues to be solved, requiring scientific advances and profound changes in public awareness, support, and action. We try to address a broad array of issues in an engaging manner to encourage such action.

Additionally, sometimes tackling difficult problems can yield important benefits along the way. Though we have not yet been to Mars, early work on the Mars Viking spacecraft led to the development of technology to monitor the health of astronauts that was eventually transformed into the insulin pump now used for diabetes control.[4] While Mahatma Ghandi did not resolve all the ills of oppression and violence in the world, the principles of nonviolent protest he established became the most powerful tools in the fight for equal rights for African Americans in the United States[5] and for many other oppressed peoples. There seems to be much to be gained by taking difficult steps forward even if we have a very long way to go.

WHAT THIS BOOK IS AND IS NOT

We have attempted to write a book that covers child maltreatment in a way that is direct, honest, and productive while still being interesting and engaging. To accomplish this we chose to weave together, culture (e.g., stories, songs), historical accounts, current media stories, and the very best and most recent scientific research. We have chosen to write a book that is targeted primarily toward the general public and policy makers. While we are certainly not opposed to the book being used in the classroom, instructors may find this book strays significantly from more traditional approaches in content and organization. This is on purpose.

Another decision we made early on was not to follow the well-established path in child welfare research of focusing mainly on foster care. This is not to say that foster care is unimportant or that we avoid the topic altogether. There are, however, many books (a few referenced here) and numerous journal articles focused either solely or largely on those relatively few maltreated children who end up in foster care.[6-10] In contrast, there are few works outside of academic volumes[11,12] or personal accounts[13] that focus solely or primarily on the millions of children who may experience abuse or neglect but will never enter foster care.

This book is grounded in five decades of research along with historical and policy documentation that goes back over 100 years. Because of the vast differences in how child maltreatment is defined and responded to internationally, this book is largely about child maltreatment in the United States. That is not to say we cannot learn things from other countries, and we do sometimes reference such work, but it would be impossible to do justice to the many issues like child labor that are central to many international contexts but are not part of the current discourse about child abuse and neglect in the United States.

In some cases the research on a particular topic has a very long history, and in other cases it is just emerging. Where there is academic consensus based on the latest and most rigorous findings in the former case, we have chosen to focus on this rather than review all the different, and sometimes conflicting, studies that may have come before. We do, however, warn you when this is done. When there is ongoing debate, we have endeavored to do justice to all sides to allow you to form your own opinion based on what we know. While the book is extensively cited, we have compiled some additional readings, song and movie listings, and other resources in an appendix for those readers who wish to delve deeper.

Earlier we mentioned that we would also talk about myths and misconceptions. We are not using the term "myth" in the traditional sense of fictitious explanations for lived experiences like how the Greek writers explained sunrise and sunset by imagining a chariot pulling the sun across the sky. By "myths" we mean common misconceptions (e.g., cracking your knuckles causes arthritis, or the United States is becoming more violent[14]) or beliefs based on prior knowledge that have been over-turned by recent science (e.g., the age should you give your child peanut butter for the first time). Finally sometimes there are points of view that have been repeated until they seem true even though we cannot quite remember where the idea came from. We have highlighted such misconceptions and compare them to the best cur-rent knowledge.

In other cases controversy is the result of honest disagreements. Not everyone in our society sees children and families in the same way nor do we all share the same values. Sometimes values conflict with each other, and this can make societal decision-making difficult. As we point out, such dilemmas are not uncommon. For example, if a mother, who is a domestic violence victim, is unable to protect her child from a boyfriend who is a threat to both, how should we respond to that? Where such debates exist, we try to provide a balanced view of both sides so you, the reader, can assess the issue.

Finally, sometimes there is difficulty moving ahead when a topic is hard to discuss because it is unpleasant or appears intractable. Child abuse and neglect can be a traumatic subject that often evokes strong emotions, particularly when a child dies. Too much of today's child abuse coverage is sensationalistic and does not result in continued discussion of problem solving. While we do discuss fatalities, we are most interested in creating a sustained discussion about the range of issues and experiences impacting all maltreated children.

OUR OPINION?

Clearly, we have a point of view. Over 50 years ago, a pediatrician named Kempe wrote an article that put child abuse and neglect on the map. That was a beginning (one of many), but we believe that important work remains to be done. We also believe that this work will not happen until a well-informed public becomes involved. So while we make a range of possible suggestions here and there and especially in the final chapter, we offer them as starting places to prompt ideas rather than as a strategic plan. Any change that will be of practical value will need sufficient public support and funding. These things are more likely to arise from a chorus of informed voices. Whether that debate results in incremental reform and enhancement or the radical creation of a new approach is up to you. We hope this book provides the information and inspiration to engage you in a public discussion that will result in a society that provides a safe, stable, and nurturing environment[15] for our children.

AFTER THE CRADLE FALLS

1

A Brief History of Child Abuse and Neglect

FROM NURSERY RHYMES TO MARY ELLEN TO TODAY

THE WORLD WE live in today is very different from the world of a few centuries, or even a few decades past. This is especially true if you happen to be a child. Children live different lives now, are seen differently by adults, and are parented very differently. Consider the following familiar nursery rhyme, illustrated in Figure 1.1: "There was an old woman who lived in a shoe, she had so many children she didn't know what to do. She gave them some broth without any bread, then whipped them all soundly and put them to bed."[1] Perhaps you recall hearing this nursery rhyme as a child, but maybe you didn't hear the final original line. We've known for a long time that parenting can be overwhelming, particularly for a family experiencing material want. The rhyme also reflects the wisdom of the day—recommending harsh discipline as a form of good parenting.

THE EVOLUTION OF CHILDHOOD AND PARENTING

Views of childhood and parenting have not been static across time, nor are they the same across cultures. History is full of records of child abuse, sacrifice, abandonment, and the exploitation of children for labor, war, sex, and other purposes.[2] In western culture, until quite recently, childhood was only a short period, perhaps less than 10 years. After that children were expected to enter the work force and take on adult roles. This was particularly true among the lower socioeconomic classes in the

FIGURE 1.1 The Old Woman Who Lived in a Shoe

United States, and persists today in many parts of the world.[3] Many religions have ritualized passages for the transition from childhood, which were generally meant to occur prior to or during early adolescence, well before the age that modern readers in the United States would consider to be the onset of adulthood. Philosophical debate about beating children as part of their education and about the meaning and purpose of childhood became more common in western culture in the 1700s.[4] However, issues like child labor and child well-being did not become the focus of public attention in the United States until the late 1800s.[5] During that time, the formal response to child maltreatment in the United States began—though it would not look similar to our present-day approach for decades.

Indeed, despite the passage of more than a century, we still have a long way to go in defining what child maltreatment is and how we should respond. But, we think it's easier to understand where you are if you know where you've been. So we begin our conversation in the United States during the late 1800s.

A Side of Vocabulary

Periodically we pause to discuss various terms used that are particularly important to understand relative to a given issue. So here is the first pause. Sometimes people use the word "maltreatment," sometimes they use the phrase "child abuse and neglect," and sometimes people just use the words "child abuse." The words "child abuse" are often, but not always, used to refer to physical or sexual abuse alone. We try to avoid using the words "child abuse" because it is easy to forget about neglect, which we will learn is a serious mistake. Now we invite you to go back in time with us to the birth of US child protection.

MARY ELLEN AND THE BIRTH OF US CHILD PROTECTION

Over the years, the story of Mary Ellen Wilson has been told and retold. She is the American "patient zero" for child maltreatment. Hers was actually not the first case to draw court attention, much as Rosa Parks was not the first person arrested for protest of the segregated transportation policy, but Mary Ellen is, like Rosa Parks, unquestionably the best remembered. Importantly for our purposes, her case also provides a very clear illustration of the complex relationship between factors like poverty, despair, misfortune, mental health, and maltreatment. Thanks to a wonderfully well written and painstakingly researched pair of books by Shelman and Lazoritz,[6,7] anyone can read the complete story for themselves. We paraphrase (indented sections) from their work, pausing to point out particularly interesting or currently relevant aspects of the case.

> Mary Ellen is born to a loving, but poor couple during the Civil War. The husband dies in the war, which forces her mother to go to work. The job requires long hours, and, lacking family, she turns to a nice and childless woman who provides child care for many women with husbands at war—a kind of 1860s day care business.

If you were to pause there you might be tempted to think that that is where the abuse begins, with a stranger who lacked attachment to the child. But no, the caregiver actually becomes very attached to Mary Ellen who, according to all accounts, is an easy child to care for with an engaging personality. So what happens?

> Faced with unresolved grief and increasing long hours away from her daughter, the biological mom becomes depressed and turns to alcohol. She realizes she is having problems, so she gives the caregiver her widow's pension card to make sure Mary Ellen remains well cared for. As her alcoholism progresses, the mother remarries a man who frequents the same bar. One day they show up in not terrific condition at the caregiver's house to retrieve the child. Fearful that Mary Ellen will be in danger due to their obvious incapacity, the caregiver hides the child and says she is dead.

It may sound odd to a modern reader that the mother took this at face value, but you have to remember that infant and child death were common in that period. A 1900 census record shows a rate of death among infants of 149 per 1,000—mostly due to infectious disease.[8]

As the war ends, there is a decreasing need for child care, and the pension office stops the widow's pension when it is discovered that the real mother has remarried. By this time the caregiver has no idea where the mother is and realizes that the child will starve if she keeps her. So, at nearly 2 years of age, Mary Ellen is turned over to the poor house.

Perhaps you are now conjuring images of Little Orphan Annie or the Victorian tales of Charles Dickens. Some evil or at least unfeeling orphanage staff person begins the story of abuse and neglect. Not really. For the third time, Mary Ellen is cared for by a rather remarkable woman, a staff person determined to improve the lives of children left at the house.

Meanwhile, in another part of town, a butcher and his wife lose their third child to disease. [Recall this is not unusual at that time and is not an indictment of the family.] He wants more kids, but she has had enough. One gets the sense she was not a particularly eager mother before the deaths and clearly has no interest in a new child. He decides secretly to adopt. He also decides that the only way to make this work is to come up with a story that he has cheated on his wife and fathered a child whose mother recently abandoned her.

Clearly, the butcher's plan is not a great way of inviting a woman already disinterested in motherhood to care for a child. People do stupid things sometimes.

The butcher accidentally encounters Mary Ellen in a play area when he visits the poor house and is enchanted. He pays the head of the poorhouse to create a fabricated record to support his story of being her father. The staff person overhears and is horrified. She tries to put in place some insurance by mandating annual visits to make sure Mary Ellen is OK—this is put in the amended contract.

For those of you familiar with Sleeping Beauty, the image of the orphanage staff person trying to put together a backup safety plan is a bit like the third good fairy, who can't undo the curse of the sorceress but does do something to alter the outcome.

Mary Ellen is taken home, loved by one adopted parent and increasingly hated by the other. A secretive pattern of abuse begins whenever the husband is at work. Then, the husband gets "the fever" and dies. The widow has no interest in remaining single and in poverty and, although she clearly hates Mary Ellen, she sees some potential in the child as a future servant. So she keeps her. The adoptive mother begins a pattern of locking Mary Ellen in a closet when out, feeds her very little, and buys her no new clothes. The physical torture escalates.

The rest of Mary Ellen's life might have become a tragic tale of suffering and hardship like some of the children portrayed in the novels of Charles Dickens. The real story, however, takes a complex turn.

The adoptive mother remarries. While the new husband isn't happy with the way she treats the child, he looks the other way. He gets a better job, allowing them to move to a nicer place. There we encounter yet another very nice woman—the landlady. The landlady begins the slow process that will eventually result in rescue. She and her family know there is a child, but they never see the child outside. The landlady makes some excuse to visit with cookies and sees Mary Ellen's condition. Horrified, the landlady tries to confront the adoptive mother. The mother (who clearly has what today we would call "serious anger management issues") comes unglued, rebuffs the concerned neighbor and decides to move. The landlady happens to have a grown son in law enforcement. She consults him but he has no idea what to do (there was no formal child protection role for police then). She does get her son to follow the family when they move so they know where the little girl lives.

We told you it was a complicated story. Possibly the drama and human interest of the tale had something to do with why it gained such notoriety.

There are two very nice unrelated people who now become important. One is an attorney who is developing a society for the protection of cruelty to animals (the New York SPCA), for which he is generating funds and encouraging political action. The second is a faith-based social worker who does charitable home visits among the slums for families within her parish. The landlady comes into contact with the social worker and tells her about the girl. The social worker turns to the church, but they say there is nothing to be done.

Once again a rather amazing coincidence occurs that offers hope.

The social worker happens to visit a dying woman who lives across from Mary Ellen and her family. Because the neighbor is so ill, she is home all day and hears the child's screams and offers to do whatever she can. The social worker is stuck until she recalls hearing about the attorney who is volunteering for the animal protection group. She goes to him and tells him about Mary Ellen. She suggests that the child is technically an animal so why couldn't his group help? After using his staff to investigate the situation and taking a sworn testimony from the dying neighbor, the attorney goes to court to get permission to remove the child.

This situation gave rise to a popular myth that still endures. Many of the people who have heard of Mary Ellen believe that she was rescued under animal protection laws. This is false, but she was helped by the attorney working with the animal protection agency. There were actually a few laws in place addressing the serious abuse of children, which judges could use as a basis for action. The problem was that there was no system in place to bring cases to the court's attention. The animal rights attorney's actions allowed this to happen.

After some evidence gathering, a police officer is dispatched. Mary Ellen is so tiny and fragile and covered in wounds and bruises that he uses a horse blanket to pick her up. The adoptive mother goes to jail, the indifferent husband seems to disappear, and Mary Ellen is adopted by the social worker's sister, who lives on a farm. Mary Ellen recovers, goes to school and eventually marries. By all accounts, despite the long history of trauma, Mary Ellen became a wonderful parent.

In thinking about Mary Ellen's story, there are a lot of "what if" questions that might be asked. What might have happened if there had been some help for Mary Ellen's biological mother right after the father died in the war? Failing that, what might have happened if there had been some help for the first poor caregiver so she could continue to act as a surrogate mother? What might have happened if the poorhouse director had been unwilling to take the bribe to create the illegal adoption? There were lots of places in this story where processes might have been interrupted before the maltreatment began.

Mary Ellen's "happy ending" could easily not have come true. She might have been hit just a little harder, or she might have gotten sick, or she might have continued to live in the abusive home, growing up uneducated and essentially a slave. Unfortunately, such bad endings were undoubtedly experienced by many other children who were not so "fortunate." More importantly from a national perspective, she was also the particular case used by activists to get people concerned about child protection.

Is this all ancient history? After all, many bad things happened in the 1800s. It would be tempting to assume that such situations simply don't occur anymore. As we move forward in this book we track both what has changed in regard to protecting children and supporting families and what has not. Unfortunately, however, we do not arrive at the conclusion that abuse or neglect is a thing of the past. First, though, let's round off Mary Ellen's story by noting a few other things that were going on at the time that impacted how people responded to her case so we can better understand how the modern response evolved.

CHILD PROTECTION IN AMERICA: THE LATE 1800S

After the Mary Ellen case, there was an explosion of what we would today call "non-profits," "charity organizations," or, in modern international contexts, "nongovernmental organizations" (NGOs). These included the American Society for the Prevention of Cruelty to Children (ASPCC), the American Humane Association (yes, animal protection and child protection remained related), and countless other private agencies and charitable societies. This was not all about Mary Ellen, or even about child maltreatment per se. There were many adults concerned about street children such as those depicted in famous photographs by Jacob Riis (see Figure 1.2). There were also individuals appalled by conditions impacting immigrant and

FIGURE 1.2 Urban Child Poverty in the late 1800's

poor families. These concerned people responded by creating settlement houses and employing visiting social workers[9] (for a brief and interesting overview of this practice in New York we recommend: http://www.unhny.org/about/history).

Was all this activity purely motivated by a desire to care for children? No. There were other motivations, like creating jobs in factories for adults by figuring out somewhere else to put children, or decreasing problems related to street children like juvenile crime, or supplying labor to rural communities. Nor were all approaches benevolent or equally applied to children of various racial and ethnic groups (which we explore further in chapters 2 and 10).

So why did this activity burst forth in a relatively short time? The late 1800s were a time of tremendous change across a number of domains. The period of the industrial revolution was marked by many people moving from agricultural lifestyles to urban labor in crowded cities. At the same time there was mass immigration from other countries by people either seeking opportunity or escaping hardship who also tended to move to urban centers. The new reality had some serious downsides for children in the cities, such as crowded, inadequate housing; unsafe child labor conditions; and lack of supervision while parents worked long hours.[10] Charles Dickens had become concerned about this much earlier in England and popularized the plight of poor children with works like *Oliver Twist*. This was also a period of advancement in wealth (which could sponsor charitable efforts) and science. Child mortality began dropping fast during the latter part of the century because of improvements in healthcare and sanitation (see *Victorian America* by Thomas Schlereth[11] for an interesting account of this period).

Interestingly, such rapid shifts to urban living related to industrialization have also created conditions that negatively impact children in other countries. For example, in the late 20th century, advocates drew attention to the street children of Latin America who flooded the streets to make money for their impoverished families as they moved to the cities.[12] This was not unlike the conditions for poor children in US cities in the 1800s immortalized by photographs like the one above (Figure 1.2). Another contemporary example is the phenomenon of the "left-behind children" in China. Advocates are currently trying to call attention to the needs of children in rural areas who are left, often to their own care, while their parents seek work in the cities.[13]

Various new approaches to the vulnerable and the poor also emerged in the late 1800s. In the United States, the educational system moved from a series of small locally funded and run schools to something resembling the education system we know today. Orphanages were replacing almshouses for children. Juveniles were separated from adult offenders in new courts and separate confinement facilities. Of course, ineffective and highly questionable practices also emerged.

One of the better known practices implemented by a set of nonprofit organizations was the so-called orphan trains (see Figure 1.3). The basic idea was that homeless or abandoned children in the cities could be relocated to the pastoral countryside, where they would be cared for by "loving families" (see the *National Orphan Train Complex* website for a more complete history). This was consistent with the (then) contemporary view that there were innate health, moral, and developmental advantages to growing up in the country. To be fair, positive outcomes were obtained for some, but certainly not all, of these children. Eventually the idea

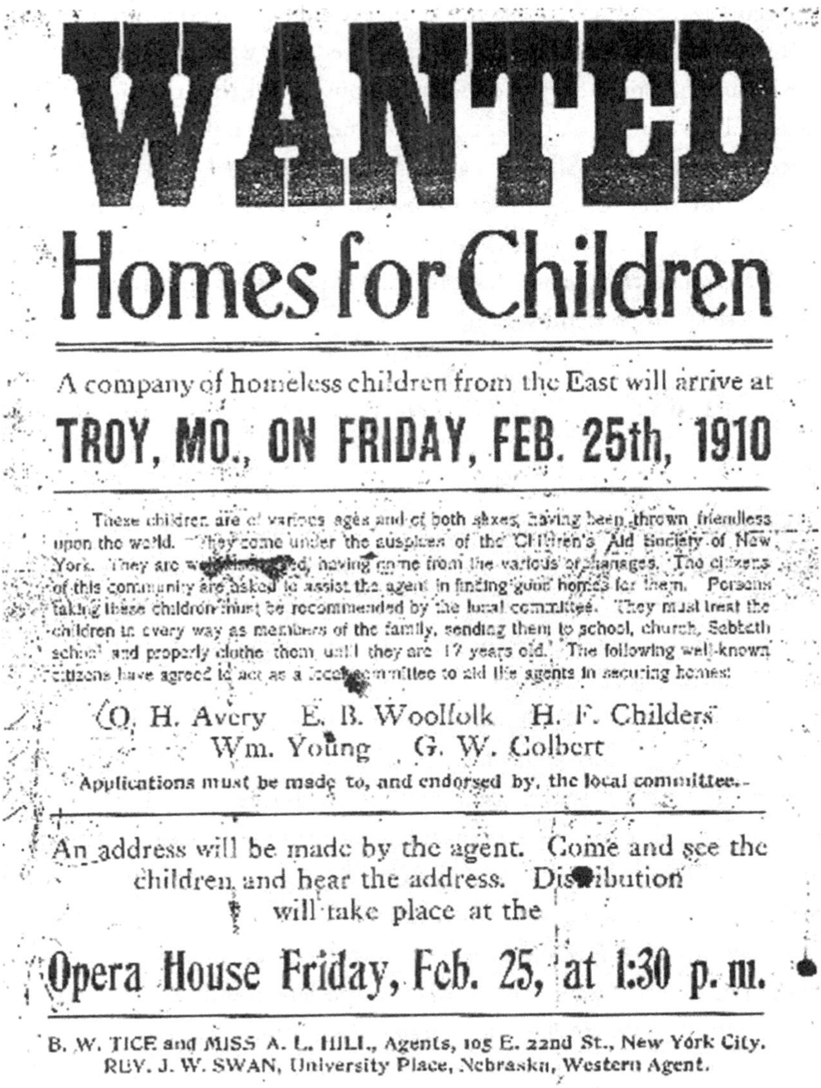

WANTED

Homes for Children

A company of homeless children from the East will arrive at

TROY, MO., ON FRIDAY, FEB. 25th, 1910

These children are of various ages and of both sexes, having been thrown friendless upon the world. They come under the auspices of the Children's Aid Society of New York. They are well disciplined, having come from the various orphanages. The citizens of this community are asked to assist the agent in finding good homes for them. Persons taking these children must be recommended by the local committee. They must treat the children in every way as members of the family, sending them to school, church, Sabbath school and properly clothe them until they are 17 years old. The following well-known citizens have agreed to act as a local committee to aid the agents in securing homes:

O. H. Avery   E. B. Woolfolk   H. F. Childers
Wm. Young   G. W. Colbert

Applications must be made to, and endorsed by, the local committee.

An address will be made by the agent. Come and see the children and hear the address. Distribution will take place at the

Opera House Friday, Feb. 25, at 1:30 p. m.

B. W. TICE and MISS A. L. HILL, Agents, 105 E. 22nd St., New York City.
REV. J. W. SWAN, University Place, Nebraska, Western Agent.

FIGURE 1.3 Orphan Train Flyer

was abandoned as problematic on a number of levels. There is a great historical fiction novel that covers this period in a very interesting way for those who wish to learn more—*Orphan Train*, by Christina Baker Kline.[14]

Change, of course, rarely proceeds in a strictly linear fashion; there are steps forward and backward, as well as periods of no change. While Mary Ellen's case and others may have called attention to physical abuse and the need to guarantee adequate care, a strong voice had the opposite effect on awareness and response to child sexual abuse. Sigmund Freud presented work in 1896 stating that mental illness was often associated with childhood sexual abuse. His ideas were not well received by peers. Freud also doubted that so many men could be perpetrators of sexual abuse. So he took back his argument and instead stated that women (and men) who had recalled abuse had not *really* been sexually abused, but that they had *imagined* it. Because of Freud's reversal, therapists for the next several decades would be taught to expect that a child's recall of sexual abuse was just normal child fantasy—nothing more. The "discovery" of child sexual abuse was postponed for over fifty years. For a charitable review of these events, you can look at the writings of the psychoanalytic author Jean Laplanche.[15] For a less charitable view, you might see *The Assault on Truth* by Jeffery Moussaieff Masson.[16]

CHILD PROTECTION IN AMERICA: FROM 1900 TO 1962

History has its little oddities, including a tendency to repeat itself. Perhaps you have heard something in recent years like "We need to talk about the whole child," referencing how various aspects of a child's life, such as family, school, and community, are interconnected. Interestingly, this is not new; the reformers at the turn of the century were quite holistic. The "silos" between service systems that people talk about dismantling today were not so evident then. Early private charitable organizations and societies covered everything from poverty to child labor to child maltreatment and maternal and child health. In 1909, the White House Conference was an attempt to develop a national agenda related to children. At the time, it was not unusual for a single conference to include issues of poverty, health, education, and maltreatment.[17] The debates we are having today about how and if poverty and contextual issues are associated with maltreatment[18-20] would have seemed quite foreign then. Sometimes we forget and have to relearn things we once took for granted.

By the mid-1920s, organizations began to specialize, and the siloing of different functions within different agencies became the norm. The child labor and infant mortality crusades split off from organizations focused on "child welfare." Child labor was integrated into the movement toward compulsory education. Why?

Parents in poor families in industrialized America worked long hours and there was a need to occupy their children. At first, many children either took care of other children or worked, but as attitudes toward child labor soured, public education was seen as the logical solution.[21] Maternal and child health concerns became largely associated with medicine and the emerging profession of public health.[22] This was accompanied by a cultural shift in favor of using hospitals and doctors in formal settings as compared to handling the healthcare needs of a family, including childbirth, at home.[11] Additionally, many roles, like medicine and education, became increasingly professionalized, spurred on by famous critiques like the Flexner Report on medical education.[23] The last areas to split from the general umbrella of child welfare would be issues of delinquency and disability. So we now use terms like "health system," "child welfare system," "educational system," "juvenile justice system," and so on. These services are usually housed in separate buildings, are operated under separate policies and separate parts of government, and have different goals but often serve the same families. These siloes are now considered quite problematic.

As the Great Depression took hold, the responsibility to intervene around the issue of poverty increasingly shifted from nonprofits to the government.[24] The level of economic crisis during the Great Depression simply made it impossible for charitable institutions to respond. The shift was seen in child welfare as well. Children's Bureau research activities in the mid-to-late 1920s indicated that most states were establishing formal government-operated child protection systems, often at the county level.[25] This is changing again, and we get to that in chapter 10.

CHILD PROTECTION BECOMES A FEDERAL POLICY ISSUE

We now fast-forward through World War II, the Korean War, and the birth of the civil rights movement to the early 1960s. Gone are the horses and buggies, gone are the orphan trains, television shows like *Leave It to Beaver* paint an idyllic picture of everyday family life. Sherriff Andy Taylor (*The Andy Griffith Show*) showed us that even a working single dad could be a great parent without (apparently) too much trouble. We are reminded in *Families as They Really Are*, however, that this apparent "golden age for children was not really that golden."[26p59] [A more detailed discussion of political and policy shifts in this period can be found in *The Politics of Child Abuse in America*.[27]] Nevertheless there is an interesting gap in progress toward addressing child maltreatment during the time between the Great Depression and the 1960s. It's not that everyone forgot about child abuse and neglect, nor is it the case that organizations concerned with child maltreatment went away. The issue simply lacked visibility. It took someone with some clout to raise the issue of maltreatment as a large-scale issue that required national public action—in this case, that someone was a medical doctor named Henry Kempe.

In 1962, in his landmark "Battered-Child Syndrome" article in the *Journal of the American Medical Association*, Kempe provided medical evidence that serious child physical abuse was more common than was generally believed. He gave advice to physicians about what to do if they encountered child abuse:

> The principal concern of the physician should be to make the correct diagnosis so that he can institute proper therapy and make certain that a similar event will not occur again. He should report possible willful trauma to the police department or any special children's protective service that operates in his community. . . . The physician should acquaint himself with the facilities available in private and public agencies that provide protective services for children.[28p11]

Kempe's article was to the modern understanding of maltreatment as the novel *Uncle Tom's Cabin* was to the antislavery movement—it was a turning point in mobilizing national attention and changing policy. Child abuse became a diagnosable medical condition and a federal public policy issue. In 1974, the Child Abuse Protection and Treatment Act passed, instituting nationwide mandated reporting and broad child protection guidelines.

How can a single article have that much influence? Sometimes well-publicized articles can have more impact than you might think and not always for the better. For example, think about the fairly recent measles outbreak in the United States.[29] This was linked to parents who refused to immunize their children, many out of fear that the vaccines might cause autism. That fear was largely generated by a single article based on what scientists call "fabricated data" and what normal people call "lies." Indeed, in 2011, the journal that published the original article was still backtracking and trying to undo the damage that had been done.

> A now-retracted British study that linked autism to childhood vaccines was an "elaborate fraud" that has done long-lasting damage to public health, a leading medical publication reported Wednesday. An investigation published by the British medical journal BMJ concludes the study's author, Dr. Andrew Wakefield, misrepresented or altered the medical histories of all 12 of the patients whose cases formed the basis of the 1998 study. Britain stripped Wakefield of his medical license in May. . . ." The now-discredited paper panicked many parents and led to a sharp drop in the number of children getting the vaccine that prevents measles, mumps and rubella. Vaccination rates

dropped sharply in Britain after its publication, falling as low as 80% by 2004. Measles cases have gone up sharply in the ensuing years.[30]

Put simply, what doctors, researchers, and the media say can make a big difference in children's lives.

MOVING AWAY FROM A PURELY MEDICAL MODEL: BRONFENBRENNER AND BELSKY

Kempe tells us, "The principal concern of the physician should be to make the correct diagnosis." Our focus on maltreatment in the modern era was rejuvenated by thinking of it as a disease. What about other issues like poverty? Well, professionals tend to see things in accordance with their training and their time. Medical doctors often contribute to knowledge building through understanding specific illnesses or diseases in individuals and cataloging how problems are caused, detected, and treated. Child maltreatment was not, however, to remain solely within the provenance of the medical profession for long.

In the 1970s and early 1980s, two key figures once again expanded how we view child maltreatment—Urie Bronfenbrenner[31] and Jay Belsky.[32] Bronfenbrenner provided a simple and elegant way to remind us that we can't understand someone (or a situation) unless we also understand the context in which that person lives (or the situation obtains). Bronfenbrenner went even further, noting the impact of societal influences, like the effects of an economic downturn. A visual representation of Bronfenbrenner's ecological framework (first introduced in 1974) can be seen in Figure 1.4.

Bronfenbrenner was not, however, focused on maltreatment. It was Jay Belsky, a professor at Penn State, who adapted some of Bronfenbrenner's ideas to the study of child maltreatment. His 1984 paper "The Determinants of Parenting: A Process Model"[32] became perhaps the most influential theoretical paper in the area of child maltreatment and moved the field from a "disease" framework to a multilevel and multidetermined model.

These, then were the forces that laid the foundation for the modern US response to child maltreatment. Mary Ellen brought child abuse to the public's attention. For the next 40 years, charitable societies were the force behind policy and practice. Public awareness, policy, and practice were transformed and greatly expanded by the "medicalization" of maltreatment following Kempe's article, which also initiated some of the first national-level policies. Then Bronfenbrenner and Belsky helped move the issue into the broader social context. This helped spawn an array

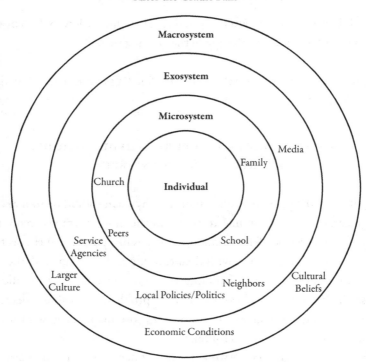

"**Mesosystem**" is a term applied to interactions between parts of the Microsystem

FIGURE 1.4 Bronfenbrenner's Ecological Framework

of approaches to maltreatment prevention and intervention that recognized that abuse or neglect is usually influenced by problems at multiple levels from individual stressors and negative coping mechanisms, to lack of parenting knowledge, to living in a neighborhood impacted by severe poverty. We pay special attention to individual stressors in chapter 3, when we discuss physical abuse, and poverty in chapter 4, when we discuss neglect.

MOVING ON

As you read on we will try to help you sort through the complex issues related to child abuse and neglect. Throughout the book, we examine how our folklore, media coverage, conventional wisdom, and policies do or do not align with empirical knowledge. Our goal is to make this an interesting journey that includes discovering a few new things or rethinking ideas you had taken for granted about child maltreatment that simply aren't true. Often we have no choice but to say there are aspects of child maltreatment (both cause and intervention) that we know little or nothing about. For those readers who prefer a story that is completely resolved at the end, this journey may be less than satisfying.

Next, we move on to an overview of the present-day child protection system. After that, chapters turn first to consideration of what exactly child maltreatment is, then to related issues and controversies and critical appraisals of the current system, and finally to a menu of possibilities you can use to consider how to best become involved in making sure the story of child maltreatment in the United States has the best possible ending.

2

A Crash Course in Child Protection in the United States

THERE ARE MANY stories about threats children face and the ways adults protect (or fail to protect) them. In the modern version of "Sleeping Beauty," an evil sorceress casts a spell that will lead the newborn princess to prick her finger on the spindle of a spinning wheel and die on her 16th birthday. The distraught parents try to get rid of all spinning wheels and reluctantly agree to allow fairies to raise the child in secret and return her after the danger is gone.[1] The value of protecting a child from strangers or witches or wolves is pretty straightforward. It becomes more complicated when we start to think about protecting a child from the actions (or failures to act) of their own caregivers.

More than 80% of child maltreatment occurs at the hands of a biological parent.[2] The Brothers Grimm seemed to understand this, even if today we prefer not to think this way. For example, in the 1812 version of "Hansel and Gretel," the children's mother persuades their father to abandon them in the woods. The original "Snow White" villain was her biological mother, who wanted to kill her out of jealousy. Not the versions you remember? That's because the Grimms later changed the characters to stepmothers—maybe because people preferred not to believe such things about biological parents.[3] This preference for stories of unrelated or distantly related adults treating children in overly harsh, abusive, or neglectful ways continues. We have orphans mistreated by orphanage staff (*Annie*), evil stepparents who are emotionally abusive and neglectful (*Cinderella*), and so on. Such stories place distance between child abuse and neglect and biological parents. That's probably a gap that

16

we need to close. Admitting that parenting is challenging for most of us from time to time[4] may help us confront the question of how to better support families who are struggling.

We would be remiss to say, however, that the concept of child abuse and neglect by parents is absent from popular culture. We reference some of these popular songs (e.g., "Hell Is for Children"), movies (e.g., *Precious*), and books (e.g., *Matilda*) that talk about maltreatment in the family in later chapters. Relatively few stories or songs talk about the child protection response after this occurs and, when they do, the images are often not positive. In fairness, few people not employed by child protective services (CPS) have a good understanding of what CPS is or what it does. So before we explore what maltreatment is and related controversies and complications, we think it important to finish our discussion of child protection by understanding how it works today. This chapter is your "crash course" in the modern US child protection system.

THE ABC's OF CPS

The many terms related to child protection can create some confusion. For example in the popular press, words like "child welfare" may be used, but they are often talking about only children in foster care. As we learn later in this chapter, only a small portion of all children who encounter the CPS system enter foster care. Hopefully the definitions in Box 2.1 will help as we move ahead.

Modern Policies and Processes for Responding to Maltreatment

Today the concerned landlady in Mary Ellen's case would have a very different experience. There would be a number to call (and a telephone) and a set of people with defined roles that fill the gap between the concern about a child and the need, if any, for court involvement. You might recall that during the 20th century efforts to address child maltreatment became increasingly government led. This, however, was largely local rather than federal until the mid-1970s. By the time the federal government formally required that each state establish a mandated reporting system through the Child Abuse Protection and Treatment Act (CAPTA) of 1974,[5] all 50 states had already established a hotline. However, CAPTA was still a landmark law. It built the foundational organizational and research "infrastructure" needed for the new response to maltreatment. People like Mary Ellen's landlady can call a number, explain their concerns, and CPS will decide how to move forward.

Over the next 20 years a series of laws were added to guide CPS. A few years after CAPTA (1974), the Indian Child Welfare Act (ICWA)[6] established standards for

BOX 2.1

A LAND OF CONFUSION

There is surprisingly little agreement about the most basic terms in child welfare.

Child Welfare is a vague term that could mean "helping kids do well" in general or could refer to your state's official CPS agency in particular. It could also mean an area of research or policy.

Child Well-Being sometimes means the same as "child welfare" or may mean "ways in which children do well apart from the issue of abuse," such as succeeding at school or not being depressed.

Child Protective Services (CPS) is a relatively consistently used term meaning the public state or county level organization tasked with protecting children. Just to confuse things a little, though, states have different official names for these organizations, like "Division of Child and Family Services." Police and the family court are not CPS. States may also contract services out to private agencies, further confusing the term.

Family Court is called different things in different states and is the (noncriminal) judicial system that works with maltreated children. They also handle things like juvenile delinquency and divorce.

Child Maltreatment means "child abuse *and* neglect."

Child Abuse means "child sexual abuse *and* child physical abuse," and sometimes includes some other forms of abuse (like emotional abuse). Sometimes people use "child abuse" to even include neglect, which makes it the same as "child maltreatment."

Test on Friday.

child welfare regarding American Indian/Alaskan Native (AI/AN) children (which we discuss further later). About two years later, the Adoption Assistance and Child Welfare Act[7] established the three primary foci of the child protection system that still exist today; safety, family preservation/reunification, and permanence. Another focus of child protection was added in the later 1990s as part of the Adoptions and Safe Families Act[8]—"child well-being."

There were a number of other laws and changes to child welfare policy that we do not go into detail about here, many of which have focused on the issue of permanency timelines or improvements to foster care.[9] [Interested readers are encouraged to check out chapter 2 of *The Child Welfare Challenge: Policy Practice and Research*.[10]]

During the first 20 years CPS hotlines were available (roughly 1965–1985), the number of child abuse reports multiplied rapidly. There were over half a million children reported as potential victims of maltreatment in 1976[11] rising to over a million in 1980, and then doubling to two million children reported in 1985.[12] By the

1990s, the number of children investigated for possible child maltreatment rose to over 3 million per year and then more or less leveled off.[2,13] Did maltreatment really grow that much, or were more people picking up the phone? We think the most likely answer is that more people were picking up the phone. We have no reason to believe that parenting *per se* was getting worse. Amazingly enough, despite the approximately 3.6 million reports made each year, most sources still agree that maltreatment is underreported in the United States[15] and across the world.[16]

Who Reports Child Abuse and Neglect?

In the United States, reports of suspected maltreatment are made both by the public (family members, neighbors, bystanders) and by professionals. Children may also report themselves, but that is relatively rare.

- **The Public's Role:** Perhaps you suspect a child has been abused or neglected and decide you want to help. In most states, you *may* call CPS *if you want to*. The key word for most of this paragraph is "may"—your role as a citizen is usually completely voluntary. Nearly 40% of reports are from "nonmandated" sources.[2] In a few states everyone is required to report,[17] although it's clear from one study that most residents in such regions are not aware of this.[18]
- **The Professionals' Role:** If you are a teacher, medical professional, law enforcement officer, or other professional who has contact with children you are almost certainly a "mandated reporter." This means you *must* call CPS if you reasonably suspect abuse or neglect. Mandated reporters make slightly over 60% of reports, and over half of these are made by educators or law enforcement.[2] Of course, some professionals ignore the law (see chapter 8) or are ignorant of their responsibilities.

The Role of the Public and Professionals After a Report Is Made

Members of the general public can do other things besides calling the hotline. Many people decide to serve as a foster parents, providing usually temporary homes to children who cannot remain with their parents. In most cases, the state pays an unreasonably small amount of money to reimburse the foster parents for care of the child (from a low of about $9 a day to a high of over $30 for special needs and older children[19]). Others become adoptive parents. Finally, in some states, volunteers may serve as a court appointed special advocate (CASA) or as a guardian ad litem to help represent the wishes of children already in care or at imminent risk of entry in court.

Professionals are also involved beyond their reporting role. Social service or mental health professionals may work for agencies that provide services to maltreated children and/or their families after they are reported. Others, like medical or education professionals, may report suspected maltreatment but continue with their regular role with a child regardless of the outcome of the report. Still other professionals may work for public child welfare agencies or family courts and be involved in case management, family support services, or foster care following a report.

Who Works for Child Protective Services?

Most people have no idea who makes up the CPS workforce. In some states, CPS investigators are social workers with master's degrees and a good deal of training; in others, they may have only an undergraduate degree in an unrelated field with no prior experience with children or families. Some states take a middle course. Missouri, for example, requires that candidates for bachelor's level CPS positions take about 10 classes in areas related to children and families. Only about 40% of the child welfare workforce is composed of professional social workers.[20]

Salaries vary wildly along with requirements. As we wrote this, Mississippi posted an opening for a CPS "Family Protection Specialist" position requiring a bachelor's in social work with a starting salary of $27,615.55 per year. That translates to about $14 per hour, less than the national minimum wage that the recent presidential candidate Bernie Sanders was promoting, and far less than the average first salary for a college graduate (about $50,000 as of fall 2015). In contrast, in Los Angeles County they require a master's degree and pay more than twice as much.

Positions in CPS include roles ranging from the individuals who screen hotline calls (we talk more about screening later), to those who go out to check on the concerns, to those who provide services to families, to those who work in the area of foster care and adoptions. Often, the latter two groups have master's-level educations.[21] Once a person is hired, the level of training prior to beginning the position again varies widely. Usually CPS workers belong to "units" of a half-dozen to a dozen workers under an experienced supervisor (Box 2.2).[4,22]

Why does all this matter? Well, it turns out that most CPS workers do not feel they are adequately prepared to do this work, and this is true both in the United States and in other countries with similar systems.[23–25] As we talk more about what they do, it becomes apparent why this is a big problem.

Other Government Roles

While CPS (operated at the state or county level of government) is the main entity charged with making sure children are safe and providing most in-home services (when offered), other facets of government play roles in the process following a report. Typically, if a child must be removed from the home, a police officer will

BOX 2.2

A TYPICAL CHILD PROTECTIVE SERVICES UNIT

One of the authors was a member of a CPS unit in California during the 1980s. His team included a rather typical cross-section of workers, including a couple of fresh-faced and very young MSWs (himself included), and a very kind but very no-nonsense former cop. There was a rather burned-out worker who had just moved to the area and didn't last long, and an intellectual older worker who was new to child protection but had held many social service positions over the years. He was later able to supplement his meager government salary through appearances on nationally televised TV quiz shows. There was also a young PhD psychologist who was working for the county while he built his practice, and finally, a true veteran who had done child protection practice since the early days of the 1960s. This mix of older and younger workers is pretty typical, as there can be a lot of early turnover in a child protection career, but there are also a few people who find their place and stay for decades.

accompany CPS to officially take the child into state custody.[26] This role hasn't changed that much since the police officer rescued Mary Ellen over 100 years ago.

Once a child enters foster care or is at "imminent risk" of entry into care, the family court (sometimes called juvenile court) system becomes involved. In addition to a judge, a child's interest is represented by a form of legal counsel (often from the district attorney's office) and possibly a guardian ad litem (usually a volunteer attorney) or a community volunteer serving as a CASA. The parent's interest is represented by the parent with or without legal counsel. While a CPS worker advises the court about the case, it is the judge who makes the decisions about remaining in care, going home, or moving on to another permanent setting like adoption. We have relatively little research about family court judges, but what we do have suggests substantial variation in selection processes to be a family court judge, how much child welfare–specific training they receive, and individual case decision-making.[27–29] While a child is in foster care, CPS is responsible for their care and safety, but the court retains a supervisory and decision-making role. If an incident of child abuse or neglect involves criminal charges against the perpetrator, than the criminal court system will also be involved in the case. Finally, for certain children, there is one more layer.

Tribal Nations: The Indian Child Welfare Act

In the United States many AI/AN tribes are separately recognized sovereign governments. Some tribal nations have their own CPS agencies, while others work with state agencies. While the reporting process is similar, the processes related to foster care are not. Foster care processes are guided by the mandates of the ICWA.[6] The development of the ICWA is rooted in very disturbing historical practices that impacted a large number of AI/AN children—including the Indian boarding schools.

In the 1800s, many AI/AN children were relocated to schools run by churches or the government. Some of these children were not allowed to return to their own communities and were forced into placements with white families. This was not done because the children were abandoned or being mistreated, but because it was deemed necessary to assimilate them.[30] An infamous quote highlighting this intent by Richard Pratt (a founder of this movement) was "Kill the Indian in him and save the man."[31] Figure 2.1 shows children attending the Carlisle School, perhaps the most well-known of these institutions. This experience is now seen as an example of, at a minimum, attempted cultural genocide and, at worst, a horrific example of institutional child abuse. Many of the schools employed intensive child labor and brutal punishment practices.[32] In addition to many reports of physical and sexual abuse at some schools, many (the exact number is not known) children died due to the poor living conditions and brutal treatment.[33]

Even after this use of boarding schools ended, AI/AN children who required out-of-home placements were still commonly not placed with kin or within their tribal community. The ICWA was put into place to remedy this in 1978 (Box 2.3).[34] More recently, additional guidelines for implementation were issued to improve adherence to the policy.[35]

FIGURE 2.1 Carlisle Indian Boarding School

BOX 2.3
THE ICWA DECLARATION OF POLICY

"The Congress hereby declares that it is the policy of this Nation to protect the best interests of Indian children and to promote the stability and security of Indian tribes and families by the establishment of minimum Federal standards for the removal of Indian children from their families and the placement of such children in foster or adoptive homes which will reflect the unique values of Indian culture, and by providing for assistance to Indian tribes in the operation of child and family service programs." (Declaration of Policy: Indian Child Welfare Act, 1978)

The ICWA was established to meet two simple goals. First, the rights of federally recognized tribes were to be protected in child welfare proceedings to prevent unnecessary separations of native children from their families and tribes. Second, the ICWA is intended to reduce unnecessary removal or harmful switching of children from one home or one system to another. The law has a number of complexities we won't go into, but in general, the ICWA has the following effects:

1. Tribes may establish their own child welfare systems and courts and are entitled to federal assistance for doing so. Optionally, they may work with state agencies.
2. The ICWA applies to children who are (1) members or eligible for membership in a federally recognized tribe *and* who are (2) involved with child custody proceedings. By "child custody proceedings" we mean court action related to foster care, not divorce-related conflicts over child custody.
3. State agencies must make serious and timely efforts to make sure that any tribal relationship is discovered and that the tribe is contacted. The tribe may either take complete jurisdiction or remain involved in other ways during the decision-making process.
4. There is an emphasis on *active efforts* to prevent removal. "Active" is a legal term here and is meant to be a higher standard than "reasonable," which applies to the non-ICWA foster care decisions.

The ICWA is the only federal child welfare policy we are aware of that explicitly includes communities as stakeholders in cases involving particular children. Under the ICWA, the interests in the case go beyond the child or parents—the tribe also has standing and rights. There is a long and very interesting history of the development of this act and continued issues with implementation that goes beyond the scope of the present book. A good resource is *Facing the Future: The Indian Child Welfare Act at 30.*[36]

It is important to point out that many states still fail to follow the requirements of the ICWA. A recent egregious example occurred in South Dakota.[37] We provide the link to the online news series here (http://www.npr.org/2011/10/25/141672992/native-foster-care-lost-children-shattered-families). Stories like these spurred renewed efforts to enforce the ICWA, including the newly issued guidelines mentioned earlier.[35]

HOW THINGS WORK: NUMBERS AND PROCESSES

We have now reviewed the "who does what" part of CPS and move on to discuss the how and when. In chapters 8 and 10 we go into more detail about some barriers and misconceptions around reporting. For now we just talk about the big picture.

What Happens After a Report?

Not all reports result in an official response. Of the roughly 6 million children currently reported per year, over 3 million kids in about 2 million families are officially investigated.[2] These cases are described as "screened in," and there is a great deal of variance among states in how often this occurs. If you live in Alabama, CPS will respond to any report with enough information (they screen in 98.4%), but move north to South Dakota and only 16.2% of all calls get screened in.[2] This may have caused you to think, "Wait, . . . what?"

Reports are "screened out" for a number of reasons. Sometimes a call is made because someone is concerned about a child, but what the person is seeing does not meet the state's criteria for what CPS can respond to as abuse or neglect (see discussion of state's rights below). Sometimes an act is actually a crime rather than maltreatment. For example, if a stranger hits your child, that's assault, not abuse, and the case is handled by law enforcement, not child protection. Quite often reports aren't pursued due to lack of information. An example might be, "I saw a person who hit a child. They got into a green car about an hour ago and were driving by City Park." On one hand, it is laudable that the concerned person took responsibility to make the report. On the other hand, there just isn't a practical means of trying to find this child. There are a lot of green cars. Rarely, people report out of malicious intent— we talk about this more in chapter 8. The number of intentionally false reports is so small that only 10 states even bother to report them nationally. Among those 10 states, the highest rate of investigated cases judged to be intentionally false is about 5% (Idaho).[2]

State's Rights and Defining Child Maltreatment

A word about state-level policy variation is important here. Recall that by the time the federal government passed the law mandating a child maltreatment reporting system, all states already has systems. We did not say they all had the same system, or even similar systems. This relates back to a key principle written into the US Constitution—the limitation of the federal government in making decisions for states. State's rights (see Box 2.4), although markedly reduced after the Civil War, still represents a core American value, and shows itself in things like determining who gets health insurance, the way public schools are funded, which curricula are used, and the definitions and procedures that relate to CPS response to child abuse and neglect.

While CAPTA set broad guidelines requiring reporting of major types of mal-treatment (e.g., physical, sexual, and neglect), states can decide what specific acts or situations fit into these categories or add additional categories. For example, if you live in Oregon a child witnessing domestic violence can be classified as maltreat-ment, but not in Missouri.[38] We talk a lot more about such issues in the coming chapters.

BOX 2.4

THE TENTH AMENDMENT

"The powers not delegated to the United States by the Constitution, nor prohibited by it to the States, are reserved to the States respectively, or to the people." (Tenth Amendment to the US Constitution, full text)

"Traditional" Versus "Alternative" or "Differential" Response

If a report isn't among the 40% screened out,[2] then someone is sent to take a look at the situation. Sometimes there isn't anything worrisome happening and the case is quickly resolved. Such cases are often honest misunderstandings. As mentioned in Box 2.2, one of the authors was formerly a CPS investigator, and once responded to a report of a young child seen in his front yard suffering from serious facial bruis-ing and bleeding. It turned out that the child's face was covered in chocolate ice cream and raspberry sauce. Apologies were made, case closed. Besides such simple misunderstandings, there are a number of medical conditions of the skin that can appear like fairly serious physical abuse.[39] For example, some healing skin infections can look like cigarette burns. Slate gray patches or "Mongolian spots" (dark skin

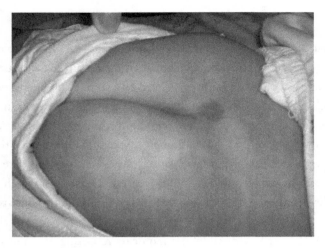

FIGURE 2.2 Example of Mongolian Spots

pigmentation like a birthmark) naturally occur, particularly in nonwhite populations (Figure 2.2). These can seem like severe bruises and might raise great concern
if noticed on an infant.

In the past, all screened-in cases followed a similar path. A social worker was dispatched to figure out what was going on, and then to close the case, set up ongoing services, or (rarely) to take a child into protective custody if there was no other
choice. This is called a "traditional" response system. All states still do this, but some
states have added an additional type of response.

Twenty-six states have adopted what is called either "differential response" (DR)
or sometimes "alternative response" (AR).[2,40,41] Alternative response is not really a
single model. States can (and do) choose different ways of implementing AR. The
key principles, however, are the same. Hotline reports are divided into what appear
to be more serious reports (usually sexual, severe physical, and neglect cases that
pose a serious and immediate threat) that go to the traditional track and apparently
less serious reports (other cases) that go to the assessment track.[40] We use the word
"apparently" because CPS cases are rather like a "box of chocolates." You don't really
know what's happening until you see the actual situation, so cases can be transferred
between tracks as needed. Which approach is better? We talk more about that in
chapter 10.

Decisions

Making sure the child is safe is always the first and most important task, but a CPS
worker must also prioritize preserving the family. This sounds very straightforward,
but workers often respond on the basis of relatively little information. In addition,

in all but emergency cases, the caregiver's response is voluntary. In a totally voluntary case, if a family does not want to cooperate then the case is usually just closed. Even when a worker gains access to the home and can take a look at the situation, it can be hard in a single visit to make all the right choices.[23] Overreaction can lead to missing an opportunity to work with and preserve the family (which is a key policy mandate). Underreaction can lead to leaving a child in a situation that might result in serious harm or death. Both can result in public outcry and even legal intervention.[42,43]

Cases that receive what we have called a traditional investigation, have two decision points: (1) whether to "substantiate" the allegations or not, and (2) whether to offer services. If a case is substantiated, the perpetrator's name may be placed in a child abuse registry. These registries are one source employers use to check the backgrounds of employees or volunteers who wish to work with children in an attempt to avoid placing a child at risk of harm. In contrast, cases that are assigned to an assessment track have only one decision point, whether to provide services or not. There is no substantiation decision for the assessment track. So why is this important?

Let's return to the ABC's for a moment. There are few terms so misunderstood and misapplied as "substantiation" (some states say "founded") in child protection. In the annual federal report on child maltreatment, statistics are generated about "nonvictims" and "victims." The words "victim" and "substantiated" are used as synonyms. This is also often the case in media stories or even in research. The problem? Research shows child outcomes for substantiated and unsubstantiated cases are pretty similar—kids are at roughly the *same* risk of negative outcomes (e.g., poor school performance, mental health difficulties, risky sexual behaviors, etc.) and repeated maltreatment no matter which label their case receives.[44–46] Substantiation actually means that, in the CPS worker's judgment, there was both sufficient harm and enough evidence of maltreatment present at the time of investigation.[47] What constitutes "enough evidence" is decided by the state. The legal standards for evidence required for CPS substantiation range from "reasonable" (lowest standard required), to "probable cause" (fair probability of something) to "preponderance" (mostly sure) to "clear and convincing" (substantially sure). "Unsubstantiated" is not the same thing as "nothing happened," but sometimes people think that's what it means.

A CPS investigation is not like what happens in fictional crime shows on television. For example, Columbo was the lead homicide detective in a very long running crime show in the United States. The show always ended in finding all the needed evidence to convict the "killer"—often right after a commercial break. In Columbo we start off knowing there has been a crime and we assume there will be evidence. Let's think about how this may differ for CPS.

CPS workers do not know if maltreatment has occurred until they are able to investigate it. Substantiation requires BOTH evidence and harm—one can exist without the other. For example, imagine responding to a case in which a young child is suspected of being sexually abused. If the abuse includes fondling alone, the child is too young to communicate, and there are no other injuries apparent, the only evidence may be an admission by the parent.

Quite honestly, TV does not do a good job representing the truth about homicide investigations either. Homicide cases often lack sufficient evidence to link a person to a particular murder. In the United States, one in three murders go unsolved— each year several thousand people literally "get away with murder."[48]

What proportion of cases are substantiated? There is a wrinkle here related to the track issue. Since assessment track cases cannot receive the substantiation label (unless they switch tracks), rates of substantiation decline in states that have this dual track system. Nationally, the adoption of the two-track approach was largely responsible for the drop in substantiation rates between 2000 and 2015—dropping from 32.4% to 17.3%.[2] These are not differences in what's happening "on the ground", just changes in policies and terminology.

To Serve or Not to Serve?

It may surprise most readers to know that only about 35% of screened-in CPS referrals receive postinvestigation/assessment services.[2] Like much of we have talked about so far, this varies markedly from state to state. Further, substantiated cases are twice as likely to receive services.[2] So what exactly do families receive if they are served? The answer is, "it depends".

Child protective services workers who provide postresponse services typically provide case management (referrals and occasional check-in visits). This is sometimes called family-centered services (FCS). A few specialized caseworkers provide very brief, but intense, direct services (worker is available 24/7 for about 6 weeks) to a small proportion of families when a child is deemed at high risk of removal. This is known as intensive in-home or family preservation services (FPS). The national annual report does not break out type of in-home service provided, but about 38% of children with screened-in reports in Missouri received FCS, and about 4.5% lived in families that received FPS.[49]

What if a child needs foster care? We talk a bit more about the myths and realities of child removal in chapter 10, but provide a brief overview here. In most states, law enforcement (usually police or sheriff deputies) must be present with CPS to sign off on the decision to take a child into state custody. This triggers a federally required court review within a few days (weekends are off the clock). Then a family court judge determines whether the placement continues to be needed or sends the child home.

In 2015, about 4 million CPS referrals were made, including 7.2 million children. About 3.4 million children were subjects of screened-in reports and about 680,000 children were substantiated. In 2015, about 23% of children with substantiated cases and about 2% of those with unsubstantiated cases entered foster care.[2] Two things are important to note. First, many children enter care for the first time after several reports of maltreatment, but the national data just tell us how many entered in a year. Based on two studies using California data, the rate of foster care entry for children over the age of 12 months is less than 5%.[50,51] Second, many people don't realize that children also enter foster care for reasons not related to abuse or neglect, including parental death, incapacity, incarceration, or the parent choosing to relinquish the child. In California between 2012 and 2014, almost 6% of entries into foster care were not related to maltreatment issues.[52]

What happens after placement? The majority of children placed into care will return home—many in less than 3 months.[53] If a child cannot return home, there is an emphasis on exit to a permanent home through guardianship or adoption whenever possible.[10,50] About 5% of youth are in care with the goal of being there until they emancipate or "age out" at age 18 to 21, depending on the state.[54]

That's a lot of decisions to follow, so we have summarized major decision points by track in Figure 2.3. Again, in emergencies, a child may be taken in to foster care at any point.

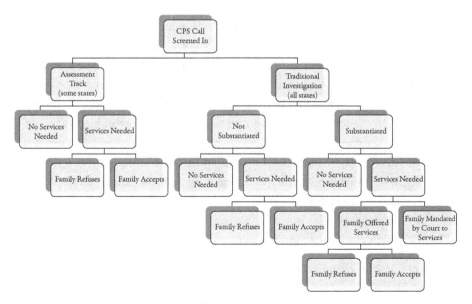

FIGURE 2.3 CPS Decision-making Flow Chart

Other Case Outcomes?

Recall early in the chapter we mentioned that a fourth goal for child protection, "well-being," was added in the late 1990s. The idea is that the system should also focus on the health, mental health, and education of the child. No one really defined what achieving "well-being" in those areas was supposed to look like, so child protection agencies were not sure how to achieve it or measure it.[55,56] Hypothetically one could meet the goals of safety and permanency and not do a great job attending to the other needs of the child. The federal government still audits states' compliance with this goal as well as the other three through federal Child and Family Services Reviews (CFSRs).[57] Predictably, states often fail the "well-being" part of the audit.

We are big proponents of promoting the long-term adjustment, health, and life satisfaction of children who have experienced maltreatment, but there are important issues to consider. First, CPS does not provide health or education or mental health care, so meeting needs in these areas is dependent on the availability of high-quality effective services in the community. Second, most families encounter CPS for a relatively brief time, lasting from a few days to a few months. It is difficult to markedly improve child well-being in such a brief time.

Child maltreatment fatalities are the most extreme examples of failing to achieve child safety. There are about 1,500 official child maltreatment fatalities per year,[2] a number that many fear is an undercount of the true incidence.[15] These cases tend to capture the attention of the media and authorities.[40] The Commission to Eliminate Child Abuse and Neglect Fatalities (CECANF) was established by Public Law 112-275, the Protect Our Kids Act of 2012, to develop a national strategy and recommendations for reducing such fatalities across the country.[58,59] In reviewing the final report,[58] we were struck by how many of the recommendations were aimed at the larger group of families known to CPS rather than narrowly focused on assessing risk of death. Since we wrote this book to focus on this larger group, we found this heartening. On the other hand, preventive suggestions require public will to implement, and we are concerned that such conversations often lapse when a given news cycle ends. As Parent[4] writes in his book about his work in children's services, "You never forget—I didn't forget, you won't forget. But at some point, you stop thinking about it, and that's the whole problem."[(p.119)]

What About the Child Protective Services Workers Themselves?

As you are probably beginning to notice, there are a fair number of decision points involved in the formal response to maltreatment, significant variation in policies and practices across states, and potential conflicts between valuing child safety and preserving the family. It is perhaps not surprising that CPS workers experience significant stress and emotional and even physical harm.[23,25,60, 61] In an extreme example, it made national news when a mother, angered over losing custody of her son, shot and killed the CPS worker she held responsible.[61] There are two books written by CPS workers about working in child protection: *No One Would Believe It* by Evelyn Norman[21] and *Turning Stones* by Marc Parent.[4] Both books describe at least one case in which the author/worker was in fear for their own safety. Here one worker responds to concerns from a worker in an adjoining county and ends up helping a woman and her children escape from a violent husband:

> "I thought we had escaped until the father suddenly tried to open the passenger door. The mother had not locked it. He attempted to drag her out of the car. I put the car in reverse and hit the gas. I actually knocked him to the ground! The mother closed and locked the door, and I drove away. We all escaped."[21,p.11]

While few cases involve this level of action, workers also suffer psychological harm as a result of intervening in some very troubling situations.[23,60] Marc Parent[4] eventually left the profession after being unable to recover from his final case, in which an infant he and his partner chose to leave in the home died. In short, this is not an easy job.

YOU MAY NOT BE TALKING ABOUT IT, BUT YOU ARE PAYING FOR IT

There isn't a lot of sustained public discussion about child maltreatment. There is almost no conversation about child protection policies and services outside of foster care or child fatalities. Just because we are not talking about it, however, does not mean it is not directly impacting us—at least economically. As we write this, we are in the midst of a change in federal leadership with a lot of public discussion focused on the economy. Setting aside the moral issue and the societal interest of raising healthy children for a moment, let's talk dollars.

We spend about 30 billion dollars per annum on child protective services at the federal, state, and local levels.[62] Of that 30 billion dollars, the majority goes to foster care. As with many things, we have structured our fiscal child welfare policy to be light on prevention and heavy on remediation. The costs of responding to child maltreatment pale compared to the costs associated with longer term outcomes of child maltreatment when we fail to effectively intervene. A recent CDC study estimated that we end up paying out over 140 billion dollars total lifetime costs on a *single year's cohort* of maltreatment "victims" (substantiated cases). Those costs go up dramatically when we include unsubstantiated cases, with estimates ranging from $250 and $500 billion.[63] To place this in context, the upper-end estimate is roughly the same as the estimated federal deficit for fiscal year 2017.[64] Keep this in mind, especially as we think through some options for improving our response to child maltreatment in the final chapter.

WHERE DO WE GO FROM HERE?

In chapter 1, we argued that in the last 150 years we have generally moved in a positive direction in terms of valuing children, but there remains much to be done. We agree with Jagannathan and Camasso[65] that our child protection policies and preventive approaches must reflect the needs and situations of all children who are maltreated. To make lasting change and build a better future for our children, all people (not just researchers or child advocates) need to be part of the discussion. The rest of this book focuses on helping you become fully aware of what maltreatment is, some of the factors that complicate addressing the problem, and finally some ideas to consider as we move forward.

3

Good Parenting or Physical Abuse?

WHILE THE MODERN CHILD protective system is less than 50 years old, the identification of physical abuse goes back centuries and crosses many cultures. About 2,500 years ago, Plato wrote, "Disobedient children are treated as a bent and twisted piece of cord and straightened with threats and blows."[1] Folk tales and fairy tales also illustrate the long-standing presence of physical abuse in everyday lives. Shannon[2] briefly retells "The Haunted Forest," a folk tale from Lithuania:

> In the story a girl suffers abuse for some time and finally runs away and finds new magical friends who create a clay model of her that they place back in her home so that no one will look for her. The clay doll has a poisonous snake inside. The model continues to be abused but cannot feel it and this further infuriates the caregiver who one day threatens her with a whip at which point the model explodes and the snake bites the caregiver who dies. The girl continues to live happily ever after in the forest.[(pp35–36)]

With such a long history of talking about physical harm to children, you would think people would be very clear about what physical abuse is or is not. They're not. For many people, "physical abuse" brings to mind images of a badly beaten child with multiple serious injuries, as can be seen in a photograph of Mary Ellen (Figure 3.1) taken after her rescue.

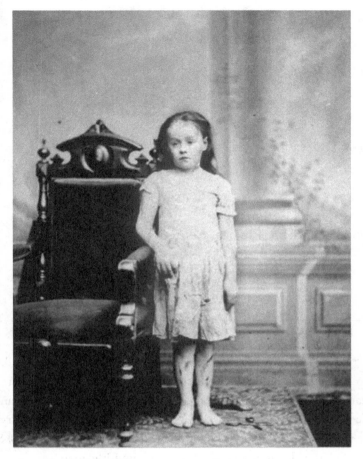

FIGURE 3.1 Mary Ellen Wilson

For others, physical abuse also includes harsh discipline. In some states, manufacture of a controlled substance in the presence of a child is labeled physical abuse. We'll talk about what we know about physical abuse and then work through the problem of where to draw the line between discipline and abuse.

HOW BIG A PROBLEM IS PHYSICAL ABUSE?

Today, physical abuse is the second most frequent type of reported maltreatment after neglect,[3] comprising about one in six official reports. Generally, physical abuse includes some sort of violent action against a child ranging from abusive head trauma (also known as "shaken baby syndrome") to hitting, biting, burning, lashing, or similar acts that may injure a child. In 2015, 117,772 children were substantiated for physical abuse, and 583 died.[3] Because of problems in the ways we code reason for death, many researchers think deaths due to physical abuse are closer to a thousand per year.[4]

The good news is that most abusive incidents do not result in severe physical harm, and there are some indicators that in the last 25 years we might be doing better. Rates of reported physical abuse seem to have fallen by about half since 1992.[4,5] Most people don't realize it, but this is consistent with data indicating that homicides, assaults, rapes, and other forms of violent crime are only about half as common as they were 25 years ago.[6] While we know poverty is associated with risk of maltreatment, rates of physical maltreatment did not go back to prior levels during the recent Great Recession[7]—though the declines we saw prior to 2010 do appear to have stopped.[8] Maybe, on average, we are abusing children a little less.

Of course when we say things like "on average," that means that patterns may not hold for everyone. For example, though research says violent crime is going down,[6] if you live in Chicago now, that is not true for your city (see www.citylab.com/crime/2016/09/where-crime-is-rising-in-2016/500690/). Averages can also mask shorter-term changes (like a short-term rise or fall in a stock compared to a 15-year trend) and have to be constantly updated as trends change. For example, like physical abuse, pediatric drowning hospitalization rates dropped significantly between 1993 and 2003 but since have largely stabilized.[9] The take home? Although physical abuse has declined compared to 25 years ago or more, it doesn't seem to be continuing to decline, and remains a large problem.

Who Abuses Children and Why?

Our stories often portray someone who abuses a child as a scary, hostile adult, possibly with strong sadistic tendencies (e.g., Marcus Eaton in the very popular *Divergent* books). Such people do exist, of course, but they aren't the norm. Honestly, other than poverty (which crosscuts all forms of maltreatment) we do not have a clear demographic profile for physical abuse perpetrators, and sometimes different sources disagree. While conventional wisdom might point to young, unprepared parents as more likely to be abusive, research indicates the rate is higher for the 25–34 age range.[3,4] Gender differences? Well, women are more commonly officially reported as perpetrators of physical abuse than men,[3] but studies suggest that this may be a serious undercount of males as perpetrators.[4] Why might this happen? Many children reported for abuse and neglect live in single-parent (usually female-headed) families, and most maltreatment statutes require a perpetrator have "care, custody, and control." Because of this, noncaretaker perpetrators, like a visiting boyfriend who hits a child, might not be listed as the official perpetrator.

What Causes a Parent to Abuse a Child?

A lot of people have tried to answer the question "What causes physical abuse?" While personal traits may play some role, factors like stress and poverty (recall the "Old Woman in the Shoe" from chapter 1) seem to provide better (more scientifically well supported) explanations for most cases of physical abuse. Let's briefly explore some ideas about why abuse occurs.

Are You Predestined to Abuse Because You Were Abused?

As a prior child abuse investigator, one of the authors recalls a fair number of cases, maybe 1 in 10, in which the call was based on a clear mistake, like a child being reported for severe facial bruising when the child just needed a wash. In such cases, you wind up meeting with a family that is obviously doing fine with no concerns present. Apologies are made and, quite often, an adult family member took the opportunity to ask questions about parenting or child abuse in general. One of the most common questions was "If I was hit as a child am I going to hit my child?" Despite having never hit their own child, many people harbor a fear that because they were hit they are somehow doomed to hit their own child. In academia, this idea is sometimes called the "cycle of violence" (Box 3.1) or "intergenerational transmission of abuse" and has to do with repeating what we have "learned."[10,11]

For the vast majority of such parents, this is of course, ridiculous. While there may be increased risk (which we talk about later) there is nothing like predestination at work. Propensity for violence comes from many sources working together, including biology (e.g., genetic differences in reactions[12]), learning, stress, and, perhaps most importantly, the lived environment. This complex array of factors means that a similar history of physical abuse (a single cause) may lead one person to act violently as an adult, another person to become addicted to drugs or alcohol but not be violent,

---

BOX 3.1
TWO DIFFERENT "CYCLES OF VIOLENCE"

In domestic violence, the "cycle of violence" refers to a repeating pattern where an abuser physically attacks a partner, followed by a conciliatory "honeymoon period," followed by increasing tension and then cycling back to violence.

In child maltreatment, people sometimes discuss the "cycle of violence" as an *intergenerational* cycle, where people abused as children might, in turn, abuse their own children many years later. These are very different ideas and should not be confused with each other.

while a third person may not develop any harmful behaviors and become a healthy, nonviolent, productive adult. Scientists' word for this is "multifinality"—many outcomes from a single cause. Another wrinkle in the intergenerational transmission of violence idea is that it predicts that one would repeat the same behavior, and this does not seem to be the case. Even when a person who was physically abused as a child later maltreats their children, it appears just as likely that they will neglect not physically abuse their kids.[13,14] Recall that our maltreatment "patient zero," Mary Ellen, became a loving, nonabusive mother[15] It was amazing how relieved many parents were upon being told this—tears sometimes flowed.

Stress and Coping

It is perhaps unsurprising to anyone who has felt overwhelmed with stress that research also indicates this is a risk factor for physical abuse.[16] Strong coping skills and social supports, however, offset this risk. For example, perhaps a parent has a bad day and later their child does something wrong. A person with strong coping skills and resources (e.g., social support) might take a deep breath and approach the behavior with an appropriate nonviolent response. Remove those positive skills and resources, and that same person may become angry and use physical force to respond to their child's behaviors. This theoretical connection between stress and physical abuse underlies many of the materials designed to prevent a parent from shaking a baby to stop the child from crying.[17] The old advice to "count to 10" when angry is really similar to the "take a break, don't shake" message in public service announcements in this area.[18] The good news is that coping skills like these can be learned and supportive resources built. We talk more about this in the final chapter.

Cognitive Distortions

We all know that two people can see the same situation differently. This can lead to different emotional or even physical responses. Theoretically, some parents prone to abusive behaviors may perceive their child's behaviors differently than parents who see the same behavior but are not prone to abusive behavior.[19] This is sometimes called "cognitive distortion." It is quite normal for an infant or toddler to cry in response to range of issues like being hungry, or tired, or ill, and so forth. Some parents may interpret this behavior wrongly as a deliberate attempt to make them miserable or evidence that the child does not love them. Such a misinterpretation can lead to negative emotional responses that may result in violence. The good news is that we can teach "cognitive restructuring" to help parents reframe their perceptions based on understanding normal child behavior. Letting people know what's normal, and helping them to identify when they're misinterpreting their child can go a long way. This is a component of many evidence-based parenting programs mentioned in chapters 9 and 11.

Context Matters

Recall from chapter 1 that we tend to use an ecological framework to understand maltreatment. The broader context like peers or neighborhood values, norms, and conditions may also influence parenting behaviors. One mechanism for doing this has to do with the way we learn behaviors and the way we learn to control behaviors.[20] Social control theories suggest that there are norms and rules of conduct that work to control our behavior and prevent us from doing negative things. Social learning suggests that people do bad things because somebody models a negative behavior that appears to achieve some goal. Alternative behaviors only develop if those are also modeled. In other words, abusive behavior is related to what I have learned (sort of like intergenerational transmission), but that learning can occur based on various contexts (peers, community) not just my own family's behavior. My implementation of a negative behavior is offset if I see other positive viable behaviors modeled and/or there are sufficient social controls to prevent my acting on what I may have learned.

"Collective efficacy" theories suggest that there is an influence on parenting exerted by the community.[21] Healthy communities share values that make all forms of violence and social disorder less likely—which sounds a lot like social control. The idea goes beyond that, though, to suggest that such communities also build social supports and interpersonal efficacy that help produce positive outcomes. Sort of akin to the "It takes a village" idea.

Putting It Together

Perhaps aspects of several of the ideas above made sense to you, and if so, you are in good company with current scientific thought. Current research tends to look at physical abuse (and other forms of maltreatment) through a risk and protective factor lens.[22] This means combining many of the preceding ideas within that ecological framework we introduced. In other words, abuse occurs due to stressors like mental health problems, domestic violence, poverty, coping skills and social supports, and risk and supports at the community level.[23-26] Overall, the notion is that heightened risk (across contexts) has to be countered with sufficient buffers or protective factors (across contexts) to prevent negative outcomes.

No matter what explanation or set of ideas sounds right to you, it is really important to understand that increased risk is not the same as predestination. To use an illustrative example, most people killed by tornadoes in the United States live in the Midwest, but most people in the Midwest aren't killed by tornadoes. Living in a place where tornadoes are more common places you at greater risk, but does not mean that you will experience a tornado, much less die from one.

DISCIPLINE OR ABUSE?

Having thought a little about the "who" and the "why" first, now we turn to the "what" and "when" part of our discussion. While not all physical abuse is associated with discipline, it is common for these two issues to be intertwined. In the United States, we are still wrestling with when we should draw a line between physical discipline and abuse. When an injury is severe or a child dies, little debate exists, but recall that most incidents do not result in serious physical injury. All children, no matter how angelic, will at some point behave in a way that is embarrassing or even maddening to their parents. For example, one of the authors had an acquaintance whose child (who was normal and happy in all respects) threw a tantrum right in the middle of a storefront window on a busy street. It requires a great deal of patience to be a parent in such circumstances so effective intervention can be calmly administered as the child calms down.[27]

Many people feel that there are times when physical discipline can be okay. Others strongly oppose corporal punishment for any reason. It's not only individuals who disagree—different cultures within a country, and entire countries, can have *very* different beliefs or even policies about where discipline ends and abuse starts. Some of this is grounded in tradition. Perhaps some readers have heard things like, "Whoever spares the rod, hates their children" (Proverbs 13:24). This view of the necessity of physical punishment to correctly raise a child is not uncommon or limited to a particular religion. Let's look at two recent examples from two very different places.

> "Tiger Mother" Amy Chua may have been strict with her daughters, pushing academics ahead of sleepovers, but she's practically a kitten compared to "Wolf Dad" Xiao Baiyou, who has written a bestselling book in mainland China originally called *Beat Them Into Peking University*, reports NPR. Xiao boasts of having more than 1,000 rules for his four children—from how to hold chopsticks to how to sleep and use a quilt. "If you don't follow the rules, then I must beat you," Xiao says. He uses a feather duster, however, not a belt. . . . "From 3 to 12, kids are mainly animals," he says. "Their humanity and social nature still aren't complete. So you have to use Pavlovian methods to educate them."[28]

Xiao needs to brush up on his psychology a bit. Punishment is "operant" not "Pavlovian" conditioning. That aside, endorsement of physical punishment of children is widespread. While not endorsing such extremes, Pope Francis recently weighed in positively on corporal punishment, saying: "One time, I heard a father in a meeting with married couples say, "I sometimes have to smack my children a bit, but never in the face so as to not humiliate them. . . . How beautiful! He knows the sense of dignity! He has to punish them but does it justly and moves on."[29]

How Do Americans See Corporal Punishment?

It turns out that the pope's view is pretty mainstream. The General Social Survey of the University of Chicago is one of the largest national surveys regularly given. It asked people, "Do you strongly agree, agree, disagree or strongly disagree that it is sometimes necessary to discipline a child with a good, hard spanking"[30] Seventy percent of Americans "agreed" or "strongly agreed" that good, hard spankings were necessary in 2012, down from 84% in 1986. Some groups were a little more likely to endorse spanking (Republicans, Southerners, Black respondents, and evangelical Christians), but the differences were not large. Almost all groups shared the same downward trend over time.

How do people actually behave? A person might approve of spanking generally and not do it. It turns out if you ask people what they have actually done, you get answers that are very close to, although somewhat lower than, the numbers we just saw. Combining the findings from several large studies,[31] researchers found that the percentage of parents saying they slapped or spanked their child dropped from about 76% in 1975 to about 62% in 2002. The bottom line is that while corporal punishment is decreasing in popularity, most Americans approve of spanking and most Americans with children report using some form of physical discipline, at least sometimes. Of course, physical discipline can include more than spanking, but before we go there, let's understand the law.

How Does the Law View Corporal Punishment?

The legal line between discipline and abuse can be vague to the point of invisibility, and once again, varies by state as seen in the following state statute definitions from the Child Welfare Information Gateway.[32] In Alabama, physical abuse is broadly defined as "harm or threatened harm to the health or welfare of a child through non-accidental physical injury." In Indiana, on the other hand, it isn't physical abuse unless "the child's physical or mental health is seriously endangered." In Indiana "reasonable corporal punishment" is not abuse. In Minnesota, some acts are physical abuse whether they cause an injury or not, such as punching or hitting a child in the head if that child is under a year of age. As a very general rule, in most places, hitting or spanking a child isn't against the law, but hurting (leaving marks or injury) a child is.

Is This Physical Abuse? The Adrian Peterson Case

Mary Ellen's example involved injuries that were quite serious over a long time, and there was no doubt in the courts or public opinion that a line had been crossed. Now we turn to a recent case that for many is not so clear. For a time, the Adrian Peterson case dominated the news and rekindled debate about the line between discipline and abuse.[1] Unlike the Mary Ellen case, there is no additional factor of poverty, the injuries are not so severe, and the parent is clearly intending to discipline, not torture.

On May 18, 2014, in Spring, Texas, a 4-year-old child pushed another child who was playing a video game. His father, pro football running back Adrian Peterson, saw this and felt that it was his responsibility as a father to give the boy a "whooping" with a "switch" (a narrow stick or branch). He saw it as his job as a father to use this approach to correct his child's behavior, so that his son would grow up to be a good person. These details and those below are taken from reporting by Nick Wright, a local CBS reporter.[33] Publically released photographs of the child taken by investigators show a series of linear bruises and cuts to the 4-year old's legs (Figure 3.2). Additional injuries were spread across the child's back, buttocks, ankles, legs, and scrotum. There were also defensive injuries to the child's hands, presumably as he tried protect himself from his father.

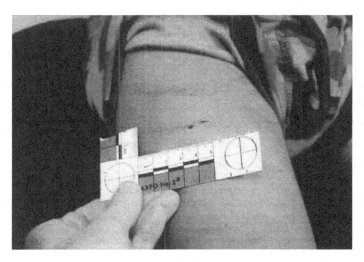

FIGURE 3.2 Leg Injuries to Child, Adrian Peterson Case

According to the child, Peterson has a "whooping room," "likes belts and switches," and put leaves in his son's mouth during this particular "whooping," presumably to muffle his screams. The child reported that he had been hit on the face by Peterson before and that he feared Peterson would punch him in the face if he told authorities. After the whipping, Mr. Peterson appeared to be a little surprised by the damage he did, allegedly texting the child's mother (who was in Minnesota, where she lived) that she might be:

> "mad at me about his leg. I got kinda good wit the tail end of the switch." Peterson is alleged to have also texted the child's mother that he "felt bad after the fact when I notice the switch was wrapping around hitting I thigh" and "Got him in nuts once I noticed. But I felt so bad, n I'm all tearing that butt up when needed! I start putting them in timeout. N save the whooping for needed memories!" Peterson allegedly also texted her that "Never do I go overboard! But all my kids will know, hey daddy has the biggie heart but don't play no games when it comes to acting right."[33]

It turned out later that this was not the only time Peterson had been alleged to have committed child abuse. According to ESPN,[34] there was a prior event in 2013 involving Mr. Peterson punishing a young child in a car, which resulted in a minor head injury. On November 4, 2014, Peterson pleaded "no contest" to a misdemeanor charge of "reckless assault" and received probation, a $4,000 fine, and 80 hours of community service, and was required to attend parenting classes.[35]

Mr. Peterson's Perspective

To us, the most interesting aspect of the Adrian Peterson case was the window into what he was thinking. This is available to us because of a very admirable quality of Mr. Peterson's—his honesty. ESPN reports that he was unusually open and direct with authorities during the investigation process.[34] Apparently this was a man doing what he thought was right, but who later acknowledged that, by accident, he might have gone a little too far. He described his point of view in a press release provided through the Minnesota Vikings on September 15, 2014:

> "I have to live with the fact that when I disciplined my son the way I was disciplined as a child, I caused an injury that I never intended or thought would happen. I know that many people disagree with the way I disciplined my child. I also understand after meeting with a psychologist that there are other

alternative ways of disciplining a child that may be more appropriate. But deep in my heart I have always believed I could have been one of those kids that was lost in the streets without the discipline instilled in me by my parents and other relatives. I have always believed that the way my parents disciplined me has a great deal to do with the success I have enjoyed as a man."

We would point out several things. First, he is repeating a parenting approach from his own childhood not because he is mentally ill or sadistic, but because he sees it as effective. He sees physical discipline as a part of loving his child. He is apparently conflicted about the injuries he inflicted. He attended the mandated parenting training and alludes to seeing value in learning about new approaches. Given his continued belief that corporal punishment made him a good person, however, it is unclear how he will choose to use such skills in the future.

The Public's View

The public response was varied. At first, the NFL imposed very light sanctions, then reversed themselves. According to the *Minneapolis Star Tribune*, this was because the team was "facing a revolt from corporate ad partners"[36] protesting the team's handling of the case. Another perspective is provided by outspoken former NBA star Charles Barkley in an exchange with sports radio talk show host Jim Rome. We include this because we feel the following conversation captures the public debate rather accurately.

BARKLEY: we spank kids in the South. I think the question about whether Adrian Peterson went overboard—Listen, Jim, we all grow up in different environments. Every black parent in my neighborhood in the South would be in trouble or in jail under those circumstances.

ROME: My thing is: I don't want to tell anybody how to raise their kids and I really don't want anybody telling me how to raise my kids. But let's make a distinction between "child rearing" and "child abuse." That was child abuse. There's no fine line here.

BARKLEY: I think there's a fine line. Jim, I've had many welts on my legs. I've gotten beat with switches—and I don't even like the term. When the media talks about it, "beating a child"—

ROME: But that's what that was, Charles.

BARKLEY: We called it "spanking" or "whipping" our kids.

ROME: If I see open wounds or bruises on a body that is a beating.

BARKLEY: Sure. I think those pictures are disturbing. And I think Adrian said, "I went overboard." But as far as being from the South, we all spanked our kids—I got spanked, me an my two brothers—

ROME: But then, Chuck, not now, right? 1964 is one thing, 2014 is another. Maybe we need to rethink this thing.

BARKLEY: And I totally agree with that. But I think we have to really be careful trying to teach other parents how to discipline their kids. That's a very fine line.[37]

There's a lot in that exchange. First of all it's implied that "whipping" children is something everyone does. That's wrong. As far as we know, whipping a child until he or she bleeds has not been the norm in America for a very long time. The national survey we mentioned earlier asked about "spanking." If they had asked about "whipping to the point of leaving welts" we suspect fewer would have seen that as acceptable. Barkley says that physical discipline is more common in the South and among blacks (which may still be a little true, but only a little, and again the survey was about spanking). Rome states that it's 2014, not 1964, and that our society isn't so violent toward kids as it used to be. This is true. Finally, and probably most importantly, Rome and Barkley agree that we are uncomfortable telling others how to raise their children.

But not all feel uncomfortable taking a different stand. We compare Mr. Barkley's statement with that of another prominent sports figure from the Vikings who, like Mr. Barkley, grew up with corporal punishment as the norm but reacted very differently to the Peterson case. The following is an excerpt from a commentary by Cris Carter (NFL).[38]

"This is the 21st century. My mom was wrong. She did the best she could, but she was wrong about some of that stuff she taught me. And I promised my kids that I won't teach that mess to them. You can't beat a kid to make him do what you want to do."

We believe it is likely that this struggle between what one thinks is okay in regard to their own parenting and limiting others' parenting behavior is part of what makes talking about physical abuse hard.

What Does Science Tell Us About Corporal Punishment?

There's been a lot of work done in an effort to understand corporal punishment and whether it is a good or bad idea, and we do have some answers. Recently science lost one of the pioneers in this area, Murray Straus (see a tribute to him at http://pubpages.unh.edu/~mas2/). In his 2001 book *Beating the Devil Out of Them: Corporal Punishment in American Families and Its Effects on Children*,[39] he makes the case that even minor violence toward children is a major driver of violence in society. While his work advanced our understanding of violence in the American family significantly, we promised to offer a balanced perspective based on current science.

Recent research suggests that children who are physically disciplined (at lower levels) do not do much worse than kids who aren't physically disciplined, but they don't do any better either.[40,41] It appears that many of the children who are physically punished and who have bad outcomes have other things going wrong in their families, like lack of warmth, stress, and other risk factors.[42,43] Further, disentangling what happens in the home from exposure to violence in other contexts like the school and community can be very difficult.[44] In other words, recent research suggests that low levels of corporal punishment that occur in an otherwise positive family and community context do not appear to be highly toxic, but it certainly doesn't appear to be beneficial either.

Indeed, virtually all social scientists and professional organizations agree that the bulk of the evidence argues against corporal punishment for several reasons. First, sometimes physical discipline can get out of hand. Many physical abuse cases start with an intent to "lightly" physically discipline a child, but the punishment either escalates or is administered harder than anticipated, as in the Peterson case. You have also probably heard advice like "You should never discipline while angry." Sound advice, but a large proportion of physical punishment is done by angry parents to children who perceive the punishment as an expression of anger.[45] When we are angry we have neurochemical reactions that can increase the perceived need to act and impair judgment—albeit usually briefly.[46] Unfortunately, a brief out-of-control moment can have tragic results. In child homicide cases[47,48] the fatal injury is often accompanied by anger or extreme frustration and hands are the most common weapon.

Norms may also come into play to support the extreme use of physical punishment. There is a long history of seeing rather severe corporal punishment as a valuable tool in raising children.[1,2] As Rome said, this is 2014, but some groups still adhere to very old ideas. For example, there has been a lot of press recently about the book *To Train Up a Child*, given away for free in some churches as a guide for parenting.[49] The book (at least the earlier edition) has been associated with more than one child's death.[50] Let's look at a couple of suggested approaches to discipline given in the book and imagine what might happen with the added burden of anger or frustration.

- Beating older children with rulers, paddles, belts, and larger tree branches
- "Training" children with pain before they even disobey, in order to teach total obedience

In 2013 a CNN news story was done about this book, triggered by the death of a 13-year-old child.[51] In the story, the authors quote the biblical passage we cited earlier in the chapter as their rationale for corporal punishment, but deny this should be done in anger. As Ateah and Durant[45] state, "the finding that maternal anger following the child misbehavior predicted physical punishment indicates that although few parents endorse the use of physical punishment by an angry parent, in reality, anger is a primary precipitant of it."[(p180)]

Another problem is that when you hit someone, you can miss. Mr. Peterson comments about accidentally hitting his son's private area. One of the authors saw a number of cases where a parent meant to "lightly swat" a child with something in "safe area," but the child moved and ended up with facial or eye injuries.

In addition, promotion of these kinds of physical punishment practices are also keeping parents from learning discipline strategies that actually are far superior in terms of results and do not result in this type of harm. Sadly, as a quote from the American Academy of Pediatrics nearly 20 years ago illustrates (Box 3.2),[52] this is not new information. The science on this is very clear—physical punishment just isn't a very practical or effective option in teaching or managing children.

Here we ask the reader to excuse us as we leave our objective balanced stance to offer a final note about corporal punishment and age. To our surprise as we were doing research for the book, a recent study of US parents indicates that spanking is fairly commonly used with infants.[53] We would like to make it absolutely clear that very young children should never, ever, be physically punished. Infants and toddlers have

---

BOX 3.2

THE AMERICAN ACADEMY OF PEDIATRICS AND CORPORAL PUNISHMENT

"Despite its common acceptance, and even advocacy for its use, spanking is a less effective strategy than time-out or removal of privileges for reducing undesired behavior in children. Although spanking may immediately reduce or stop an undesired behavior, its effectiveness decreases with subsequent use. The only way to maintain the initial effect of spanking is to systematically increase the intensity with which it is delivered, which can quickly escalate into abuse. Thus, at best, spanking is only effective when used in selective infrequent situations." American Academy of Pediatrics. (1998). Guidance on effective discipline. *Pediatrics, 101,* 726.

soft bones and skulls that haven't knitted together yet, which means that when a very young child is shaken or hit, serious consequences from fractures to permanent brain damage or even death can occur.[54,55]

CAN WE DO A BETTER JOB DEFINING AND RESPONDING TO PHYSICAL ABUSE?

Are there ways we can clarify the murky line between discipline and abuse? Coleman and colleagues[40] suggest there are, at least in terms of legal parameters. They suggest three metrics be used to assess whether an act is abuse: reasonableness (including understanding the child's behavior and developmental age), intent, and the likelihood of functional impairment. For example, a news story recently captured a mother in Baltimore hitting her apparently teenage son as she moved him off the streets after he threw rocks at police.[56] This was hailed as an example of positive parenting. Viewed according to Coleman and colleague's criteria, most might agree the amount of force was "reasonable," given the context and the age of the youth, the intent to get her son out of a possibly dangerous situation seems clear, and there was no apparent risk of functional impairment. In contrast, Mary Ellen's adoptive mother intended to hurt the child, the nature of the violence was clearly unreasonable, and there was potential for functional impairment. So it works for differentiating those two cases.

On the other hand, let's imagine a CPS referral made early on about the child that died in the story covered by CNN above.[51] She was 13, which is a "reasonable" age for corporal punishment in most states.[57] The parents reportedly intended to discipline. Death followed as a function of cumulative physical trauma and eventual exposure rather than a single serious blow.[51] So if a CPS call had been made after a single incident early on, Coleman and colleagues' approach might lead us to call this reasonable discipline even though the outcome was tragic. It is complicated.

Of course, from a prevention standpoint, Coleman and colleagues'[40] criteria cannot be used at all. It only works after the fact. There may be ways of better defining what is and isn't physical abuse after it occurs, but this will not help us understand which situations or set of risks may escalate to abuse.

What Policy Options Do We Have?

We could make corporal punishment illegal—a form of child abuse in all circumstances or specific to certain ages.[31] At least one legal scholar has suggested that states can and should pass laws against corporal punishment generally, and that this would likely be judged constitutional by the Supreme Court.[58] About 30 years ago,

Sweden changed its corporal punishment laws and engaged in a concerted effort to improve parent training and provide effective public service announcements. Approval for the use of corporal punishment went from 53% in 1965 to 11% about 30 years later, and the few existing studies of actual behavior indicate a similarly dramatic decline[59] in physical punishment and abuse. Many, however, would argue that banning corporal punishment by parents violates core American principles of the primacy of the family as well as any number of different and long-held cultural traditions within our population.[60–62] And, there are as we said, cases of physical abuse (like Mary Ellen's) that occur outside of corporal punishment.

Another option would be the funding of a widespread public awareness campaign of alternatives to and the risks of corporal punishment rather than calling corporal punishment abuse. There have been some attempts at this, and we are not really sure how well they work outside the Swedish example,[63] but it is an interesting idea.

Our View: It Isn't Just "Why Not"—It's Also "Why?"

After studying child maltreatment for decades and working in various roles related to prevention or intervention, it seems to us (the authors) that the question around corporal punishment has been incompletely framed. The debate to date has essentially been between whether it results in enough short- or long-term harm for concern and whether we have the right to tell others what to do. We think there are two excellent reasons to stop corporal punishment that are hard to argue with: First, it doesn't work as well as available alternatives. There has *never* been a scientifically validated effective parenting intervention that relies on physical punishment. Second, if improperly used or used in the context of other family risk factors, physical punishment can do accidental and serious harm.

CONCLUDING THOUGHTS

Is help available? Anthony Biglan, in *The Nurture Effect*,[64] does a good job of summarizing advances made in evidence-based parenting approaches from infancy through adolescence. Some parents may believe that such programs won't work on their children, particularly if those children have difficult temperaments or behavior disorders. But actually most current evidence-based parenting programs were designed *specifically* to work with difficult children. In addition to parenting approaches, there are educational approaches and even population-based public health approaches being developed and tested. We talk more about parenting intervention in chapters 9 and again in 11. For now, suffice it to say that, yes, help is available.

All parents struggle from time to time and can benefit from books or parenting classes or helpful social support. Parents who are already engaging in abusive or very high risk parenting behaviors need immediate help. If you have concerns about a child being physically abused, reporting these concerns to CPS is important. If there are parenting concerns but not current abuse, you can help a parent reach out to resources like 2-1-1 hotlines that connect people to specialized services depending on their specific needs. More generally, we, as a society, need to continue to wrestle with our views on what we call physical abuse and work toward improving prevention efforts and the systemic response after it occurs. For now, however, we turn to a very different parenting issue that focuses not on action but rather lack of action. So let's read on about child neglect.

4

What Neglect Is and Why It Isn't "Just Poverty"

AS WE MENTIONED IN CHAPTER 2, the original version of "Hansel and Gretel" involved their biological mother persuading her husband to abandon their children in the woods because they did not have enough food for them.[1] Not having enough food is not neglect, that's poverty. Choosing to abandon children to their death in the woods to solve your food problem, however, *is* considered neglect. This perspective is not new. By the dark ages there were already signs of seeing forms of neglect like this as wrongful behavior. The Visigothic code required parents to pay a child back in some way if, after being abandoned, they later made themselves known again to their parents—if they did not atone, the parents could be exiled.[2] Notice that neglect does not involve directly inflicting harm, it is an omission of care that could cause serious harm.

While poverty has been clearly associated with all forms of maltreatment,[3] it is most strongly associated with neglect.[4-8] We struggled with whether to talk about neglect alone in this chapter or combine it with a discussion of poverty. In the end, we decided that these issues are so intertwined that it is best to explore them together. So first we briefly discuss poverty (the topic of entire books by itself) and why it is related to, but not the same as, neglect. Then we move on to talk about neglect specifically.

THE ISSUE OF CHILD POVERTY

The idea that poverty is a serious problem for families is not new. It was a major concern of the first White House Conference on Children at the turn of the century (1909).[9] Later, in the 1960s, poverty was an integral (though less frequently discussed) part of the thinking behind the civil rights movement.

> Martin Luther King Jr was embarking on a campaign more specifically focused on poverty at the time of his death because he and others recognized it as such a serious social problem. . . . King was pushing an idea that might be considered among his most radical: Not only should poverty be eradicated, he argued, but everyone should be guaranteed an income that would prevent them from falling into poverty.[10]

So how are we progressing with ending poverty?

Child poverty dropped considerably during the mid-20th century, but has been fairly stable for the last 50 years. Poverty varies a great deal by race in America. Overall, Black, Hispanic and Native American children are much more likely to live in poverty than Whites and Asians. Figure 4.1 shows the percentages of poor children by race since 1980.[11] As the figure shows, more than one in three Hispanic and Black children currently live in poverty.

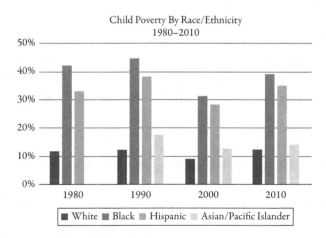

FIGURE 4.1 Percentage of Poor Children by Race since 1980

What Has Poverty Got to Do with Child Maltreatment?

Sometimes we hear that "maltreatment" is just a word people have come up with to describe the behaviors of poor parents. In other words, the link between poverty and maltreatment is merely an illusion based on some type of social class bias. Many people, including some child abuse scholars, supported this view in the past. In the last few decades, it has become clear that poverty and maltreatment are not the same,[12] but poverty does increase the risk of all forms of abusive or neglectful behaviors.[3,7,13–15] Keep in mind we are talking about risk again, not predestination. While poverty increases the risk of child maltreatment, most parents who are poor do not maltreat their children.

In the first chapter we introduced the story of the "Old Woman in the Shoe," who had too many children to be able to adequately care for them. This seems a clear reference to poverty, as she also has to send them to bed with only broth for dinner. We feel empathy for the woman's obvious distress, but then modern reader almost certainly wonders why she "whipped them all soundly." Did poverty cause her to beat her children? It's not that simple. There are a lot of ways in which poverty makes it difficult to parent. Let's revisit the story of Mary Ellen to think about this further.

Poverty and depression caused Mary Ellen's mother's descent into alcoholism; this could have resulted in her becoming neglectful or abusive, but the second caregiver intervened and took over her care. Poverty forces the second caregiver to relinquish Mary Ellen to the poorhouse (this is not abandonment, as she is seeking good care for the child). Eventually, Mary Ellen ends up in a situation where her adoptive mother, albeit not wealthy, has enough means to care for the child. In addition to beating her, she chooses to neglect Mary Ellen's need for education, clothing, and sufficient food. This choice not to provide care is key to differentiating poverty and maltreatment. Sometimes this is an active choice, like Mary Ellen's adoptive mother. Sometimes it is a passive choice that stems from other problems associated with poverty, like the alcoholism of Mary Ellen's mother, that lead to a parent's incapacity.

How Might Poverty Lead To Maltreatment?

There are two main lines of thought. First, poverty can be overwhelming and degrade someone's ability to parent. The second idea is that both poverty and maltreatment are caused by a third factor. Actually, either of these explanations may be true—just for different families.

Money Is Protective

Poverty means not having some of the resources that most of us depend on to adequately raise our child. Among these are medical and child care, the ability to hire help (such as a babysitter) in times of emergency or high stress, reliable transportation, and safe housing.[16] While it may be true that "Money can't buy happiness," it can certainly buy quality day care or fix a flat tire.

If you are a family with two children living in poverty, what does this look like? The most recent federal poverty guideline for a family of four is an annual gross income of $24,250.[17] That translates to about $2,020 a month. Without government benefits, let's see what your family can afford. Although you won't pay income tax, there is still some Social Security and Medicaid withholding –about $121.00 per month. In the United States, the median gross rent is $905.00 per month.[18] Now you have utilities and phone costs, either public transport or a vehicle payment (or at least occasional repairs and gas). Let's say that you only use public transportation and get a pass for $20.00. Then let's be really conservative and only spend another $200 total per month for utilities.[19] It's hard to imagine spending less on food than the lowest national food stamp amount of $611.00 a month.[20] This leaves about $160.00 a month to cover everything else from child care to clothes, to diapers, and so forth. In fact, the official poverty level is so low that children can qualify for federal school lunch programs with family incomes between 125% and 185% of this level.[21]

How much you earn also impacts where you live. Living in a low-income neighborhood may compound the already serious effects of individual poverty.[22] Figure 4.2 illustrates the overlap in poverty, violent crime, lower education levels, and fire department calls in Springfield, Missouri. In this figure, darker colors are worse. Clearly the lived experience is different by neighborhood.

Poverty Causes Stress

Economic hardship has been found to place increased strain on caregivers and children as well as adult relationships, all of which can impair parenting.[23–26] As we discussed in the last chapter, stress without commensurate resources and coping skills can alter our behavior. For some this may lead to violence, but for others like Mary Ellen's biological mother, it may lead to depression or unhealthy coping approaches that lead to one neglecting the care of one's children. A recent article about two families losing children to gun violence in high-poverty neighborhoods describes the overwhelming situation:

> In the months that followed Jamyla's death, the women have confronted crime, lack of transportation, health issues, a loss of utilities and debt. At times they are able to offer the kind of love and support experts say can help children avoid the dangers of toxic stress. . . . Other times, they find themselves paralyzed by their situations and on the edge of "losing it."[26]

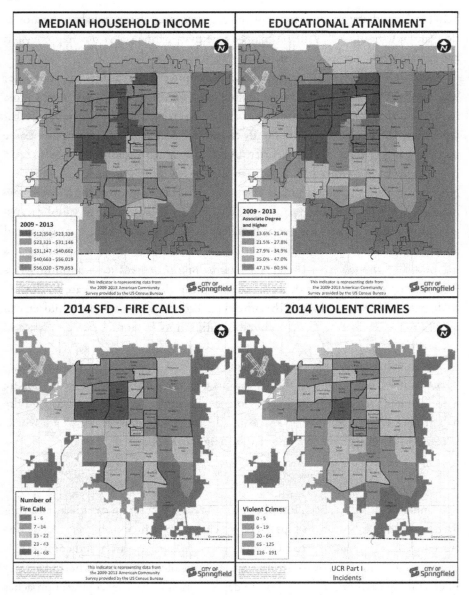

FIGURE 4.2 Geographic Overlap in Income, Educational Achievement, Fire Calls and Violent Crime

While traditionally much of the focus on poverty and parenting has been on urban areas, a recent study of rural poverty indicates that there is a similar path between early family hardship, maternal depression, and report of poor health (without prior underlying illness) as well as reduced sensitivity in parenting behaviors.[27]

So back to our "old woman in the shoe." Clearly the shoe is a tiny living space for so many children; she is tired and overwhelmed and is having difficulty feeding them. Maybe at some point she will become paralyzed like the woman in the news story. If that does not resolve or other help does not arrive, it is a recipe for neglect.

Poverty as a Manifestation of Underlying Problems

Another line of thought is that sometimes preexisting issues place a parent at risk of both poverty and abusing or neglecting their children.[28,29] For example, let us imagine a young girl becomes a parent at age 16. Becoming a parent as a teenager decreases your likelihood of completing your education, which severely impacts earnings.[30] You may not yet know much about parenting or child development and may not be emotionally ready to handle the stresses of parenting. The consequences of becoming a teen parent may be both ongoing poverty and maltreating behaviors.[31]

CAN WE TELL THE DIFFERENCE BETWEEN POVERTY AND MALTREATMENT?

Scientists, activists, and the public sometimes critique child protective services (CPS) for having high proportions of low-income families on their caseloads.[24,32] Some worry that low-income families are more visible because of their involvement in service systems. Therefore, low-income families are reported more than medium- to high-income families. This is one type of "surveillance bias." This idea is simple, elegant, and just doesn't pan out.

First, and most importantly, CPS investigators only respond to the calls that other people make. Blaming CPS for the overrepresentation of low-income families among reported cases is like blaming a firefighter for spending his time putting out fires in the part of town where all the 911 calls are coming from. Nationally, CPS does screen out about 40% of all calls they receive[33] and could perhaps favor investigation of the poor that are reported, but we have no evidence this happens. The person screening the report does not inquire about income, the report has to include information that meets the state definitions of possible maltreatment and harm and, as you will recall from chapter 2, some states do not screen out any reports (according to national data) and others screen out most.

Okay, so what about calls made by other service systems that serve the poor? If low-income families are being differentially watched by professionals providing poverty-related services (income assistance, free health clinics, etc.), then they should have very high numbers of reports by these kinds of reporters. Mandated reporters (recall from chapter 2 that most professionals are required to report) do make about 60% of all reports, but the kinds of reporters who are poverty-related service providers are a fairly small portion of all reporters—for example, *all* social service and medical sources combined only account for about 20% of all reports.[33] There just aren't enough reports from these sources to drive the massive overrepresentation of the poor in official records.

There are a few other checks we can do. First, if poor people were being reported more just because of surveillance by mandated reporters, then there would have to be a much higher proportion of mandated reporters among all reports for poor people when compared to all reports for wealthier people. There isn't. In fact, richer people have a slightly higher proportion of reports from mandated reporters than do poorer people.[29] Second, if reports are merely made because some low-income families are unlucky and are reported for no other reason than they are poor, then you would expect the outcomes for poor and reported children to be pretty similar to poor and not-reported children. Across a number of behavioral and health outcomes this is simply not the case.[12]

SO WHAT IS CHILD NEGLECT?

Neglect is the most common form of maltreatment, being present in over three-quarters of reports nationwide[33]—a trend that has been consistent for some time.[34] If a child is reported more than once, neglect is often present in subsequent reports no matter the type of maltreatment the first report included.[35] Neglect is often broken down into separate types, as shown in Table 4.1. However, as illustrated by the shaded area, not all types of neglect are "reportable" in a given state.[36]

At first glance, some of the examples in Table 4.1 may seem utterly trivial. For example, under the category of "medical neglect," we see "delaying healthcare." This is not referring to an occasional missed dental check-up or forgetting to get your child a flu shot. This category includes children whose health has been severely impacted (e.g., stunted growth, severe untreated cavities resulting in an abscess, or lack of treatment for a serious injury or illness). Similarly, lack of supervision (the most common kind of neglect by far) is only an issue when there has been or there is significant potential for harm- such as a 2-year old wandering in the street alone. Another term that is sometimes used by CPS workers related to neglect is "dirty house." This is not referring to what your kitchen may look like if you didn't have time to do dishes for a day, but referring to conditions like those noted in a case study:[37]

"The house was cluttered with dirty clothes, debris, and dirty dishes. Dog feces were found in the children's bedroom. One bathroom had a toilet that was broken, and dirty clothes were piled in the bathtub."[(p379)]

TABLE 4.1

General Definitions of Child Neglect Subtypes

Category	Overall definition
Physical neglect	Abandoning the child or refusing to accept custody; not providing for basic needs like nutrition, hygiene, or appropriate clothing
Medical neglect	Delaying or denying recommended healthcare for the child
Inadequate supervision	Leaving the child unsupervised (depending on length of time and child's age/maturity); not protecting the child from safety hazards, providing inadequate caregivers, or engaging in harmful behavior
The following are only considered neglect in certain states	
Emotional neglect	Isolating the child; not providing affection or emotional support; exposing the child to domestic violence or substance abuse
Educational neglect	Failing to enroll the child in school or homeschool; ignoring special education needs; permitting chronic absenteeism from school

Despite our argument that poverty and maltreatment are not the same, it can be challenging sometimes to disentangle poverty and neglect in a given case. In the definition used by the National Child Abuse and Neglect Data system, neglect includes lack of care even though the parent is able to do so or offered resources to be able to do so and still does not. You may live in a state where the law makes the divide between poverty and neglect explicit. For example in Delaware: "Neglect" or "neglected child" means that a person who is responsible for the care, custody, and/or control of the child has the ability and financial means to provide for the care of the child but doesn't.[36] Let's look at a recent news report that helps illustrate what neglect involving basic needs, hygiene, educational neglect, and the so-called dirty house can look like in its most extreme form (a word of warning, this may be hard to read).

PLANT CITY—The family had lived in the rundown rental house for almost three years when someone first saw a child's face in the window. A little girl, pale, with dark eyes, lifted a dirty blanket above the broken glass and peered out, one neighbor remembered. Everyone knew a woman lived in the house with her boyfriend and two adult sons. But they had never seen a child there, had never noticed anyone playing in the overgrown yard. The girl looked young, 5 or 6, and thin. Too thin. Her cheeks seemed sunken; her eyes were lost. The child stared into the square of sunlight, then slipped away. Months went by. The face never reappeared. Just before noon on July 13, 2005, a Plant City police car pulled up outside that shattered window. Two officers went into the house—and one stumbled back out. Clutching his stomach, the rookie retched in the weeds. Plant City Detective Mark Holste had been on the force for 18 years when he and his young partner were sent to the house on Old Sydney Road to stand by during a child abuse investigation. Someone had finally called the police. They found a car parked outside. The driver's door was open and a woman was slumped over in her seat, sobbing. She was an investigator for the Florida Department of Children and Families. . . .

She lay on a torn, moldy mattress on the floor. She was curled on her side, long legs tucked into her emaciated chest. Her ribs and collarbone jutted out; one skinny arm was slung over her face; her black hair was matted, crawling with lice. Insect bites, rashes and sores pocked her skin. Though she looked old enough to be in school, she was naked—except for a swollen diaper.[38]

Of course, thankfully, most cases are nowhere near this severe. Danielle's story, however, does indicate issues that extend far beyond lacking financial resources and go far beyond a temporary lapse in care. None of the rest of the family is starving and the other adult children of the parents do not appear to have suffered a similar circumstance (which is not typical) . . . something else is wrong.

WHY IS NEGLECT SUCH A PROBLEM?

It may come as a surprise to many, but even less severe cases of neglect can result in pretty devastating consequences. Research suggests that the outcomes that can follow neglect are just as bad as they are for physical abuse or sexual abuse.[39,40] Neglect is the most common form of maltreatment noted in fatal child maltreatment cases, with over 80% of fatal maltreatment including issues of neglect alone or in combination with other maltreatment types.[33] Nor is the recognition of neglect as a serious problem a new concept; such concerns were commonly raised in the early years of the child welfare movement over 100 years ago.[41]

To better understand why neglect can be so damaging, let's turn briefly to a discussion of basic human development. In the mid-20th century, a psychologist named Abraham Maslow[42] developed a visual hierarchy of needs that many readers have probably seen before (see Figure 4.3). The lower levels reflect basic needs that must be satisfied in order to move to the upper levels. This idea and picture has endured perhaps in part because of its common sense. It makes sense that most people can't move on to achieving abstract life goals while they're starving. Such a fact is even more pronounced for children.

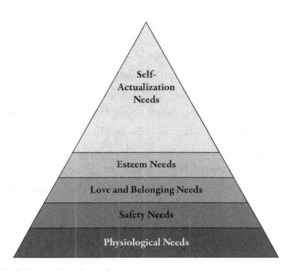

FIGURE 4.3 Maslow's Hierarchy of Needs

Neglect includes varying degrees of deprivation of needs in the bottom three layers of the pyramid. Compared to other mammals, humans are especially vulnerable to various kinds of deprivation early in life. Unlike many other animals, humans are born with relatively underdeveloped brains. Perhaps you have seen a calf born on a farm or a fawn born on a nature show. Within minutes the young animal is up and walking and figuring out how to nurse. In contrast, people take much longer to learn and need assistance with learning the most basic things, how to grab objects, move around, and interact with others. Human brains take decades to develop (longer than the entire life span of most mammals) and so physical and psychological nurturance is critically important for us. Of course, the importance of nurturance is not limited to the early years, but it is easiest to start thinking about the consequences of neglect with young children.

Basic Needs: Brain Development, Stimulation,
and Later Intelligence

While the brain continues to develop in significant ways throughout adulthood, there are particularly important timeframes often called *critical periods*. A critical period is a time frame during which absence of proper care and input may lead to delays that are difficult or impossible to make up for later. The well-known "thalidomide babies" of the late 1950s are a good example of a critical period in physical development. If thalidomide was taken by a pregnant woman during the critical period for fetal limb development, those limbs never formed.[43] Critical periods also exist for certain aspects of brain development.

Figure 4.4 compares images of brains of a typical 3-year-old child next to a similarly aged child who experienced severe neglect in a Romanian orphanage during their earliest years. This level of utter deprivation of needed stimulation is not typical in cases of neglect in the US, but what about Danielle? Danielle was adopted by a loving family and has no detectable underlying physiological disability, but displays significant difficulties with attachment to others and with language.[38] Although she was over 6 years old when found, hospital staff reported, "she couldn't chew or swallow solid food. . . . She didn't know how to hold a doll, didn't understand peek-a-boo." Danielle may always have significant deficits because certain critical periods in her neural development passed and, even with therapy and a loving home, are beyond our current ability to revisit.

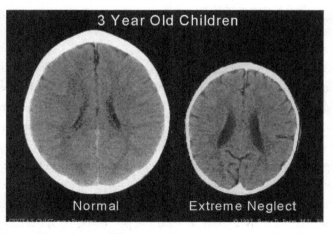

FIGURE 4.4 Brain of Typical 3-year-old Compared to a 3-year-old Severely Neglected Romanian Child

The good news? Most parents attempt to provide their young children with new experiences such as going outside, talking to them or reading to them, or providing toys that make noise or have different textures. These activities have a profound impact on the developing brain. Further, most development is not associated with narrow critical periods. In many areas our brains remain "plastic," meaning that experiences continue to shape our brain. Only a couple of decades ago, many evidence-based texts and articles would have said our brains were "mostly done" by adolescence, but that is no longer believed to be the case.[44] While this plasticity does not appear to apply to certain basic skills, some exciting work is being done trying to see whether such windows can be reopened.[45] For now, we have a long way to go before we can address the harm caused by the deprivation that Danielle experienced. While most children do not experience such extreme conditions, even poverty alone has been found to impact brain development, especially in the absence of nurturing behavior.[46]

Basic Needs: Physical Development and Health

Children need medical care for both preventive purposes (like vaccinations) or for treatment of conditions like injury or illness. While medical neglect is rare compared to other forms of neglect (about 3% of all cases, 7% of fatal maltreatment cases) it does occur.[33] According to the news account, Danielle had never seen a doctor. "She weighed 46 pounds. She was malnourished and anemic."[38] Lack of appropriate nutrition, even apart from deficits in parenting, can impact neurological and physical development.[47,48]

Children also require a certain level of cleanliness or hygiene in their environment. Here we refer back to that phrase "dirty house." If you were to glance at our family room on any given day you might notice a pressing need to sweep up the dog hair from our ever-shedding furry family members, scattered DVDs needing to be put away or even, a pair of dirty socks (son's, husband's?) that did not make it to the hamper. This is not what "dirty house" means to a CPS worker. Let us revisit the description of Danielle's environment.

> "The pile of dirty diapers in that room must have been 4 feet high," the detective said. "The glass in the window had been broken, and that child was just lying there, surrounded by her own excrement and bugs."[38]

At what point does messiness become neglect? As noted in a court review of a California child protection case, "chronic messiness by itself and apart from any unsanitary conditions or resulting illness or accident is not clear and convincing evidence of a substantial risk of harm."[49] Of course, people can hold differing opinions about where to draw the line between housing that is so dirty that it poses a risk to a child and what is not ideal but acceptable. During training to be a CPS worker, one of the authors was shown a series of pictures of a very, very dirty house, with rotting food, garbage piled everywhere, and other things best left unmentioned. The trainers made the point that the family court judge was not willing to rule that the house was severe enough to pose a risk to the child, and since the family was uncooperative, the case was dropped. On a subsequent visit a live rattlesnake was found inside the home. At that point, the judge's opinion changed.

Safety Needs: Structure and Guidance

Supervisory neglect is the most commonly reported type of neglect.[33,35] We've all noticed that child in the supermarket whose parent seems not to have told them to avoid pulling things off the shelves. This, albeit annoying, is not what lack of supervision means in CPS. Supervisory neglect occurs when lack of normative expected parental supervision places a child at serious risk of harm. Not everyone will agree when such behaviors cross this line.[50] For example, the legal standard for when a child can be left alone is rarely set by age but rather ability.[51]

Young children can seem like a "danger magnet," leading to a host of child-proofing products like covers for electrical outlets, rubber furniture bumpers, cabinet door locks, and gates for stairs. Why? Because a young child's "job" is to explore. Perhaps the most well-known expert on child development, Jean Piaget, famously said, "Play is the work of childhood." Once children are mobile there is a natural curiosity about their environment that kicks in prior to their brains being developed enough to understand what is dangerous. Parental supervision is a critical in preventing serious harm like suffocation, drowning, and poisoning. Dangers also change in relation to the environment. For example, accidental crushing by flat-screen TVs has become a new threat with the advent of large but thin TVs that can be easily pulled over.[52] Supervision, however, remains an important part of parenting, even as the child becomes more capable of avoiding physical threats.

Despite differences in opinion about when lack of supervision should be a child protection issue, the recognition of the importance of supervision is not a new, "majority culture" idea. Nor is the need for supervision limited to very young children. The following is an excerpt from a Native American legend that illustrates the idea of lack of supervision for older children.[53]

"The Deserted Children"
There was a camp. All the children went off to play. They went to some distance. Then one man said, "Let us abandon the children. Lift the ends of your

tent-poles and travois when you go, so that there will be no trail." Then the people went off. After a time the oldest girl amongst the children sent the others back to the camp to get something to eat. The children found the camp gone, the fires out, and only ashes about. They cried, and wandered about at random. The oldest girl said, "Let us go toward the river." They found a trail leading across the river, and forded the river there. Then one of the girls found a tent-pole. As they went along, she cried, "My mother, here is your tent-pole." "Bring my tent-pole here!" shouted an old woman loudly from out of the timber. The children went towards her.

They found that she was an old woman who lived alone. They entered her tent. At night they were tired. The old woman told them all to sleep with their heads toward the fire. One little girl who had a small brother pretended to sleep, but did not. The old woman watched if all were asleep. Then she put her foot in the fire. It became red hot. Then she proceeds to kill the children one by one. . . . The little girl jumped up, saying, "My grandmother, let me live with you and work for you. I will bring wood and water for you." Then the old woman allowed her and her little brother to live.

What is interesting about this story is that it highlights two reasons why even older children are dependent on adults. Not only do they still need help with shelter and obtaining food, but they also require protection from bad things, like the evil old woman, in the wider environment. Not wanting to leave the reader hanging regarding the folk story, it has a happy, if rather typically violent ending for children in an early folk tale. The children eventually get rescued by nature, and the evil woman gets eaten by a water monster.

Social Needs: Nurturing and Attachment Theory

Attachment theory is credited to Mary Ainsworth and John Bowlby,[54] who, interestingly enough, were writing about the need for a secure attachment between caregivers and infants about the same time the Kempe article alerted us to child abuse. Attachment is particularly related to responsiveness to a child's needs and nurturing during the early years of life.[55] Perhaps you saw some variant of the picture in Figure 4.5 in a high school or a college psychology course, or perhaps in the popular book *Love at Goon Park*. The image shows one of Harlow's baby monkeys clinging to a parent surrogate that is covered in a soft, fuzzy towel, instead of clinging to the one that provides food. This surprised scientists, who felt that the monkey would cling to the wire mother given the strong survival drive related to food. This remarkable need for the feeling of comfort per se was a way in which Harlow (the scientist who

FIGURE 4.5 One of Harlow's Monkeys

conducted the experiment) illustrated the deep-seated need for attachment. Those of Harlow's monkeys that were denied a comforting parental figure to attach to developed a range of very unpleasant health and behavioral outcomes. Similarly, in humans, a variety of later relationship problems have been associated with insecure attachment.[56–58]

Some research suggests neglected children are more likely to have insecure and/or disorganized attachments[59] compared with nonneglected children. This is particularly likely for children like Danielle who experience neglect for a very long time with no other positive caregiver relationships.

NEGLECTING NEGLECT?

Hopefully now you have a better idea of what neglect is and why we should be concerned. Given the broad potential impacts of neglect across various areas of development (i.e., cognitive, emotional, physical, etc.) it is not surprising that neglect has been linked to later cognitive problems, poor school performance, delinquency, relationship issues, and mental health problems.[39,60–63] What can be done about it? Unfortunately, despite the prevalence of neglect and its relevance to child development, neglect has received relatively little attention in policy and research compared to other forms of maltreatment. This has popularly been termed the "neglect of neglect."[64]

Another problem is that neglect tends to happen in families also experiencing other forms of maltreatment either simultaneously or over time.[35,65,66] Types of maltreatment over time have been described as a "rolling iceberg."[35] If you look at an iceberg for long enough, it will often roll over as it melts unevenly. The same iceberg can appear completely different as what was underwater now becomes visible. Second and later reports to CPS will often contain different forms of maltreatment. No matter what type the first report mentioned (e.g., sexual or physical abuse) the second report (if there is one) is most likely to be neglect.[35] It's not clear whether subsequent types were always there (like the submerged part of the iceberg) or whether new forms of maltreatment emerge over time. It's likely a bit of both.

What Do Neglecting Families Look Like?

Danielle's story is an extreme example of child neglect. So what is going on in most families that neglect their children—besides poverty?[8] In a sample of 1,089 families in which both biological parents resided in the home when the target child was between 3 and 5 years old, rates of paternal and maternal depression were twice as high in families in which child neglect was present.[67] Among women, neglecting behaviors were found to be related to current drug use, maternal history of sexual abuse, low self-reported perceptions about parenting skills, and difficulty obtaining child care.[68] Negative social relationships with family, domestic violence, and increased social isolation predicted substantiation of neglect in another study.[69] Even within an entirely lower income study sample, children reported for neglect lived in substantially poorer neighborhoods and the primary caregiver was less likely to have completed high school.[5]

WHAT SHOULD WE DO ABOUT NEGLECT?

While neglect is not poverty, poverty makes it hard to parent and has a number of negative effects for children. Emerging research indicates that even poverty alone without maltreatment can create long-term changes in the developing brain.[70,71] This makes the fact that neglect and poverty tend to co-occur particularly disturbing. So what should we do?

Almost all of the issues mentioned here fall outside the realm of what CPS can directly provide. This makes an effective response complex and dependent on the availability of quality services for the family in the community. Services may also be needed on an ongoing basis to adequately address family functioning.[72] This can be a barrier to getting people the help they need, since longer-term services are costly, but, not to be too repetitive, the cost of current poor outcomes associated with maltreatment is likely much greater. Currently, only one program has received enough research attention to be considered effective with families reported for neglect, Safecare.[73] Child neglect prevention programs exist,[74] but we need more research done to understand how effective they are.

What would happen if fewer people were poor? There is new evidence that economic interventions can improve child outcomes[75] and even reduce the risk of maltreatment.[76] We talk more about these ideas in chapter 11, but suffice it to say that we have done surprisingly little work in terms of intervening to attempt to remediate poverty compared to the volume of work linking poverty to poor outcomes. That being said, while economic intervention may help a good deal of families avoid neglecting behavior, there are cases like Danielle's and others in which significant issues outside poverty exist.

In the meantime, talking about the realities of neglect is a good place to start. It is important to help others understand that neglect is not just poverty and that its consequences can be severe and long-lasting. Suffice it to say that it is time to end our "neglect of neglect" and this will require your help.

5

Child Sexual Abuse

"STRANGER DANGER" OR A DANGER CLOSER TO HOME?

WHEN MOST PEOPLE hear the words "sexual abuse," they think of a threat from outside the family. Children's stories referencing sexual abuse and sexual assault date back hundreds of years. "Little Red Riding Hood" (written by Charles Perrault in the late 1600s) is probably familiar to most readers. A young girl in a red cloak is being sent on a path through the woods by her mother to visit and provide food for a sick grandmother (Figure 5.1). Her mother warns her to stay strictly to the path and her task. Along the way she is tricked into talking to a wolf, who learns about her destination. The wolf uses this information to get ahead of her to attack and possibly eat her—depending on the version. Modern commentators point to Perrault's story as a veiled reference to the sexual assault risks faced by young girls centuries ago.[1]

"Sexual abuse" is a form of child maltreatment perpetrated by someone who has "care, custody or control" of a child (a parent or relative, for example) while "sexual assault" is a crime perpetrated by someone who is not a caretaker (an acquaintance or stranger). We tend to pay more attention to prevention and even popular discussion of children being sexually assaulted. For example, it is much less likely that you are familiar with Grimm's story, written about 200 years after Little Red Riding Hood, called "All Kinds of Fur." This story is about incest—another word for sexual abuse.[2] In this story, a king's wife lays dying and makes him promise that he will only remarry if he finds someone equal to her in beauty. After a period of mourning the king realizes that his young daughter is the only person who is sufficiently beautiful and therefore a suitable choice. The court advisors are appalled, signifying

FIGURE 5.1 The Tale of Little Red Riding Hood: An Early Attempt to Protect Young Girls?

recognition of child sexual abuse as wrong even then. The daughter tries to evade him, then attempts to run away, and finally has no choice but to marry him (for the complete story, see http://www.pitt.edu/~dash/grimmo65.html). Clearly the princess has fewer options for self-protection than the young girl leaving to see her grandmother.

As pointed out by Professor Mintz of Columbia University, child sexual abuse is not new,[3] but the contemporary discussion of child sexual abuse has been greatly confused with sexual assault by strangers. This has significant consequences regarding how our society sees both. For example, a good proportion of the child sexual abuse prevention work to date trains children to avoid strangers, not members of their family.[4]

The situation is reminiscent of an old joke. A man walking down a city street happens upon a stranger who is on his hands and knees under a lamppost. The traveler asks the man, "What are you doing?" and the man on the pavement says, "Looking for my keys." The traveler offers to help look for the keys and soon both men are on the ground. After several minutes of searching, the newcomer asks, "When did you last see your keys?" To which the first man responds, "When I dropped them in that dark alley over there." The helper then asks, "Why aren't we looking over there?" And the reply is, "The light is better here and it is easier to search." Similarly, it is easier to think about preventing or intervening following sexual actions toward a child when the perpetrator is a stranger (or a wolf) than when the perpetrator is someone a child trusts (like the king), often in their own home. Addressing the prevention of and intervention following child sexual abuse requires that we look for "the keys" in the dark alley rather than where it is easier to see.

WHAT IS CHILD SEXUAL ABUSE?

Child sexual *abuse* and sexual *assault* may involve similar physical actions but are quite different socially and legally. If you molest your own child, that's child sexual abuse. If you molest someone else's child, that's sexual assault. A nearly identical situation exists in differentiating physical abuse (e.g., hitting your own child) from physical assault (e.g., hitting someone else's child). While most of the time the abuse is at the hands of an adult, abuse by a sibling (we look at a recent example of that in a bit) can also fall under the category of sexual abuse.

Child protective services (CPS) generally does not deal with sexual assault cases because these are considered crimes—handled by the police. Like so many other things we have talked about so far, however, there are exceptions. CPS might be involved in a sexual assault case if there is a need to check out the alleged perpetrator's own children's safety. CPS could be involved if there is an allegation that a sexual assault occurred due to lack of supervision by a parent (which would actually be a neglect case). Finally, CPS is sometimes involved in cases you might have heard called "statutory rape."

Not all sex involving minors is considered abuse (or assault) requiring outside intervention.[5] For example, about half of all American girls report having consensual intercourse by age 18 with someone outside their family.[6] In most states, a child cannot consent to sex prior to age 16, although that depends on the age of the two individuals having sex.[7] If the age difference is too large or one is an adult and another a teenager, this may be classified as "statutory rape" and may be reported to CPS, law enforcement, or both, depending on the state. Sometimes this is classified as child sexual abuse if it is perpetrated or allowed by a person who is responsible for a child's care.[8] Knowing what is not legal and must be reported to CPS or law enforcement can be ridiculously complicated. For example, in California, if two 13-year-olds have sex, that does not have to be reported under the law. If one of them has a birthday the next day and they are again intimate, this is not legal and mandated reporters are required to report. Now if the younger person has a birthday on the following day and they once again have sex while the same age, then no report is required.[9]

What about marriage, as in the story of the king and his daughter? Child marriage remains an accepted practice in some cultures, despite the custom being labeled as abusive by UNICEF due to issues of age and consent.[10] In the United States, the age at which you can marry does vary a bit by state, but in most cases if you are under 18 you need a parent's or a judge's consent.[11] In the United States underage marriage, if such consent is obtained, would not be abuse.

Putting aside issues of consent and age, there is variation in what specific acts are labeled child sexual abuse in the United States. Several states specify various acts such as fondling, oral sex, intercourse, and so forth, as sexual abuse. Sometimes, sexual exploitation is also included. Sexual exploitation includes allowing a child to engage in prostitution or in the production of child pornography or similar acts. In seven states, the definition of sexual abuse includes trafficking of children for sexual purposes.[12] In cases of child sexual abuse, however, sex trafficking (children required to do sexual acts for money or other needs) refers to the child's caregiver being the controlling party, not trafficking by a stranger.

The response to child sexual abuse in determining harm differs from other forms of maltreatment. As we noted in chapter 3, there is disagreement about how much force is used and what kind of harm must occur before something like corporal punishment is deemed physical abuse. Sexual abuse isn't like that. There's a pretty clear agreement in our society, and in most societies, that any sexually motivated act (from exposure to pornography to intercourse) toward a child is wrong. Injury per se is not required to consider child sexual abuse serious.

How Often Does Sexual Abuse Occur Compared to Sexual Assault?

We wish it were easy to provide a clear-cut answer to how often child sexual abuse occurs, but this is complicated by how often our measures combine child sexual assault and child sexual abuse. Sexual abuse may be the least well understood form of child maltreatment in a statistical sense. For example, an article in *Lancet*, one of the world's premier scientific journals, reported that child sexual abuse happens to between 2% and 62% of women.[12] Providing such a huge range is basically the same as saying, "We have no clue whatsoever." You would think that this appalling lack of specificity might be due to children being afraid to disclose abuse. Actually that isn't the main problem. The main problem is how it's measured. Imagine asking three different questions:

1. Did you have sex prior to becoming an adult? or
2. Did you have sex with an adult family member prior to age 18? or
3. Were you molested or sexually exploited in any way by a parent when you were a child?

Someone responding to the first question might conceivably report sexual assault, sexual abuse, and/or consensual sex. The second question excludes consensual sex, but this could still be assault if the adult family member did not live with them— say a visiting cousin. The third question is probably better, but whom do we ask? If I was abused at a very young age, I might not remember. When individuals who self-reported child sexual abuse changed their mind in a subsequent survey were asked why, misunderstanding questions was one of the most common reasons.[13] We could ask parents, but, if the parent is the perpetrator, will they report? Let's look at some of the best estimates we have.

We start with cases that are formally reported to the police. The federal government's National Incident Based Reporting System (NIBRS) tracks incidents of sexual assault and child sexual abuse reported to the police. This probably includes about a third to a half of all actual cases, possibly less for child sexual abuse. Table 5.1 shows some of these data from the most recent report we could find (2000) that breaks this down by age and relationship to the perpetrator.[14] You can see that very few reported sexual assaults against children are carried out by strangers—about 7%, or 1 in 16. Strangers constitute a far larger proportion of assaults against adults (about a quarter). Other research tells us that for younger children, about half of all sexual acts against children are committed by family members (child sexual abuse), but for teens, this changes. About two-thirds of sexual acts perpetrated against teens are committed by acquaintances (assault not abuse), and this continues into adulthood.[15]

Several studies provide estimates of sexual abuse that also include assault. The National Crime Victimization Survey shows rates of rape/sexual assault to be about 2 or 3 per year (depending on age) per 1,000 children between 12 and 17 years of age.[16] Of course this omits younger children, and we can't disentangle abuse from assault without information about the perpetrator. A recent large-scale review of 120

TABLE 5.1

Offenders

| Victim Age | Total | Offenders | | |
		Family Member	Acquaintance	Stranger
All victims	**100.0%**	**26.7%**	**59.6%**	**13.8%**
Juveniles	**100.0%**	**34.2%**	**58.7%**	**7.0%**
0 to 5	100.0	48.6	48.3	3.1
6 to 11	100.0	42.4	52.9	4.7
12 to 17	100.0	24.3	66.0	9.8
Adults	**100.0%**	**11.5%**	**61.1%**	**27.3%**
18 to 24	100.0	9.8	66.5	23.7
Above 24	100.0	12.8	57.1	30.1

studies of self-report of sexual abuse found an average prevalence of 20% for women and about 8% for men for North America (which includes Canada).[17] Again, it is not clear whether the studies reviewed limited questions to familial abuse or might have included actions by other adults. Finkelhor and colleagues[15] conducted a national phone survey with adolescents and reported a rate of 26.6% for females and 5.1% for males, but the number includes both childhood sexual assault and abuse.

Another way to measure child sexual abuse is to ask mandated reporters about how often they see sexual abuse or look at official reports to CPS. The most recent National Incidence Study (NIS-4) asked mandated reporters how often they encountered child sexual abuse and found a rate of .6 per 1,000 boys and 3.8 per 1,000 girls within a 1-year time frame.[18] The same study reported that 37% of cases involved a biological parent, another 23% involved a nonbiological parent or partner, and 40% involved an unrelated person.[18] It is difficult to know whether the cases involving the unrelated person should have been labeled assault rather than abuse. The NIS-4 estimate is about twice the 57,286 officially substantiated sexual abuse reports in the annual national child maltreatment report.[19] Both of these sources are reporting single-year estimates. A more recent analysis of official reports linked over multiple years indicates a prevalence of close to 6% for females and close to 3% for males prior to age 18.[20]

Why are official report rates so much lower than self-report? Some estimate that perhaps a third to a half of all sexual abuse cases are reported to CPS.[19] Why? While we said a child's willingness to report was not the "main" problem leading to variations in rates of known sexual abuse, it is still a problem. As is true of any kind of maltreatment, sometimes no one suspects and a child says nothing (we talk about

this more in chapter 8). Even if someone suspects abuse and tries to elicit information from a child, a child may not disclose. It is unclear how often this occurs.[21] So
based on comparing self-report and multiyear analyses of sentinel reports, we are left
with an estimated prevalence for sexual abuse in the range of 6%–20% of girls and
3%–8% for boys. This is more specific than the range in the Johnson[12] article, but it
is still wider than we would like.

Who Is Most at Risk for Sexual Victimization?

We use the word "victimization" here, because it is difficult to separate sexual assault
from sexual abuse in terms of research on who is at risk. Figure 5.2 shows that in
sexual assault data from about 16 years ago,[14] younger boys are at higher risk than
older boys, and older girls are at the highest risk of all. It is interesting to note that for
both males and females, there is a peak vulnerability during the preschool years (age
4) that continues to decline for males, but that peaks again for girls early in their
teen years. These data come as a surprise to most people, who believe that young
adult women, not teenage girls, are at higher risk of sexual victimization. We don't
often think about it this way, but it can be fairly claimed that "children are the most
victimized segment of the population."[22] One more caveat, emerging research suggests that while females are generally more at risk, among sexual minority youth that
difference may be attenuated.[23]

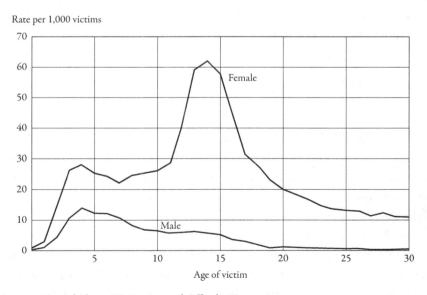

FIGURE 5.2 Sexual Abuse: Victim Age and Offender Types

There are also other factors that contribute to children's vulnerability to sexual abuse. Low-income children appear to be at higher risk of sexual victimization—about three times as high.[18] Children living with both biological parents have lower risk.[18] It is not clear whether this latter issue results from more exposure to paramours in single-parent households or just the difficulty inherent for one parent alone to provide adequate supervision with other competing demands of work, other children, and so forth. There is some data that indicate persons with cognitive and communication disabilities are at greater risk, but the data on this are really poor and rates vary wildly across studies.[24-26] Finally, the rates may be higher for sexual minority youth, with a prevalence of 32% reported in a recent study.[27]

What Happens to Survivors of Child Sexual Abuse?

Child sexual abuse has been linked to immediate health concerns related to injury and sexually transmitted disease[14] as well as an increase in risk of a range of longer-term problems such as conduct disorder and delinquency,[28,29] poor school performance,[30] sexual revictimization,[30,31] mental health and substance abuse problems, sexual risk behaviors,[32] health problems like obesity and higher healthcare utilization,[31,33-35] teen pregnancy,[36] and later parenting difficulties.[30,37] Similar to other forms of maltreatment, there is an indication that repeat instances of sexual abuse are associated with greater risk of negative outcomes.[38] Of course, not all children who experience sexual abuse will have negative outcomes. Social support and intervention services may play a strong role in promoting resilience/recovery.[39-41] We talk more about resilience in chapter 9.

WHO WOULD WANT TO HAVE SEX WITH A CHILD?
PEDOPHILE AND NONPEDOPHILE SEXUAL OFFENDERS

One of the most difficult things about understanding sexual abuse is understanding why someone might want to have sex with a child. Our understanding of perpetrators of sexual abuse and assault against children is rather like watching figures emerging from fog. We know something's there, we see outlines, but most of the details are still obscure. Among reports to police, women were perpetrators in about 1% of adult assaults and about 6% of childhood abuse cases.[14] As we mentioned earlier, by definition child sexual abuse is committed by a family member or someone who has care, custody, and control. We will cover what is well known, and pay less attention to areas in which science, as yet, has little or nothing to offer.

Let's start with a word that gets thrown around a lot when people think about child sexual abuse—"pedophilia"—and put it in the context of what we know about the broad spectrum of child sexual abuse and assault. In 2014, Pope Francis made news, quoted as stating that he thought about 1 in 50 priests, bishops, and cardinals were pedophiles (Box 5.1).[42]

BOX 5.1

TWO PERCENT OF CLERGY ARE PEDOPHILES: POPE FRANCIS

(NEWSER)—Pope Francis has offered an estimate on "the level of pedophilia in the Church," Sky News reports: He puts it at 2%, basing his information on aides' figures. "That 2% includes priests and even bishops and cardinals," the pope tells *La Repubblica* newspaper of Italy. "Others, more numerous, know (about the problem) but keep quiet. They punish without giving the reason," he says, per the BBC. The figure would suggest that some 8,000 out of 414,000 clergy members worldwide are pedophiles, the BBC notes. He adds: "This needs time, but there are solutions, and I will find them."

What Does This Actually Mean?

"Pedophile" is a medical (psychiatric) term referring to a person who has strong sexual feelings towards younger (prepubescent) children. A pedophile is someone who wants to have sex with children, not just because they happen to be available, but because they are sexually attracted to children. Currently, you can only be officially diagnosed with pedophilia when those desires translate to actual behavior or serious psychological problems.[43] Placed in the context of the pope's statement, it is unclear whether he was referring to the desire or those who acted on this urge. Only the latter would be, technically, pedophiles. Note that a pedophile could be someone who sexually assaults strangers' children or someone who abuses their own child. Research suggests that many, perhaps most, child sexual abusers do not fit the definition of pedophile (Box 5.2).

Michael Seto is a researcher who has made understanding sexual offending against children his life's work. We rely heavily on his book *Pedophilia and Sexual Offending Against Children*[44] and his recent (2015) meta-analysis (study of studies)[45] in the following section.

Who Sexually Offends Against Children?

Most of the focus of research has been on male perpetrators—which, as you will recall, are by far the majority of known cases. Seto's[44] synthesis of existing research

BOX 5.2

OFFICIAL DIAGNOSTIC CRITERIA FOR PEDOPHILIC DISORDER
(DSM 5, 302.2, F65.4)

A. Over a period of at least 6 months, recurrent, intense sexually arousing fantasies, sexual urges or behaviors involving sexual activity with a prepubescent child or children (generally under age 13 years or younger).
B. The Individual has acted on these sexual urges, or the sexual urges or fantasies cause marked distress or interpersonal difficulty.
C. The individual is at least 16 years of age and at least 5 years older than the child or children in Criterion A.

Note: Do not include an individual in late adolescence involved in an ongoing sexual relationship with a 12- or 13-year-old

Specify whether:

Exclusive type (attracted only to children)

Nonexclusive type

suggests that about 1 in 20 men, or less, have some attraction to prepubescent children. This is not the same as saying 1 in 20 men are pedophiles. Many of these men have other, often stronger, sexual desires for sexually mature teenagers or adults. Seto[45] suggests two broad categories of sexual offenders: the "antisocial" and the "atypical sexual interests" groups. We briefly review these types and then focus in on what we know about intrafamilial (sexual abuse) perpetrators.

Antisocial Sexual Offenders

As the label implies, these people are characterized by antisocial tendencies, which include "impulsivity, callousness, risk-taking, antisocial attitudes and beliefs and a pattern of unstable, irresponsible behavior."[45(p43)] Such a person does not have much of a conscience or care much about others, and this allows that person to act in a self-centered, rule-breaking manner without much concern for the consequences. Probably about half of all criminal (not CPS) sexual offenders fit this category, and this type of offender is more likely to offend against older children than are offenders in the next category.[44]

Offenders with Atypical Sexual Interests

There are a number of "paraphilias"—the technical term for people who are sexually aroused by atypical things, animate or inanimate, rather than other adult (sexually mature) humans. One kind of atypical sexual interest is pedophilia. Some argue that this kind of primary sexual attraction toward children may be as immutable as the attraction of adults toward other adults. These people do not tend to have high levels of antisocial characteristics.[44]

Adolescence-Limited

Within the "atypical group," but not belonging to the pedophile classification, is what Seto calls the "adolescence-limited" group.[44] These individuals offend during adolescence against younger children, but are unlikely to continue their sexual contacts with children into adulthood. The theory is that, among teenagers who are not socially competent and unable to obtain sexual partners their own age, some may look to young children to gain this kind of interpersonal connectivity. This is an understudied group. Sometimes adolescent offender cases are addressed by CPS depending on their relationship to the victim.

Where Does Incest Fit In?

While the term "incest" is used in literature and popular media, in the research world we tend to talk about "intrafamilial" sexual abuse. Seto and colleagues[45] found that people who offend against family members do tend to look different from those who look outside their own family for victims. Compared to extrafamilial offenders (those who sexually assault children), existing research indicates that intrafamilial abusers are:

- more likely to have been neglected, physically, and/ or sexually abused as children;
- less likely to display atypical sexual interests (in other words, may not fit the definition of the pedophile); and
- less likely to score high on a range of measures of antisociality.

In terms of other indicators of mental health (depression, anxiety, etc.) the extrafamilial and intrafamilial offenders looked fairly similar. Beyond this, our factual understanding of intrafamilial sexual offending against children is still quite weak.

A large number of theories about why intrafamilial child sexual abuse may occur are rooted in Freudian thought (despite the fact he retracted his original statement, as mentioned in chapter 1) rather than empirical study. We do not review them, as evidence no longer supports them. Indeed, treatment approaches for sexual offending against children that are based on nonbehavioral theories like those stemming from Freud don't work and may even make things worse.[44] While we have tried to identify differences between extrafamilial and intrafamilial abusers, it is not clear that there are cut-and-dried categories. Overlap does exist.

WHAT DOES A SEXUAL ABUSE CASE LOOK LIKE?

Let's take a look at a family recently in the news, because they serve as a good illustration of some of the more common features of child sexual abuse. The timeline information is taken from the *Washington Post*.[46] After outlining what happened in the well-publicized case of Josh Duggar, we discuss how this illustrates aspects of child sexual abuse cases generally. The timeline, as reported, goes something like this:

First Set of Sexual Abuse Events (March 2002): Josh (age 15) told his father that he had touched the breasts and genital areas of his sleeping younger sisters (unclear which) several times.

Response to First Set of Sexual Abuse Events (2002): Josh was disciplined within the family (unclear how) and authorities were not notified.

Second Set of Sexual Abuse Events (March, 2003): Josh's father became aware of more sexual abuse events, including touching through clothing while the victims were awake and also touching an unrelated babysitter (age unknown) while she was asleep.

Response to Second Sexual Abuse Events (March 2003): Josh's father brought the incidents to the attention of church elders. Josh was sent for 3 months to do construction work, possibly at the old Veterans Hospital in Little Rock. The old Veterans Hospital was then operated by the Institute for Basic Life Principles, an organization founded by the televangelist Bill Gothard. There was to be a facility called the Little Rock Training Center, which would use a "Bible-based rehabilitation program" to help troubled youth. [As an aside, Gothard has since resigned from the agency after allegations that he sexually harassed over 30 women, including minors.[47]] Josh's father then told his acquaintance, an Arkansas State trooper, who was made aware of at least one of the incestuous events. The trooper gave Josh a talking to, but apparently did not file an official report or report the case to CPS, possibly violating mandated reporter laws. That trooper is currently serving a long prison sentence for unrelated charges having to do with child pornography.

Official Involvement: December 2006: An anonymous tipster called the Arkansas Child Abuse Hotline, reporting the events. It is unclear what role CPS may have taken, as such proceedings are not usually made public. It is known that police did investigate and determined that since more than 3 years had elapsed since the first officer had been informed of the events, that the statute of limitations had expired.

Public Disclosure (May, 2015): The events became public, following the (perhaps illegal) leaking of a police file. Josh Duggar resigned from his position as the executive director of Family Resource Council Action, the legislative lobbying arm of the Family Resource Council.

So what does this story highlight about child sexual abuse?

Sexual Abuse Does Not Have to Include Having Sexual Intercourse

The Duggar case as reported is not atypical of child sexual abuse. Among cases reported to law enforcement, about half of all cases involved "only" fondling.[14,48] David Finkelhor, one of the nation's leading experts on child sexual abuse victims, has recently done a study suggesting that among all victims of child sexual abuse, perhaps only 4% experience intercourse.[49] This is entirely consistent with the experience of the author who was a child abuse investigator. Alleged reports of fondling were, by far, the most common kind of sexual abuse encountered in the cases assigned. Of course, it is critical that we not divide sexual abuse cases into "serious sexual abuse" and "sexual abuse lite." There is no evidence that fondling or other types of sexual abuse are less harmful than intercourse. In fact, a recent study showed that some outcomes seemed to be as bad or worse for children who were "just touched."[50]

Protection of the Abuser by Family Is Not Uncommon

In the popular movie, *Precious* the mother of Precious is well aware of and permits her husband's (Precious's father) sexual abuse of the girl from a very young age. She threatens to harm Precious if she tells anyone.[51] In the Duggar case it does not appear that the parents tried to silence the girls in a threatening manner. The Duggar son was protected by his family in other ways. The family did not report the case to authorities, unless you count telling an acquaintance who was a police officer who never forwarded the information. The case did not get checked out by officials until an anonymous call was made to CPS. Later statements by the family, relatives, and friends of the family continued to support Josh by casting the acts in a less negative light (e.g., by pointing out that the victims were sometimes unaware, that he was a child at the time himself) or even to attack people who have talked about the abuse.[52] We are told by Josh's father that what happened in the Duggar home wasn't really so bad—by comparison—"we've talked to other families who have had, you know, other things happen, a lot of their stories were even worse."[46]

While the Duggar's case is not atypical in terms of protecting the abuser, this is certainly not always the case. We don't actually know how often nonoffending parents are unaware of sexual abuse that is occurring, but in at least one study of adults, 71% of those who disclosed past child sexual abuse said that the nonoffending parent was completely unaware.[53] Some studies indicate that later child outcomes are improved when the nonoffending parent is supportive,[54,55] although a recent meta-analysis indicates this effect may be smaller than previously believed.[56]

Mandated Reporters Don't Always Report

As we learned in chapter 2, mandated reporting laws require that professionals, including police officers, report cases of child abuse. The law enforcement officer in the Duggar case failed to do so. Currently, in the state of Arkansas, clergy members are also mandated reporters, and it appears a decision was also made not to report by clergy in the Duggar case. Research suggests that such failure to report is not uncommon.[18] We talk more about this in chapter 8.

Intrafamilial Child Sexual Abuse Victims Are Accessible

The targets of child sexual abuse in the Duggar family were readily available in the same home. This is common.[14] Recall that this was a key difference in the location of the threat to Little Red Riding Hood compared to the king's daughter. In the Duggar case, there was no evidence of other violence toward his sisters and, again, this is not uncommon. A large proportion of abuse is fondling rather than physically invasive acts. It is not clear in the Duggar case whether there was any prelude to the molestation—which is also common.

Many abusers will insidiously worm their way in to the child's confidence and slowly ramp up the abuse beginning with seemingly "innocent" talk and touches.[57] The technical term for this behavior is "grooming." We are aware of at least two studies of child sexual offenders[58,59] that posed a simple question: How do sexual offenders go about victimizing children? Combined, the studies interviewed over 100 child sex offenders who were either in prison or in treatment and included intra- and extrafamilial perpetrators. Perpetrators said they commonly made their actions a "game" to develop trust. They gradually brought up sexual subjects or engaged in less overt sexual touching, including "accidental" touches, then escalated the sexual nature of the encounters. If children showed discomfort, most abusers would stop the approach for a while and start again later.

HOW DO WE RESPOND TO THE SEXUAL ABUSE OF CHILDREN?

Formal CPS or court responses typically begin with a report by the victim, a family member or other adult or through discovery of medical evidence, such as a sexually transmitted disease in a very young child. While any type of maltreatment may include responses from multiple systems (recall that Danielle's case in chapter 4 included law enforcement, the courts, and health care responses at a minimum), child sexual abuse provides a good exemplar of multiple points of intervention.

Child Protective Services Role

Hypothetically, an older child might disclose sexual abuse to a teacher. The teacher, if they adhere to mandated reporting laws, would contact CPS. The CPS worker would go to the school and talk with the teacher and then the child. After that, the role of CPS is largely dependent on the presence of a nonoffending parent who is supportive of the child. We do not have good data on how often this occurs, but some smaller qualitative studies suggest this is not uncommon.[56] In such cases, where the perpetrator is prevented from having further access to the child and the nonoffending parent gets the child needed help, CPS may have virtually no ongoing role.

Healthcare Role

Child sexual abuse can have health consequences aside from physical injury such as infection with a sexually transmitted disease. Not all sexual abuse cases are referred for medical evaluation—existing estimates suggest less than 25%.[60] Results of these examinations may be used to further either child protection cases in family court or to support the prosecution of offenders in criminal court. There are a range of issues that arise in the accurate medical diagnosis of sexual abuse. Pediatricians who are board certified in child abuse, those physicians who keep up to date with the research, and those who review cases regularly with an expert have been found to have greater ability in distinguishing between normal and abnormal physical examinations.[61]

Court Role

If the child is not protected by a nonoffending parent, CPS may choose to place the child in foster care. This will involve the police and family court. Only in very serious cases do intrafamilial sexual abuse cases go to criminal court, and when they do they are usually treated far less harshly than people who hurt kids outside their own family.[62] As far as we can tell, nobody knows how often familial sexual abuse perpetrators are prosecuted in criminal court. There is no way to track child sexual abuse cases that result in arrests, prosecutions, or incarcerations nationally. Lacking solid data, we attempted to use existing information to make a very rough "guesstimate." Perhaps a third or a half of all sexual abuse cases (about 135,000 per year) are reported to CPS.[18] Of those, perhaps a quarter to a half move forward to the district attorney's office.[63] Only about two-thirds of those are acted on by district attorneys.[63,64] Perhaps three-quarters of prosecuted cases result in a guilty plea (generally for a lesser charge) or a conviction, and about half of those are incarcerated.[65] Our best guess is that the number of intrafamilial child sexual abusers who go to jail is in the 1%–10% range. This is not terribly different from the percentage of rapists who go to jail.[66] This estimate of real-life criminal justice involvement stands in stark contrast to the coverage of criminal justice action for sexual abuse in news media.[67]

Mental Health Role

There is a fair amount of literature related to treatment for child victims of sexual abuse, which tends to overlap with treatment of trauma generally. We talk about trauma treatment in chapter 9. There are however a unique network of agencies that have arisen to focus on forensic interviewing and treatment that we overview here. Over the years, concern mounted that the number of people (CPS, doctors, police, etc.) who may talk to the child in the process of a sexual abuse investigation may lead to additional trauma. This led to development of formal recommended guidelines for forensic interviewers[68] and recommendations for how pediatricians and other family healthcare providers may question the child.[28] In many communities, forensic interviews and treatment services are provided by Child Advocacy Centers (CACs).[69] Sometimes these centers specialize in sexual abuse, and sometimes they respond to other kinds of maltreatment as well. They employ people specially trained to interview children in a legally and therapeutically sound manner. "Multidisciplinary teams" are commonly used at CACs and include representatives from the disciplines listed previously (and others) to further limit the trauma associated with investigation and develop the best possible treatment plan. You can check out the following website for more information and help finding a program locally: http://www.nationalcac.org/.

Support for Nonoffending Caregivers and Family Members

There is a smaller related literature on the support of other family members and nonoffending parents.[55,70] Some of the evidence-based child-centered approaches include parallel components for nonoffending parents.[71] In some cases, CAC agencies are able to provide mental health support to both the child and the caregiver.[72] While it makes intuitive sense that the support of nonoffending members of the family would be beneficial, there is insufficient research to be able to say whether outcomes are better when this occurs.

Treatment for Offenders

Interventions meant to reduce the likelihood that perpetrators will reoffend do exist.[73] There is consensus that at least in most cases juvenile sex offenders need to be assessed and treated differently,[74] which makes sense given the "adolescence-limited" kind of abuser described previously.[44,75] The relative effectiveness of approaches to treatment of sexual offenders has long been a "hot topic." Cognitive-behavioral approaches are among the most promising, with more limited data on behavioral approaches such as aversive conditioning.[44] Seto[44] reports that research finds some positive effects of both approaches on reducing arousal, with additional effects on improving avoidance strategies and reducing cognitive distortions (e.g., "the child is enjoying from this too") using cognitive-behavioral approaches. Unfortunately, research has not found profound effects on recurrence. Current thought is that approaches need to be tailored to the typology of the offender.[76]

There are some new strategies being piloted as well. One interesting, very recent, development has been the establishment of support groups or hotlines for offenders with the explicit purpose of preventing future victimization.[77] Another innovation being tested is professional outreach to men at risk as a primary prevention strategy.[78] It is still too early to assess the relative effectiveness of these newer approaches or whether such an approach is more appropriate for a particular type of offender.

SEXUAL ABUSE PREVENTION?

We mentioned earlier that much of the sexual abuse prevention literature focuses on so-called stranger danger (as in "Little Red Riding Hood"), and much of this is delivered in school settings.[57] Generally, research on the effectiveness of those programs is mixed, with positive effects on increasing children's knowledge but relatively little else.[79] Most programs focus on children learning to understand and resist inappropriate touching and dangerous situations.[80] Other common educational components include making sure that children are not alone with a nonparental adult, making sure children know what is appropriate, encouraging parents to know where their children are and whom they are with, and telling children to disclose anything that makes them uncomfortable. While some public health messaging programs aimed at parents (instead of children) that cover these skills exist, we do not know much about how effective these are.[22,81]

It is unfortunately difficult to translate these common educational approaches to stopping child sexual abuse within the family.[82] Recall the story of the king's daughter. She apparently had no other trusted adult in her life; while the court advisors thought his idea of marriage was terrible, they were afraid to stand their ground; and her attempts at evasion and running away failed. It is difficult to evade your own caregiver in your own home—particularly if there is no other trusted adult to whom you can turn. The good news is that you can be that other trusted adult who listens to a child's concerns and seeks help immediately—even if the danger is a member of your own family. Like the joke about looking for keys in the light, we need to be able to look at (and talk about) what is difficult.

6

Words Can Hurt

EMOTIONAL ABUSE

WE NOW TURN to the issue of emotional abuse. Like neglect, emotional abuse is underresearched and often ill-defined. Like physical abuse, there can be a continuum between child discipline or guidance and maltreatment. Interestingly, while emotional abuse is clearly not absent from our consciousness, as we learn, it is sometimes absent from our policies.

In the best-known version of "Cinderella," she is constantly being belittled, is given poor clothing despite her family's wealth, and is excluded from family activities by her stepmother and stepsisters. The Centers for Disease Control and Prevention (CDC)[1] breaks down emotional abuse into two categories—psychological abuse Figure 6.1 (an act of commission—something like the extreme and continual degrading of Cinderella by her stepmother and stepsisters) and emotional neglect (a lack of nurturing, which Cinderella also experiences). This split does not exist in most child welfare policies. Most states (we talk about this a bit later) that include emotional abuse just have a single category.

Remarkably, Cinderella seems to tolerate her treatment and emerge unscathed, which brings to mind the old children's rhyme, "Sticks and stones will break my bones, but words will never hurt me." This turns out not to be true for a lot of people. Human beings generally react badly to constant psychological threat, from outside or inside the family. The bullying literature reminds us that people appear particularly sensitive to emotional assault in childhood.[2,3] As pointed out by

FIGURE 6.1 "Emotional Abuse"

Abraham Maslow in the 1940s[4] and by Biglan more recently in *The Nurture Effect*,[5] human beings have a fundamental need for love and belonging.

WHAT IS EMOTIONAL ABUSE?

The American Professional Society on the Abuse of Children (APSAC) recognizes six categories of emotional maltreatment: spurning, intimidating or terrorizing, confining and isolating, exploiting and corrupting, denigrating emotional needs, and neglecting health[6] While the specific actions listed here may seem clear, emotional abuse is similar to physical abuse regarding the issue of where to draw the line between less-than-ideal parenting and emotional abuse.[6] We briefly alluded to the story of Cinderella already, but now let's turn to an early African folktale to think about the continuum of behaviors involved:

"Mosadimogolo yo o neng a tlhoka bana" ("The old lady who did not have children")

A childless woman, who lives on her own, one day chases away a bird that is eating the bran (*moroko*) she put out to dry. However, the bird implores her to let it eat the bran in exchange for the promise of children. When the woman agrees, the bird instructs her to put five sticks inside a calabash [a large African gourd] and to cover it with a winnowing basket (*leselo*). After three days, three boys and two girls suddenly appear. The woman is very happy because the five children are a great help in the house. However, one evening, on returning home drunk from a party, she verbally abuses them for being rowdy. The children are deeply hurt when she tells them that they are not humans, but actually stick people. After hearing their cries of anger and sorrow, the bird makes them disappear despite the woman's pleas for their return.[7]

In this example, we are told that there is verbal abuse of the children that results in emotional harm. On the other hand, the fact that the words appear to spoken in the "heat of the moment" may make us cringe a little. We have all likely said things to those we care about that we might regret. When we think of emotional abuse today, however, we do not typically think of a single incident as illustrated in the folktale, but rather a long-standing and harmful pattern of behavior.[8]

Let's look at another fictional story from popular US culture that illustrates this point: *Carrie*, by Steven King.[9] For those familiar with the story, the part in which Carrie wreaks violent vengeance on high school peers may come to mind first, but this is really a tale of severe emotional maltreatment by a seemingly mentally ill mother. To summarize, Carrie experiences constant belittling and emotional torture. She is locked in a closet for hours to pray for forgiveness, she is told her acne is a punishment from god, and her mother purposively forces her to wear really ugly clothes. Carrie's understandable shyness and behavioral oddities lead to bullying and exclusion by peers, and the story ends badly. Unlike the folktale, this horror story illustrates a long-term pattern of parental behavior that includes many of the aspects of emotional abuse listed in the APSAC definition: spurning, intimidating or terrorizing, confining and isolating, denigrating emotional needs.[6] These behaviors eventually lead to substantial psychological harm.

Our understanding of what is and what is not emotional abuse in a real-life context is one of the least well developed areas of child protection research, policy, and practice. In the next sections, we try to bring some clarity to this situation.

Appropriate Child Rearing or Emotional Abuse: Where Is the line?

Is pushing children to excel and belittling them when they fail abusive? The term "Little League parent" brings to mind an image of the parent screaming at their child for striking out, motivated by hope that their child will someday become a star player. This type of individual falls in the "heckler" category in a 2014 *Huffington Post* guide on parents in sports.[10] For an interesting take on pushing children to excel, we thought we would revisit a news story about the so-called Tiger mom:

Chua says she never allowed her kids to have a playdate, watch TV, participate in a school play, or choose their own extra-curricular activities. . . . When her 7-year-old daughter failed to master a new piece on the piano, Chua drove her relentlessly. "I threatened her with no lunch, no dinner, no Christmas or Hanukkah presents," Chua writes, "no birthday parties for two, three, four years. When she still kept playing it wrong, I told her she was purposely working herself into a frenzy because she was secretly afraid she couldn't do it. I told her to stop being lazy, cowardly, self-indulgent and pathetic." Chua made her daughter work into the night, denying her even a break to go to the bathroom. "The house became a war zone, and I lost my voice yelling, but still there seemed to be only negative progress, and even I began to have doubts." Then—at last—the girl made a breakthrough. She mastered the piece, and wanted to play it again and again."[11]

Some of you may think, "this is emotional abuse"; others will not. One commentator notes, "Unlike many Western parents who would have backed down, convinced that the child just wasn't ready or able to master the new piano piece, Chua believed that her child could do it. But she wasn't going to learn the piece without intense effort, and that effort wasn't going to happen unless the child was pushed."[12] Another author concludes, "The European parents, they provide their children wings so their child can fly away and be free on their own," while "The Asian-American parents are more like the wind that is beneath the wings of their child, because they're always there, supporting the child, letting the child fly and reach success."[11]

Using the legal lens of Coleman and colleagues[13] introduced in chapter 3, it might be hard to draw a line in the above case. Recall that those authors highlighted the intent of the action, a standard of reasonableness and the probability of harm as key considerations. On one hand, Chua's intent is to help her daughter develop a skill. The authors retelling her story appear to indicate a general cultural acceptance of her means. On the other hand, there is a potential for functional impairment depending on how long the inability to go to the bathroom or possible withholding of food lasts, as well as the belittling—it's messy.

Now let's look at a very different case, also from the news, that may be a little clearer.

A Minnesota woman was arrested this week after shaving her daughter's head and forcing her to pick up garbage and do windsprints wearing nothing but a tank top and a diaper. The mother allegedly imposed this punishment—which she dubbed "diaper duty"—because she wasn't happy with the 12-year-old's grades, the *Minneapolis Star-Tribune* reports. Neighbors called police after seeing the girl outside crying and begging to be let back inside. By the time police showed up, the girl had been outside in the diaper for half an hour, and they described her as hysterical. They arrested the mother, 38, and her boyfriend on suspicion of misdemeanor malicious punishment of a child. One neighborhood boy said it wasn't the girl's first humiliation either—he'd seen her and her younger sister picking up garbage in diapers a month earlier.[14]

The child does not appear at risk of physical harm, but there is evidence of emotional harm and a pattern of behavior intended to cause psychological pain. Referring back to ideas raised by Coleman and colleagues,[13] it would appear that both the reasonableness standard and the potential for functional impairment could be used to help draw a line between discipline and abuse.

Now let's explore an example at the extreme end of the continuum from an adult who reports memories from her childhood.

One woman from Indiana, PA still struggles with daily memories of her father routinely forcing her, her mother and siblings at gunpoint against a wall while he shot a ring of bullets around them.[15]

This story seems to clearly fall in the abusive category and illustrates what APSAC and the American Humane Association term "terrorizing." The family is subjected to a dangerous situation, but without physical contact or harm this would likely fall into the category of emotional abuse if it is reportable at all (we talk about this more later).

How Big a Problem Is Emotional Abuse?

A large-scale international meta-analysis (a structured review of many prior studies), estimates that between 0.3% and 36% of children experience emotional abuse.[16] You, like us, are probably shocked at the hundredfold-plus difference between 0.3% and 36%. How do people come up with such broadly different guesses? If you recall from chapter 4, we mentioned the "neglect of neglect" issue in terms of research on that kind of maltreatment. There is a similar problem with researchers and policy makers "neglecting emotional abuse," and this complicates our ability to define it and to judge how common it is. We see this issue of definition reflected in official reports as well. Table 6.1 illustrates the difference in prevalence of substantiated emotional abuse by state in 2015.[17] In some states, a quarter of all reports are classified as emotional abuse, while in others, the proportion of cases classified as emotional abuse is less than 1%. Some may think that emotional abuse is more likely to be identified in

TABLE 6.1

Proportion of All Child Protective Services
Investigations That Are for Emotional Abuse

State and Rate	
Vermont	1 per 852
Alabama	1 per 430
New York	1 per 198
Colorado	1 per 37
Montana	1 per 28
California	1 per 9
Georgia	1 per 9
Alaska	1 per 6
Wyoming	1 per 5
Connecticut	1 per 4

Source: Child Maltreatment 2015[17]

politically liberal states, but as can be seen in the table, the data simply don't support such a conclusion.

It is, of course, impossible that parenting practices vary by factors of a hundred or more simply because we cross a state line. What is different is the definition and screening practices written into state policies. By now, you may be noticing a recurring theme about state differences. The combination of defining maltreatment differently and differences in how cases are handled can lead to widely different and unstable estimates.[18]

Our failure to come up with a simple definition of emotional abuse remains a serious problem. Various definitions of emotional abuse used in policy or in research can be quite different from each other. Recall the actions delineated by APSAC (spurning, intimidating or terrorizing, confining and isolating, exploiting and corrupting, denigrating emotional needs and neglecting health.[6] Now read the screener question that is part of the Juvenile Victimization Questionnaire (JVQ): "At any time in your life, did you get scared or feel really bad because grown-ups in your life called you names, said mean things to you, or said they didn't want you?"[19] These are clearly not the same thing. The Childhood Trauma Questionnaire (CTQ) focuses on verbal humiliation and threats of harm (emotional abuse) or failure to provide love (emotional neglect).[20] The National Incidence Study separates emotional abuse from emotional neglect, but it includes things not typical for either definition. For example, emotional abuse includes "administering unprescribed substances" and "other/unknown abuse." Emotional neglect includes "domestic violence" (see chapter 7) and "knowingly permitting drug/alcohol abuse."[21] One can imagine a fair amount of variation in prevalence depending on which measure or question is used.

What Causes Emotional Abuse?

There is no well-developed causal theory or any clear data that can allow us to authoritatively say "emotional abuse happens because. . . ." For some parents, it seems plausible that forms of emotional abuse are used as discipline, as in the case from Minnesota discussed earlier. A fairly recent review found that many of the same risk factors for other forms of maltreatment (e.g., prior history of maltreatment, poverty, mental illness, lower social support) appear to increase the risk of emotional abuse as well.[22] It appears that emotional abuse crosscuts cultures around the world but, like physical abuse, may be higher or lower in some populations.[16] In short, it would appear that there are a number of potential causal mechanisms, and thus far a specific path for this behavior compared to other maltreating behaviors is not known.

HOW BAD IS EMOTIONAL ABUSE?

As we noted early in the chapter, emotionally abusive experiences appear to stand against a fundamental human need for warm nurturing[5]—particularly by a primary caregiver. Another survivor reports that her mother "called her ugly and worthless, once impulsively cutting off her bun of hair to give her an uneven chop, only to deride her for being bald. She would say things like . . . I would amount to nothing, that I would always be on the street, that no one wanted me."[15] Theoretically this may have consequences for how we think about ourselves and react to others later. Remember the discussion of attachment in chapter 4? The monkeys raised by the nonliving surrogates displayed a range of dysfunctional behaviors that carried into their own parenting behaviors later.[23] While they were not belittled as the example the adult survivor recalls, they were confined and isolated.

What Does Research Tell Us About It?

A large-scale meta-analysis used data from a number of preexisting studies examining mental behavioral health outcomes and found that emotional abuse was often equally problematic when compared to physical abuse or neglect.[24] A more recent study that tried to control for other types of maltreatment found a stronger association of emotional abuse to a mental condition called borderline personality disorder,[25] which in turn may express itself in behaviors like delinquency.[26] The experience of emotional abuse may also change the way we react to stress, which in turn impacts the likelihood someone will develop depressive symptoms.[27] Others suggest emotional abuse has a profound impact on later intimate partnerships.[16,28]

What kind of emotional abuse is worst for children? We are not really sure for a variety of reasons. There is some very new research that suggests particular forms of emotional maltreatment may have varying outcomes, but work is still quite young in this area.[29] Like emotional abuse in general, our understanding is also impacted by the measure used. One study using the CTQ mentioned earlier found that polydrug use was associated most strongly with sexual abuse and emotional neglect.[30] If the same study had used the question about emotional abuse from the JVQ, it is not clear the results would have been the same.

Another barrier in understanding the effects of emotional maltreatment is that official substantiation of emotional abuse reports actually require elements of time exposed and harm. We can report a child as physically abused after a single event, in most cases long before lasting harm has occurred. The same might be said for neglect. This isn't true for emotional abuse. Table 6.2 provides some examples from state statutes.[31] What we can see in the table is that when states do address the issue (and not all states include emotional abuse as a reportable type of maltreatment), they typically don't accept a report until after it has had long-term and serious impacts on the child. Statutes define emotional abuse based on manifestations of children's emotional or behavioral problems. If you do not see your state in the table and are curious you can go to https://www.childwelfare.gov/topics/systemwide/laws-policies/state/ and select your state and then under the topics click the box "Definitions of Child Abuse and Neglect" and select "Go!" in section three. This will provide you with the definitions for each type of reportable maltreatment. Anyway, the main point is that by the time such harm is evident and is reported, it is likely that the abuse has been going on for a long time. Therefore any study that is using official reports to define emotional abuse will have a hard time disentangling chronic exposure from the type of maltreatment. Further, early preventive intervention that could be imagined in physical abuse or neglect cases is hard to apply to officially reported emotional abuse.

Another confound in our understanding of the effects of emotional abuse is that people who suffer emotional abuse often, or perhaps usually, experience other kinds of maltreatment as well.[32,33] We also know that chronic maltreatment is particularly bad.[34-38] Very recent work indicates that while overall emotional abuse is roughly equivalent in outcomes to physical or sexual abuse, combinations of emotional

TABLE 6.2

Examples of State Definitions for Emotional Abuse

State	Definition of emotional abuse
Alabama	Nonaccidental mental injury
Alaska	"Mental injury" means a serious injury to the child as evidenced by an observable and substantial impairment in the child's ability to function in a developmentally appropriate manner
California	. . . he or she is suffering serious emotional damage, or is at substantial risk of suffering serious emotional damage, as evidenced by severe anxiety, depression, withdrawal, or untoward aggressive behavior toward self or others, as a result of the conduct of the parent or guardian
Georgia	Not included as maltreatment at all
New York	. . . a state of substantially diminished psychological or intellectual functioning in relation to, but not limited to, such factors as failure to thrive, control of aggressive or self-destructive impulses, ability to think and reason, acting out, or misbehavior, including incorrigibility, ungovernability, or habitual truancy; provided, however, that such impairment must be clearly attributable to the unwillingness or inability of the respondent to exercise a minimum degree of care toward the child.
Ohio	Harm or threatened harm to a child's health or safety' includes, but is not limited to, mental injury.
Oregon	The term "abuse" includes any mental injury to a child that shall include only observable and substantial impairment of the child's mental or psychological ability to function caused by cruelty to the child, with due regard to the culture of the child
Texas	Mental or emotional injury to a child that results in an observable and material impairment in the child's growth, development, or psychological functioning
	Causing or permitting a child to be in a situation in which the child sustains a mental or emotional injury that results in an observable and material impairment in the child's growth, development, or psychological functioning

Source: https://www.childwelfare.gov/pubPDFs/define.pdf

abuse with sexual or physical abuse may be worse.[39] And of course, like most other forms of maltreatment, emotional abuse is often accompanied by poverty.[21]

Problems in definition, measurement, and common joint experience with other forms of maltreatment all make it difficult for scientists to truly understand the direct and singular contributions of emotional abuse. While some brief and/or "pure" forms of emotional abuse undoubtedly exist, these are likely the exception. And given how we have chosen to orient our response system, child protective services are not usually involved in such cases.

WHAT SHOULD WE DO ABOUT EMOTIONAL ABUSE?

Where do we draw the line between the tiger mom and the child threatened and demeaned on a daily basis? Clearly, outcomes for the children involved are likely to be different. Unfortunately, the framework offered by Coleman and colleagues[13] to help us with an improved legal definition for physical abuse is not terribly useful in helping us draw a clear line between less-than-ideal parenting and emotional abuse. Official state definitions are unsatisfactory, since those definitions generally require that children be psychologically damaged before we can say that emotional abuse even exists. While more attention to emotional maltreatment by child welfare has been called for,[29] it seems unlikely that child protection systems will be able to intervene early as long as reporting statutes mandate that significant harm has to occur in order to report at all. Until that changes, we must look outside child protection for a preventive approach.

We also have much to learn regarding intervention. There has been some work done on developing a diagnostic framework[6] that may be helpful for clinicians and those that intervene. A focus on child safety and trauma reactions related to perceived threats of harm has been suggested,[29] but addressing this issue remains a work in progress. There are some promising approaches, at least for early childhood, that focus specifically on responsive parenting.[40] A review of existing evidence-based parenting programs suggests that few of them address emotional maltreatment directly and none of them address the entire range of related parenting behaviors.[41] As of the writing of this chapter, the first comprehensive meta-analysis of interventions specific to emotional abuse is underway but results are not yet available.[42]

It may be that the easiest course of action while we are learning more about specific interventions for emotional abuse is the promotion of positive approaches to parenting that we outlined in the chapter on physical discipline.[6] Such interventions would undoubtedly be enhanced if we could attend to the social support and mental health needs of parents.[22,43,44] In other words, there may be promise in building a healthier emotional climate, both around the parent and around the child. Anthony Biglan[5] goes so far as to say, "The quality of human life, perhaps even survival of life as we know it, depends on finding ways to make everyone's environment more nurturing."[(p213)]

Peter, Peter Pumpkin Eater had a wife and couldn't keep her. He put her in a pumpkin shell and there he kept her very well.

—AMERICAN ORIGIN MOTHER GOOSE CLUB

7

Protecting Women Versus Protecting Children

MUST IT BE EITHER/OR?

DOMESTIC VIOLENCE OR the domination of women is a familiar topic in fairy tales. For example, Peter, in the rhyme above, imprisons his wife and both Mr. Fox and Bluebeard kill women whom they lure to their castles.[1,2] Sometimes domestic violence is almost romanticized in popular culture. For example, some popular songs appear to normalize violence against women such as: "He Hit Me (It Felt Like a Kiss)" by The Crystals in 1962 or "Love the Way You Lie" by Eminem in 2010.[3] Both these songs portray violence as an unfortunate aspect of an otherwise passionate love affair. Other songs have spoken to how glad a man is to now have a girlfriend "under my thumb."[4]

Domestic violence, also called intimate partner violence (IPV), encompasses a range of behaviors from psychological control to physical and sexual abuse. Given the broad range of experiences and its enduring presence from folk tales to pop culture, it is not surprising that as many as one in three women may experience IPV in their lifetimes.[5] Why are we talking about this in a book about child abuse and neglect? Many of these women are parents. In the United States and around the world the number of children estimated to be exposed to IPV is very high.[6] Several states (which we discuss further later) now consider exposure to IPV a form of maltreatment under certain circumstances. Further, child maltreatment and IPV often co-occur.

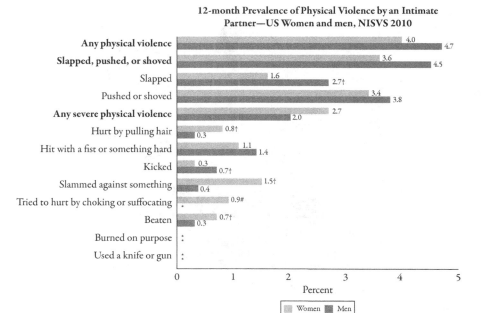

FIGURE 7.1 Lifetime Rates of Physical IPV for Men and Women: 2010
† Statistically significant difference (p < .05) in prevalence.
* Estimate is not reported; relative standard error > 30% or cell size ≤ 20.
# Formal statistical testing was not undertaken because the number experiencing these behaviors was too small to generate a reliable estimate for at least one of the comparison groups.

A NOT SO "SIDE NOTE"

Before diving into the debate evident in the chapter title, we want to acknowledge that this issue is not limited to women[7] or heterosexual couples. We know much less about domestic violence when men are the victims.[8] We have no idea how often male victims or gay and lesbian couples experiencing IPV may be parents.

Depending on the sampling used and type of violence measured, the gender symmetry of IPV varies a great deal.[9,10] Figure 7.1[11] shows the distribution of different kinds of violence across genders. Men are much more likely to be the aggressors in cases involving extreme physical violence. This could be because men, on average, are larger and stronger than women and can inflict greater physical damage. Men are, in fact, only about half as likely to suffer severe physical IPV, according to the Centers for Disease Control and Prevention (CDC), and are far less likely to experience sexual IPV.[12] Another complicating factor is that many of the researchers and advocates in the field of IPV are trained in a traditional feminist perspective, which tends to lead researchers to focus on female victims.[9] A final barrier to measuring the extent of victimization among men is that societal expectations of men to be strong and physically capable may make men ashamed to admit such abuse.[13] Some evidence

FIGURE 7.2 Child Witnessing Parental Violence

suggests that, holding the level of violence equal, judges are more likely to grant temporary restraining orders to female plaintiffs.[14] There is a growing literature on partner violence within gay and lesbian couples,[15] but, as we mentioned, we honestly do not have that much information on violence in the context of gay and lesbian couples who are parents.[16]

Witnessing any IPV between primary caregivers regardless of sex or sexual orientation can have negative consequences for children (as illustrated in Figure 7.2) and may be considered child maltreatment (which we see depends on where you live). This being said, this chapter focuses on female parents because (1) this has been the focus of the policy debate related to child welfare, (2) women are more likely to be primary caretakers of children and appear to be at more serious risk of physical harm, and (3) we just plain know more about it.

INTERPERSONAL VIOLENCE AND HARM TO CHILDREN

Rigorous research in this area is relatively new and is hard to do. Both child maltreatment and domestic violence are often unreported, making tracking them difficult. Unlike child maltreatment, there is no centralized reporting and data system for IPV. If there is an arrest or a temporary restraining order, then there is a record of that (which may have no information about children at all), but there is no centralized IPV database that tracks cases that do not become involved in the criminal justice system. While some states do include IPV as a form of reportable maltreatment, it is unclear what proportion of families with children that involve IPV are captured in these incidents. Based on the estimated prevalence, we're betting it is a pretty low number. This makes understanding how outcomes vary for children who witness IPV alone compared to child maltreatment alone or in combination challenging.

A recent review of the published literature on childhood exposure to IPV and subsequent outcomes[17] identified only 24 articles within the last 10 years from the United States or Canada. Of these only nine involved asking questions during childhood, while the remainder were adult samples using retrospective recall of what the respondent said happened to them as children. Asking people what happened to them a long time ago can be problematic.

Memories of things that happen very early in life (say before you are 2) are very unlikely to be recalled simply because of the way our brains develop.[18,19] A catchier phrase for this is "infantile amnesia." You may not believe this at first because perhaps you know someone very trustworthy who told you something like, "I recall sleeping next to Muffy, my new puppy, who we got when I was two." This is not a lie. Memory experts believe that these memories are not original, but instead, that the child was told about sleeping with Muffy when he was older (say, 4 or 5) and formed a mental picture of the event. It is that picture based on later information that is recalled and mistaken for the original memory, which no longer exists. Things like this make the lives of social scientists interested in childhood experiences difficult.

Seven of the adult studies came from the general population or had general population comparison groups, while the others were drawn from what researchers call "clinical samples." A "clinical sample" in this case means that the subjects of the study were engaged in some sort of treatment for a health or mental health problem or were participating in criminal justice or women's shelter services for IPV.[20] Most women involved in IPV do not access shelter services, and most men are not arrested.[21] Similar to child maltreatment, there is a range of types of IPV and degrees of severity in a given case.[11] Much remains unknown about the experience of women who may be at less physical risk and/or who do not seek help.

What We Know About the Effects of Interpersonal Violence on Children

Keeping in mind the caveats about current available research, according to the aforementioned review by Wood and Sommers[17] there appears to be some consensus that there are negative effects following childhood exposure to IPV. There remain several complications that limit our understanding of how such a causal path from exposure to outcome actually works. For example, child maltreatment and IPV share some underlying risk factors, like poverty, that also have direct detrimental effects on children.[22] Further, the reaction of the adult victim may also be important. New research suggests that if the child witnesses IPV but has a caregiver that is still functioning well as a parent, this may buffer some of the effect.[23] Also similar to studies of maltreatment, there does appear to be a dose-response effect. In other words, a child who witnesses chronic IPV is likely to have worse outcomes than a child who only witnesses a single incident or limited and intermittent IPV.[24,25] Overall, current science suggests that exposure to IPV can result in harm to children's development and that more is worse, but much about exposure and outcomes remains unknown.

Most research on childhood exposure to IPV has focused on emotional harm, but it is also possible for children to be harmed by being in close proximity to violence (one of the authors had a very serious case like this involving an infant). Injury can occur prenatally if a mother is harmed during pregnancy.[26] The exact prevalence of IPV during pregnancy is not known, but research suggests it is not rare.[27] There is a commonly held belief that pregnancy places women at greater risk of IPV, but researchers aren't sure whether that is true or not.[28,29] We also know from research on 911 calls that older children may be injured or at risk of injury when trying to stop the violence.[30] We actually do not know how many physical injuries sustained by children occur, because they happen to be in the wrong place during a violent episode between adult caregivers in their home. Most child protective services (CPS) data systems do not have indicators for this, and vague categories, like "assault" or classification of an injury as "accidental" in emergency room data, make this very hard to count.

THE OVERLAP BETWEEN INTERPERSONAL VIOLENCE
AND CHILD MALTREATMENT

In many families, IPV and child maltreatment co-occur.[31-33] Much of the information we have on the overlap between child maltreatment and IPV comes from large studies of children known to have been maltreated that also included questions about the presence of IPV. Early research indicates that it could be possible that IPV is present in as many as a third to a half of all families known to CPS.[34] Data are more limited on the proportion of children living in families with IPV who are also maltreated. A national phone survey found that about 34% of youth who witnessed domestic violence also said they had been maltreated in the last year, with the overlap rising to 57% for lifetime occurrence of child maltreatment.[35] Another study found that nearly 60% of adults who reported childhood exposure to IPV also reported having been physically abused.[36]

Families involved with CPS with co-occurring maltreatment and IPV tend to have a large constellation of other risk factors. For example, studies have found higher rates of substance abuse, more prior (and subsequent) instances of child maltreatment, and higher rates of poverty.[37–40] Not surprisingly, experiencing both child maltreatment and IPV has been linked to problematic behavioral, developmental, emotional, and physical outcomes.[40–42] We don't yet know exactly how strong the differences are between maltreatment alone or maltreatment combined with IPV, whether types of either matter, or the exact mechanisms that lead to a given outcome.[17,41,43]

Why and How do IPV and Child Maltreatment Co-Occur?

There is no clear evidence or settled theory about why and how IPV and child maltreatment co-occur. For example, some scientists have found that domestic violence immediately after birth predicts later maltreatment,[44] but there is very little research on which comes first or whether they develop at the same time.

There appear to be at least three ways to think about the co-occurrence of IPV and maltreatment. To keep things simple and to be consistent with a recent news story example, we are going to use a stereotypical case of the father or boyfriend as perpetrator and the mother as victim. Jouriles and colleagues suggest three possible types of co-occurrence: (1) The father engages in IPV and also abuses the child; (2) the father abuses the mother, who then abuses the child; or (3) both parents are engaged in both behaviors.[45]

Mother and Child as Co-Victims

As is illustrated by this case from Oklahoma, there appear to be cases in which the father is abusing both the mother and her children in separate instances (see Figure 7.3):

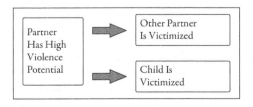

FIGURE 7.3 CM and IPV: Mother and Child as Co-Victims

She tells BuzzFeed things got especially bad when their second child was born in 2004. She says she never saw Braxton hurt their kids. But that fall, she brought their 20-month-old son to the hospital when she noticed his leg was swollen; he had a fractured femur and broken bones, leading suspicious authorities to check on his 3-month-old sister and find her injuries.[46]

This mother does not appear to be directly harming her children, nor is it clear whether she realized her child was being hurt until the child's injury was serious. We do not have good data on how often this is the form co-occurrence takes. In one study, 50% of the men who endorsed assaulting their wives also abused their children.[47] However, maltreating behaviors toward the child by the mother were not mentioned. Jouriles and colleagues[45] found only two studies that looked at this (and we were not able to find any newer ones), and the sole perpetrator model was the least common form of co-occurrence.

Interpersonal Violence Victims Abusing Their Children

Some people have suggested that domestic violence may place a level of stress on the mother that eventually leads her to be abusive toward her children,[47-50] as shown in Figure 7.4. In one qualitative study a CPS worker describes a mother who states she is hitting her child because "she was being hit by her husband so she had to make the child behave."[32] We just don't know if or how often this pattern occurs. In the Jouriles and colleagues review,[45] no studies reported this sequential type. Studies of maternal stress and behavior (not maltreatment) in the presence of IPV have found conflicting results. Some studies have found that domestic violence results in greater parenting stress and less warmth, while others have found that the mother's protective actions and warmth toward the children increased.[51]

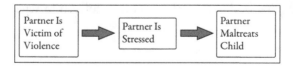

FIGURE 7.4 CM and IPV: IPV Victims as Abusers

Interpersonal Violence and Maltreatment by Both Parents

It is possible that the manifestation of violence between parents and between the parent and child stem from other problems. In such instances, IPV may be mutual and one or both parents may also abuse or neglect their children (see Figure 7.5). Both

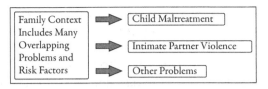

FIGURE 7.5 CM and IPV: IPV and CM by Both Parents

studies in the Jouriles and colleagues article[45] found support for mutual IPV with one or both parents also abusing the child. In another article,[43] the perpetrator of the maltreatment was not identified (i.e., one or both parents) but mutual partner IPV was the most commonly reported. Of course, as we mentioned earlier, this does not mean that the level of violence is the same between the parents or between the parent and child.

Can theories of why child maltreatment happens be extended to understanding the co-occurrence of IPV and maltreatment? It turns out that some of the well-known ideas for why child maltreatment happens such as stress particularly as related to poverty, lack of social support, community norms (approving of violence), or co-occurring issues like substance abuse, also figure prominently as causes of IPV.[22,52] There is some indication of increased risk of adult involvement in IPV associated with childhood maltreatment, but we aren't sure how exactly how this relationship manifests.[53,54]

Of course, there are some people (relatively few) who are prone to violence from their earliest years. As we mentioned in chapter 5, such individuals are often associated with the label "antisocial" or "psychopath," and tend to be arrogant, prone to impulsive action, and lacking in empathy.[55] The prevalence of individuals like this, however, is too small to account for the common occurrence of IPV or child maltreatment.[56,57] For most people, it appears that family violence grows a variety of risk factors and conditions. It is also a social phenomenon, not a disease, and therefore likely to be multidetermined.

CHILD PROTECTION'S ROLE? VIEWING DOMESTIC VIOLENCE AS CHILD ABUSE

Because of the overlap and the potential negative impact on children of witnessing IPV alone, some states (and other countries[58]) have looked to child protection to address this issue by classifying a child witnessing domestic violence as a form of child maltreatment. There are strong opinions and some data on this issue,[59] so we spend a little time talking through whether or not this is a good move for child protection.

Why Viewing Domestic Violence as Child Abuse Might Be a Good Idea

Classifying exposure to IPV as child abuse seems straightforward: (1) CPS agencies exist to protect children; (2) witnessing domestic violence may harm children; therefore, (3) child protection may have a role in responding to domestic violence, to keep kids safe and promote child well-being. We first review the case for why this might make sense.

First, creating policies that identify witnessing domestic violence as child maltreatment could be beneficial in cases in which there is significant risk of harm to the child because the parent victim is unwilling or unable to protect the child. Or, in some cases children may be at risk of harm because they become involved while trying to intervene.[60] This quote illustrates one perspective on how a parent who may "fail to protect" a child should be treated:

> In Oklahoma, a state with some of the highest child abuse rates in the nation, enabling child abuse is a felony that carries the same penalties as active child abuse. In a lot of ways, this makes sense. After all, as parents, we are programmed to protect our children. A parent who doesn't intervene when someone harms her child, or who fails to leave her child's abuser, fails in that regard.[61]

Such harm may or may not be present in an initial report of maltreatment, and most current programs are designed to work collaboratively to address both the mother's and the child's needs.[47,62] As a portion of a quote from a Canadian study illustrates, addressing the mother's needs may sometimes clash with the duty to protect.

> So the first probably two times we go out on a new case of domestic violence we're, you know, you're the victim and we recognize all that kind of stuff and how can we help you be safe and make changes for you, but then after two or three times you're like, "listen lady! You need to protect your kids and you're putting"—and you know we get, we take a much harder line because again we need to ensure kids are safe.[63(p95)]

A report of IPV exposure to CPS might also allow for an otherwise unseen risk to the child to be discovered. The next paragraph describes a case in which a call to CPS did not result in any attempt to intervene because the state did not consider domestic violence as a form of child abuse.

The December 2014 report was still pending when Jonchuck's (the father's) own lawyer called DCF one last time the day Phoebe died. Jonchuck, DCF was told, was "driving all over town in his pajamas" with Phoebe in the car. "The father seems depressed and delusional," the report added. Agency administrators acknowledge they failed to gauge the seriousness of that report. Shortly after midnight on Jan. 8, 2015, Jonchuck raced toward the iconic Sunshine Skyway Bridge in his white Chrysler PT Cruiser when a Pinellas County Sheriff's deputy spotted him. Jonchuck stopped the car on a bridge approaching the Skyway. And, as the deputy drew close to him, Jonchuck cradled his 5-year-old to his chest before flinging her off the bridge to her death, the Sheriff's Office said.[64]

In Phoebe's case, domestic violence was not accompanied by maltreatment per se, but there was a more general risk to the child and perhaps intervention could have offset tragedy. While this is an extreme example, several scholars have pointed to the potential of child welfare to operate as a gateway to services for the child and the mother.[33,65]

Why Viewing Domestic Violence as Child Abuse
Might Not Be a Good Idea

There are also compelling arguments against classifying child exposure to IPV as maltreatment. One potential problem, is that a woman who is being hurt by her partner may not be able (psychologically or physically) to prevent the maltreatment of her child, and then may have the child removed from her custody because she "fails to protect" the child.[66] This very much looks like the woman being victimized twice, once by the perpetrator and once by the child welfare system. While this has happened,[67] it is not clear that this is frequent. In Canada, which has a similar CPS response to domestic violence as some states in the United States, there is not evidence suggesting that exposure to domestic violence cases involved children being placed into foster care at higher rates.[58] This is consistent with at least one study of child welfare decision making in the United States.[68] In both cases, the decision to place a child into foster care was associated with the risk related to the maltreatment itself, *not* the presence of domestic violence.

A second issue has to do with the ability of child protection agencies to respond to IPV cases. Child protection workers are often not equipped to provide services directly to the mother even when they want to. Most of the time the actions of CPS will be limited to trying to provide referrals, which the mother may not choose, or be able, to take advantage of.[63] If the violent partner is present during the CPS investigation, this may also pose a barrier to connecting the mother with whatever services exist in the region. In at least one state where domestic violence was officially classified as child abuse, the rapid increase in reported cases coupled with the inability of

child protection to respond became such a problem that the policy including exposure to domestic violence as child abuse was repealed.[59] To our knowledge, this is
the only state to reverse its approach in this way. While other states have faced problems implementing a CPS response to IPV, most have chosen to focus on improving
models for continuing to serve these families.

Interpersonal Violence as Child Abuse? It Depends Where You Live

While child protection may have a role to play in responding to IPV, it remains to be
seen exactly which approach is the most effective and/or will be adopted into policy nationally. Once again our understanding of child protection responses is con-
founded by the variation in child protection policies adopted by different states.[69] As
can be seen in Table 7.1, in Ohio the child has to be physically very close to IPV for it
to count as maltreatment, while in Arizona this is not the case. Indiana is completely
different from all other states, with custodial status being a predominant factor.

TABLE 7.1

State Definitions	
Definition of Circumstances in Domestic Violence Specific to Child Witnessing	States
Domestic violence is committed in the presence of or perceived by a child	Arizona, California, Delaware, Florida, and Louisiana
Domestic violence when the child is physically present or can see or hear the act of violence	Alaska, Arkansas, Georgia, Hawaii, Idaho, Illinois, Indiana, Mississippi, Montana, North Carolina, Oklahoma, Oregon, Utah, and Washington
"Child Witness" applies to any child who may be present or witness the domestic violence act	Arizona, Georgia, Hawaii, Idaho, Louisiana, Montana, Nevada, Ohio, Oklahoma, and Utah
"Child Witness" is specific to any child who is related to or a member of the household of the victim or perpetrator of violence	Alaska, Arkansas, California, Delaware, Florida, Illinois, Mississippi, North Carolina, Oregon, and Washington
"Child Witness" is only specific to noncustodial child of noncustodial parent	Indiana
Domestic violence act occurs within 30 feet of the child	Ohio

It is not really clear that any of these definitions are grounded in research. Why set a harmful distance of being within 30 feet of the incident as in Ohio? Are CPS workers going to be issued large tape measures? What does "perceived" violence look like as compared to "witnessed"? Many of these questions just aren't answered in law or policy, which makes case decision-making more challenging.

Legal Decision-making

Another dilemma in response to co-occurring maltreatment and IPV is that the legal process may involve at least two different courts. If CPS is terribly concerned about the child's safety, they may refer the case to a family court, but that court has no role in addressing the IPV. Child protective services also has no role in cases of noncaregiver paramours. In the Oklahoma example, you have a harm to the child (witnessing domestic violence) but CPS has no role to play regarding the mom's boyfriend, so any action is limited to the mother. So whom should the CPS worker identify as the perpetrator? Under Oklahoma law, and under the law of many states, the perpetrator listed on the child maltreatment case is the mother because she is failing to protect the child and has care, custody, and control. What happens to the perpetrator of IPV will vary by state and relationship to the child.[69] In most instances, this will also involve the adult criminal court. Table 7.2 illustrates some of the variation in the potential penalties that involved adults might face.

If the case reaches a criminal court, there is discretion in terms of how the case is handled. We return briefly to the prior news story to illustrate how the parents are treated quite differently in regard to sentencing. Let's read a little more about our earlier example.

Tondalo Hall was allegedly being abused by her boyfriend, Robert Braxton Jr. Yet when Braxton broke the ribs and femur of their 3-month-old daughter, he served just two years in prison, while Hall was sentenced to 30 years for allowing the abuse to happen. She was one of 28 mothers in similar situations uncovered in a recent BuzzFeed investigation, one of just three such cases in which the mom got a longer sentence than the man who abused the child. . . . In court during her trial, as well as in statements outside of court, Hall described the abuse she says she suffered; the judge who sentenced her acknowledged that she seemed to fear Braxton. Hall ended up pleading guilty and testifying against Braxton, though she did not get a reduced sentence in return and he *did* get a deal when prosecutors realized their case against him was going south.[46]

TABLE 7.2

State Variation in Legal Response to Child Witness Cases

Legal Consequence to Child Witnessing in Domestic Violence	States
Abuser faces increased sentence if convicted of crimes that involve domestic violence	Alaska, Arizona, Arkansas, California, Florida, Hawaii, Idaho, Illinois, Montana, Mississippi, North Carolina, Ohio, Oklahoma, Oregon, Washington
Abuser faces additional charges for child maltreatment if prosecuted for the crime that involves domestic violence	Delaware, Georgia, Utah
Abuser or abused partner may face child maltreatment charges	California, Illinois, New York
Abuser or abused partner faces investigation by child welfare agency for emotional maltreatment	Alaska, Minnesota
Abuser liable for child's counseling costs if convicted of a crime that involves domestic violence	Connecticut, Illinois, Louisiana, and Nevada
Abuser must undergo counselling	Ohio and Oklahoma

Source: Information from O'Malley et al., 2014[80]

It was certainly lucky (for the children) that the case was investigated by CPS, and CPS had no role in the criminal court's response. On the other hand, the criminal case outcome is disturbing to both child protection and IPV advocates. It is completely outrageous that a person can plead guilty to causing that type of serious harm to two children and get only 2 years in prison. It is equally outrageous that the mother who failed to intervene but herself committed no violent acts gets a sentence 15 times longer.[61]

Limitations of Interpersonal Violence Services

In our society, protecting children is something the government gets involved in, but protecting women is not a governmental function per se outside of the criminal justice response. There is no "women's protective services," although there is (since 1994) a federal Violence Against Women Act.[70] In most communities, government responses to violence against women are limited to regular police, courts, and tools such as temporary restraining orders (TROs). In a given area, services for domestic violence may range from far too little (hospital screenings and possibly some emergency shelter space) to much more sophisticated community-wide coordinated responses involving police, medical organizations, and nonprofit agencies.[69] Similar to child protection, some of these agencies have thresholds of severity. So for example, while any woman may be able to contact a crisis line and receive phone counseling or referral, only the most serious cases are admitted to shelters. Recall that CPS is largely a case management system, so another difficulty in serving IPV within a child protection framework is that the available services specific to the IPV may be sparse or difficult to access.[32]

Seeing the Problem Differently

Hester[71] describes this problem related to IPV and maltreatment in the United Kingdom as a matter of system culture. She calls her idea the "three planet model." In the United States, it is easiest to label the planets as CPS, victim/survivor protection and services, and the court system including family and criminal courts. The main point is that these "planets" evolved from differing points of view, with differing mandates and policies. This leads these groups to perceive the issue and their roles in very different ways.

For example, child protection workers may fear that domestic violence advocates will ignore the safety needs of the children and focus solely on the adult victim of domestic violence.[66] The CPS worker sees risk of harm to the child as their primary concern, even though they may be very sympathetic to the adult victim's situation.[72] In contrast, providers of IPV services see the adult victim as the focal point of their services. Anything that complicates her recovery may be viewed as unfair and an expression of societal policies that are antiwoman. There are websites where you can get tips on how to deal with the "problem of child protection" as a woman. Some of these websites have a decidedly anti-CPS slant (http://justicewomen.com/tips_bewarechildprotectiveservices.html.).

Hester's final "planet" is the court response, which is also quite flawed in many instances. Complaints range from unfair sentencing as illustrated by our news story about the Hall family[46] to fears that mothers unfairly lose custody,[58,67] to unfair responses to male victims of IPV,[13] to complaints about fairness in child visitation when maltreatment and IPV occur.[73] We do not have solid numbers on how often problems with each of the three planets occur alone or interacting with each other.

Clearly these issues impact public perception. On one hand, it is reasonable to be upset when things go wrong due to incompetence, lack of resources, or other causes.

On the other, it is hard to imagine any human or medical service system in which such mistakes never happen. There is simply a difference in orientation between assuming an entire system is biased or "evil" and trying to identify problematic areas in or between systems and address those.

ADDRESSING INTERPERSONAL VIOLENCE
AND MALTREATMENT OUTSIDE CPS?

The co-occurrence of IPV and child maltreatment is a very complicated issue and is one of the least coherent parts of the public safety approach in our country. Obviously, prevention of both would be ideal, and we address child maltreatment prevention in the final chapter.

Some see societal norms as perpetuating the occurrence of IPVs, which leads to recommendations like changing norms about how society sees violence against women through media campaigns.[52] The research on the effectiveness of such approaches is limited, and what studies do exist show relatively little impact.[74] Recently, the large number of highly visible cases of IPV and child abuse in professional sports appears to have prompted change that goes beyond passive media campaigns. The NFL has begun a mandatory training program in domestic violence, sexual assault, child abuse, and driving under the influence. While its impact remains to be seen, we this as a hopeful sign that may serve as a model for other industries.[75] You may also recall the story of successes in Sweden around changing norms about corporal punishment in chapter 3.

Four approaches to address the overlap in IPV and child maltreatment were located that fall largely outside child protection. The first approach suggests ways of extending safety prevention practices typical in IPV interventions to include child safety planning,[76] but no outcome research could be located. Another approach is to engage the batterer (in almost all cases these campaigns target the male) in seeing his responsibility toward the child and proactively rejecting violence. A component of this has been integrated into some battering intervention programs in England, but only preliminary and qualitative reports of effectiveness could be found.[77] Home visitation programs have been suggested as promising avenues for domestic violence prevention,[31] as they have been for maltreatment. Strong evidence for the effectiveness of home visitation approaches relative to maltreatment or domestic violence, however, remains to be found. Finally, there are calls for enhanced roles for medical providers (doctors, nurses, etc.) in the screening and support for victims as well as children.[70] It is not clear however how this translates into reduction of IPV and/ or child maltreatment without additional formal services as found in models like

Project SEEK designed to address maltreatment.[78] Hopefully, further research will advance our understanding of these and other prevention innovations, but improvement to the child protection response itself is also key.

REFORMING AND REFRAMING

In 1999 the Greenbook Initiative[79] was launched to try to bring together the various parties involved in IPV and child maltreatment (child protection, domestic violence services, law enforcement, etc.). There are a range of toolkits and resources available to provide ideas to improve the situation. These range from media campaigns to funding sources to practice guidelines (see http://thegreenbook.info/read.htm). Almost all reports and articles discuss the need for better collaboration between the systems designed to support women in abusive relationships and the systems designed to support children.[47,80] A few states have integrated a domestic violence consultant into their child welfare staff to advise workers about resources and approaches to talking to victims about options,[81] and similar models are being implemented in the United Kingdom.[82] Its not yet clear how effective these models are at impacting both IPV and child protection goals.[83] Another model has to do with protocol development to guide child protection workers through the process of assessment and service delivery as well as in building collaborative relationships.[47,84] The empirical testing of these variations in responding to IPV and child maltreatment is still in its infancy. There are several training programs that have shown promise in professionals' efficacy in addressing the overlap.[85] To the extent that training helps address the confusion and tension involved in the assessment process, such efforts might improve the ability of child protection to respond.[63]

A quite different approach is the construction of parallel systems. For example, some suggest that an entirely new system centered on IPV be created to address situations where child protection is of less concern and limit the engagement of CPS to cases in which the danger to the child is severe.[86] This is similar to the idea of differential response in CPS, which we introduced in chapter 2. In Canada, a form of differential response treatment for co-occurring CPS and IPV cases found that CPS involvement was more protracted, but the rates of recurrent reporting of maltreatment were lower.[65]

It remains to be seen what the most successful approach to the co-occurrence of IPV and child maltreatment from a child protection standpoint will be. It may well look different in different places because of the resources available and the level of community support. It is clear that pitting the needs of IPV victims against the needs of children is not a good idea. Nor is serving one and ignoring the other.

8

Why Didn't They Say Something?

REPORTERS WHO DON'T, CHILDREN WHO WON'T,
CHILDREN WHO CAN'T

AS MENTIONED EARLIER IN THE BOOK, several sources suggest that many cases of abuse and neglect go unreported.[1,2] Why might this be the case? Sometimes it is because no one outside the family knows and a child won't or can't (due to age or disability) report. We have conflicting messages about keeping secrets in our culture. Most of us learn at some point (usually from peers) not to be a "tattle tale." This phrase is likely from an obscure nursery rhyme: "Tell Tale Tit, Your tongue shall be slit/And all the dogs in the town, Shall have a little bit."[3] A fascination with the virtue of being able to keep a secret despite hardship can be seen in the early Hungarian folktale, "The Boy Who Could Keep a Secret."[4] In this story, a child believes he will become the king after a dream but only if he can keep this secret. For this he endures abuse at the hands of his mother and the king who adopts him and is nearly executed several times. He is, however, eventually rewarded by becoming king. Such deeply ingrained messages about keeping secrets or not tattling may compound the difficulty a child faces when deciding to tell someone about abuse or neglect at the hands of their own caregivers (Figure 8.1).

Sometimes a failure to detect maltreatment has nothing to do with the child but instead reflects uncertainty on the part of bystanders about what to do. Even among adults who understand how and when to report, some may wrestle with the decision. It is really maltreatment? Could I be wrong? Will it really help to tell someone? Will I make it worse if I say something? Will the family retaliate against me in some way? We explore reasons why children may not disclose and why adults that are aware may not report more in this chapter.

FIGURE 8.1 Secrets

WHY CHILDREN KEEP MALTREATMENT A "SECRET"

Those readers old enough to recall Pat Benatar (or those of you who listen to oldies rock n' roll) may recall the following portion of her song "Hell is for Children":

> They cry in the dark, so you can't see their tears
> They hide in the light, so you can't see their fears
> Forgive and forget, all the while
> Love and pain become one and the same
> In the eyes of a wounded child
> Because hell
> Hell is for children
> And you know that their little lives can become such a mess
> Hell, Hell is for children
> And you shouldn't have to pay for your love
> With your bones and your flesh.
> It's all so confusing, this brutal abusing
> They blacken your eyes, and then apologize
> You're daddy's good girl, and don't tell mommy a thing

Be a good little boy, and you'll get a new toy
Tell grandma you fell off the swing.[5]

The song describes children being instructed by abusive parents to keep it secret. Honestly, we do not know how many cases of abuse or neglect go unreported because the child is successful at hiding the reality of the situation.

To Tell or Not?

Most of the research on children's disclosure of maltreatment has been done on child sexual abuse, and such studies find that it is not uncommon for children to delay reporting for months or years.[6,7] On the other hand, at least one study indicates that children who are victims of physical abuse are less likely to disclose prior to a child protective services (CPS) investigation than child victims of sexual abuse.[8] Some researchers have suggested that children will choose not to report maltreatment because of not wanting to hurt their caregivers,[9] but it's unclear how common this is. It is also possible that some children won't disclose to protect themselves, but will do so to protect someone they love or feel responsible for.[10]

There is a difference between a child actively seeking to hide abuse or neglect and being uncomfortable telling someone. Research indicates that children do consider issues of being believed, self-blame, and peer response,[11] but we don't really know how this varies by different types of maltreatment. In some cases, asking the right questions in a sensitive manner may help bring out the truth.[7] Hospitals are quite sensitized to suspicious injuries and have protocols for checking that stories given by caregivers and the child are consistent with the presenting injuries.[12] The level of routine in such a process was evidenced when our oldest child broke his wrist at an end-of-the-year school party. Despite the fact he was covered in grass stains and dirt, he was asked by every medical staff person encountered from the intake person, to the nurse, to the radiologist to explain how it happened. As a maltreatment researcher, his mother realized what they were doing and was glad to see the diligence. It was, however, amazing how many times within a few hours this occurred and how frequently his mother was in the room with him while the questions were asked. This latter part was a bit troubling. If we had caused the injury, would our son have disclosed in front of us?

Of note, while asking questions following an injury to assess for physical abuse seems straightforward, the same may not true for neglect.[13] It is not clear how many healthcare providers have standard approaches for assessing possible child neglect when an injury or serious illness due to medical neglect is not apparent.

When Children Can't

Younger children and children with certain disabilities may not disclose because of communication barriers. Obviously a child who is very young and not yet verbal is completely dependent on someone else noticing a problem and reporting. We seem particularly vigilant about reporting of infants. Children under the age of 1 year have the highest rate of screened-in reports for maltreatment.[14] It is not clear whether this reflects their greater vulnerability to injury and other health consequences that trigger reports or whether people are more sensitized to looking for signs of maltreatment in young children even if an injury or suspicious health concern is not apparent. Self-report requires a child reach a certain stage of language and memory development. Generally studies of forensic interviewing suggest children are not involved in such interviews until they reach about age 3 or 4.[15,16]

Children with certain disabilities may lack the ability to report maltreatment. We do not have a clear idea how prevalent abuse is for children whose disabilities impair communication.[17–20] In clinical populations with disabilities (i.e., hospitalized children) rates as high as 60% for physical abuse have been reported, but it is not clear whether this is representative of children with disabilities living in the community.[21] While some research suggests that children with certain disabilities and chronic health issues may be difficult to parent, which places them at more risk of maltreatment,[21–24] that is not the same as knowing how often it actually occurs. Further, in at least one meta-analysis there was no strong relationship between child disability and greater risk of physical abuse or neglect.[25]

Part of the issue here is the lack of cross-reporting between systems of child protection and systems that provide services to children with disabilities. Administrative child maltreatment databases usually do not do a good job capturing information about disabilities. For example, California and Texas record data on disability services that is reported to the national child abuse reporting archive, but Florida and New York do not.[26] Similarly, special education records, healthcare providers, and regional children's rehabilitation centers do not routinely record information about trauma or maltreatment.

TO TURN A BLIND EYE OR NOT? ADULTS DECIDING TO REPORT

When the child cannot or is unwilling to communicate what has happened, detection of maltreatment is dependent on the observation of others and their decision to report. Abuse and neglect do not always occur "in the dark" without witnesses or

signs noticed by others, but there are several reasons why bystanders and even mandated reporters may say nothing.

Is Reporting in My Best Interest?

The following excerpt from a news story[27] brings up one issue: fear of the perpetrator.

> The responding officer said this in the police report about the abused three-
> year-old, "I observed multiple injuries to her lower extremities, to include her
> buttocks, legs and lower back." He went on to say, "The victim had injuries to
> her shoulders and face to include black eyes."
>   . . . their description of a three-year-old girl who weighs 19 pounds, her belly
> distended from hunger is enough. Scars, scabs and bruises cover her tiny body
> from the back of her neck all the way down to the bottoms of her feet. One
> investigator told the *I-Team* this is the worst case of physical abuse she has ever
> seen where the child actually survived.
>   Eyewitnesses told police of abuse they had witnessed including spankings
> with a belt. During another incident, a woman watched as Brian Amis beat the
> toddler with a set of 15 keys. She said, "It was so violent that she had to leave the
> residence and go outside as she started to feel sick." The woman said she didn't
> intervene because she was nine months pregnant.

In other words, the female bystander was afraid of harm to herself and her baby if
she reported what she saw. We do not have data on how often maltreatment goes
unreported due to fear of retribution. While some research indicates that women are
more likely to intervene in cases of child abuse then men,[28,29] these studies did not
ask questions about perceived barriers to intervention like fear for one's own safety.

Is Reporting in the Best Interest of the Child?

Reporting can feel uncomfortable, and even professionals face uncertainty in how
to proceed. For example, in studies of medical providers it is not uncommon to hear
that attempting to screen for maltreatment is awkward due to the setting or the
perceived conflict between the idea of "policing" as compared to "clinical care."[30,31]
There is some evidence that structured training processes can help with this problem,[32] but the research on the effectiveness of training for mandated reporters is
quite sparse. Nor is the research community immune from fears of reporting. There
is great debate about the ethics of asking children about their experience of abuse or
neglect in studies.[33-35] This is because the researchers are mandated reporters and
must report any maltreatment that child subjects disclose to them. Some researchers

choose to ask questions that indicate "risk of maltreatment" (e.g., harsh punishment, parenting stress, etc.) rather than actual maltreatment experiences, freeing themselves of any legal responsibility to report particular events.[36] Recall, though, that risk of something does not mean it will occur. Is asking about maltreatment directly harmful? There is a growing literature suggesting that asking about maltreatment in research might provide more benefits than not asking,[37,38] or might at least do no harm.[39]

What if reporting does no good or even makes it worse? There are numerous tragic tales of children who were known to child protection and yet were not protected.[40] Such stories may influence reporter behavior. For example, in a study of school social work practices, one worker expressed frustration at the apparent inaction of CPS and the futility of reporting.[41] Similar sentiments, that CPS is likely to either not respond or might make things worse, have been found in the research for quite some time.[42–44] The following is a quote from a pediatrician:

> While he [clinic social worker] advised me similarly about reporting, we agreed that nothing would be done if the case was followed by CPS at all. But we both felt that CPS probably wouldn't have done anything about the case.[42(p263)]

Similar views have been found in studies of the general public.[45]

The frustration is, on one hand, quite understandable. Most cases of severe maltreatment cited from news stories in this book had histories of more than one report to child protection. Recall from chapter 2 that many cases reported do not meet the legal standards required to respond, or once a response (investigation) happens, to compel the acceptance of services. Child protective services may also lack capacity to respond with services due to high caseloads and lack of sufficient resources in the community to meet a family's needs.[46] On the other hand, the presence of prior reports can actually increase the risk level on such assessments and make the case more likely to be pursued in the future.[47] In other words, a report that does not result in action may well be critical to passing a later threshold for intervention when another report is made.

Are there benefits of reporting even if services are not provided? This seems counterintuitive, but recall that studies of participation in research find that participants often report a benefit to disclosure. At least one study found that some victims who are believed and reported felt it was beneficial, even if the report did not "fix" the problem.[48] This is a fairly new way of thinking about reporting, however, and we do not understand to what extent a given child benefits even when services are not provided or when services are ineffective. Such perception of helpfulness may differ according to the relationship between the family and the reporter, whether the perception of the parent or the child is the focus, or even the quality of engagement with the CPS worker that responds.[49,50]

It's None of My Business

We talked about this a little in relation to corporal punishment in chapter 3 and talk about it a bit more in the final chapter, but the reality is that there is a tension between the value of the rights of the family and norms of noninterference[51,52] and the rights of a child to safety and nurturing. This tension between a child's rights compared to a family's or parents' rights is not limited to the United States.[53,54] As social work professionals, both of the authors are mandated reporters so, to some extent, this issue is resolved for us. Some argue that mandated reporting gets in the way of a more appropriate response of care by the community,[55] but it is not necessarily a natural response for other adults to intervene to support families or protect children. We found this theme expressed in several contemporary songs.

In "What's the Matter Here"" by 10,000 Maniacs, a woman notices that her neighbors are abusing their son. The woman questions how anyone could do that to their child, but hesitates to say anything because she doesn't think she should interfere.

> All these cold and rude
> Things that you do
> I suppose you do
> Because he belongs to you . . .
> And I want to say, "Hi"
> Want to say
> "What's the matter here?"
> But I don't dare say
> "What's the matter here?"
> But I don't dare say.[56]

In "Alyssa Lies" by Jason Michael Carroll,[57] the singer/narrator's daughter has a classmate that appears to lie about her injuries, and the daughter is concerned. Finally, one night after hearing his daughter pray for her classmate he decides to intervene. Unfortunately, it is too late and Alyssa has been killed by her parents, "Alyssa lies with Jesus because there's nothin' anyone would do."

Research involving self-reported victims of abuse suggests that in a fair amount of cases there is a bystander witness to abuse by an adult.[58] That same study reported that most individuals reported no impact when bystanders attempted to intervene. A study of bystander involvement in child neglect indicated that individuals that adhered to the idea that it was up to the family to decide how children were raised, were less likely to report observing child neglect and somewhat less likely to intervene.[29] That same study reported that women and adults with more education were more likely to try to offer help. Community approaches to maltreatment prevention that educate and engage large members of the community along with formal agency services may offer promise in enhancing our ability to intervene.[59] It is still too early, however, to understand how such community-based programs impact prevention of initial or recurrent maltreatment.[60]

REPORTS THAT DON'T PAN OUT: LIES AND MISTAKEN REPORTS

It would be wrong to avoid the "elephant in the room," the possibility that children or adult reporters are sometimes wrongly accusing someone of maltreatment either by mistake, or more troublingly, on purpose. First, it is possible to believe a child is maltreated and just be mistaken. One of the cases investigated by one of the authors many years ago involved a report of a series of horizontal lacerations across the sides of a child's legs. Upon arrival, the parent and child were able to simply show the investigator the thorn bush that child had ridden through on a bicycle. This was an honest mistake made by a concerned party. As mentioned in chapter 2, there are also some medical conditions that can look very much like abuse but are not.[61-62] Reports based on these observations are made without malicious intent. As pointed out in an article reviewing the New Zealand child protection system, people who report and those who screen cases reported operating with a high degree of uncertainty.[63]

Malicious Adult Reporters

There are calls made maliciously, but these are the exception rather than the rule. Sometimes such calls move ahead to the investigation phase, but many such cases are "screened out" or rapidly closed following initial assessment. Among official reports in Canada (which has a similar national system to ours), intentionally false reports were about 4% of all reports.[64] Even in instances where there are hotly contested child custody issues (commonly cited sources for such allegations), one study found that less than 25% of parents in these highly conflictual situations resorted to false allegations of maltreatment to try to win their case.[65] So does it happen? Yes. Is it common? No.

The Burden of False Reports

Despite the fact that intentionally false reports are uncommon, some have raised concerns that erroneous reports from mandated reporters drain valuable agency resources better spent elsewhere.[66] While this argument may seem commonsensical, the reality is that the proportion of child welfare funds and personnel time spent on the investigatory function is quite small.[67] This is not to say that improving the accuracy of child welfare reports is not a laudable goal. There is a lot of room for improvement. Researchers and policy makers note the great diversity in the content and frequency of training for mandated reporters, let alone the community.[68] Very little rigorous study has been done on the effectiveness of various training approaches for mandated reporting.[44] Clearly we could improve on both reducing "false negatives" and "false positives," and we need more evidence on how training impacts this. It is hard to imagine any policy, however, where honest mistakes, like the "thorn bush" report above, are completely avoided.

Children Reporting Falsely?

Many people wonder about false reports made by the child. Once again we do not have good data on how many children falsely accuse someone of maltreatment, but it is certainly rare. We do know that children (like adults) can be susceptible to suggestion. There is a vast literature related to this that has resulted in significant changes to how forensic interviews are done to avoid leading a child to a false statement or assumption.[69] On the other hand, in the study of conflictual custody families mentioned above, only 5 of the 26 false reports showed any evidence of coaching.[65] Typically the concern is the opposite; that children are reluctant to come forward.

Training for mandated reporting always emphasizes believing the child. Could this result in reporters being wrong? Sure, but ultimately it is a question of whether it is better to be wrong and apologize or be reluctant to believe a child and miss a case in which there are serious concerns.[63]

HOW COULD WE DO BETTER?

From a public health perspective, ideally we all need to gain more comfort in taking action when we suspect a child is being maltreated. Adults need to be ready and willing to listen when a child discloses and know how to report to the appropriate authorities. We need to improve training and resources to aid in detection and comfort with reaching out to families that may not need to be reported now, but without help will in the future. Calling attention to maltreatment is important, but it is the intervention that does or does not follow that will likely make the greatest difference in the life of a child.[70-72] Our last two chapters talk in more detail about system issues and reforms, but first we address one final issue that we have mentioned a bit already. We explore the reality that not all children who experience maltreatment have bad outcomes.

9

Resilience and Treatment

SOMETIMES, CHILDREN WHO suffer child abuse or neglect go on to live healthy, happy lives. We call them resilient. We used Cinderella as an example of emotional abuse in an earlier chapter, but she is also, at least in the modern Disney version, an example of resilience.[1] She is not bitter, she has no difficulties imagining a better future or obtaining it. Once her foot slides into the glass slipper, everything else is fine. We're just beginning to get a better understanding of why some people who experience stresses and trauma seem to do well and others do poorly. In this chapter we explore the idea of resilience and whether it is due to nature, nurture, or specialized care. To address the latter point, we also talk a bit about the kinds of treatment available for maltreated children.

WHAT DO WE MEAN BY "RESILIENCE"?

The American Psychological Association uses the term "bouncing back" in their definition of resilience, which makes a lot of sense (http://www.apa.org/helpcenter/road-resilience.aspx). It does, of course, suggest that before the negative experience things were going well. This does not always fit in cases where individuals appear to overcome a set of experiences that began in infancy or as least as far back as they can recall. In some cases it appears that there may be preexisting factors that allow someone to never really have a "happy beginning" and still have a so-called happy ending. So we prefer a broader definition that includes positive adaptation despite significant risk.[2] While we tend to think of resilience as all encompassing, some researchers have suggested that resilience following maltreatment may also be limited or domain specific.[3] In other words, there may be a continuum of resilience from very limited to spanning all areas of one's life.

Let's think about some familiar fictional characters as illustrations of apparent total resilience, limited resilience, and no resilience. Although they are a little extreme (most children neither grow up to save the world nor murder people), we hope that they get the point across.

- Harry Potter was seriously neglected and badly psychologically abused by his adoptive family. On the whole, he becomes a likable and functional person not markedly damaged by the maltreatment he experienced. He is able to achieve great things, develop friendships, and eventually establish his own family with children he seems to parent quite well.[4] In many ways, Harry epitomizes the idea of the completely resilient child.
- Jenny Curran, Forrest Gump's best friend, experienced ongoing sexual abuse at the hands of her father. She becomes something of a "lost child" as she moves into her teen and adult years—becomes involved with drugs, has a series of unstable relationships, moves around a lot, and contracts a fatal illness. With the exception of the illness, these issues seem to have been generally dealt with by the time she enters her thirties.[5] She is an example of a person who was hurt for years by maltreatment but was eventually able to find a degree of life satisfaction and certainly became a positive, loving parent. She is an example of more limited resilience.
- Classic silver screen villain Norman Bates (*Psycho*) grew up with a mother who was incredibly psychologically abusive (at a minimum). Norman never gets past the damage done, becoming a lonely, crazed, knife-wielding murderer whose homicidal tendencies are tied to an odd ongoing psychological presence of his mother.[6] Norman is not resilient.

How Common Is Resilience Among Maltreated Children?

Nobody has a firm estimate of how many maltreated children develop in a resilient fashion. Research estimates run the gamut from almost none to around half—partly because it depends on what outcome(s) one measures.[7,8] We've only been looking at this for about 25 years, which may sound like a long time, but in the research world that is a pretty new topic. Resilience across all aspects of functioning requires that we follow a child over many years. We've got very few studies that look at overall lifelong functioning—mainly because, by definition, that takes a lifetime to do and is pretty expensive. Few agencies or foundations are willing to fund a request for grant funding that begins with the words, "if you give me lots of money for the next several decades." Indeed some of the groundbreaking studies in this area include children who came to the attention of child protection some 40 years ago.[3]

Why Are Some Children Resilient?

As we have pointed out, some people who experience trauma do well and some do poorly. It is even possible that some people derive a psychological benefit following a traumatic experience.[9] This is kind of like the philosopher Frederick Nietzsche's famous assertion, "What does not kill me makes me stronger." We would very much like to be clear that we are not saying that harming children is a good idea because some people may derive some future benefits. We doubt that even our philosopher friend routinely invited people to beat him up just to make him "stronger." So what makes someone resilient? Does it mean everything is okay? Can we create resilience, or are we born with it?

There is some consistency in what research indicates as key ingredients of resiliency. Some of these are within the person, and some factors occur in a person's environment. We like the way a recent review[10] broke the idea of resilience down into things about the person (individual characteristics like adaptive coping skills), things about their family, and things about their community, and have provided a summary of them for you later. The children's story by Ronald Dahl (and movie) *Matilda* describes a child who despite emotional abuse and neglect by her parents and subsequent abuse by a school principal becomes a kind and talented young person.[11] In her story, we see hints of things mentioned in research on resiliency that appear in Box 9.1, she is exceptionally bright, appears to have a positive perspective on life, and is able to use other resources like reading to help her cope.[8] Matilda appears to be resilient in every way we can think of: She triumphs over those who were abusive is happy and even magical.

Another novel and film illustrates a different form of resilience. *Precious* is a 2009 film featuring an obese African American teen (Precious) who has been subjected to severe emotional, physical, and sexual abuse from a very young age by both her parents.[12] Her family circumstances impact her life across domains. She cannot read or write, becomes pregnant by her father resulting from sexual abuse, and ultimately contracts HIV. Remarkably the movie ends rather positively after caring adults become aware of her situation and intervene. She severs ties with her abusive parents, learns to read, and displays a strong determination to complete her education

---

BOX 9.1

FACTORS RELATED TO RESILIENCE (NOT ALL ESSENTIAL, BUT THEY CAN
ALL HELP)

Individual Characteristics:
- They have temperaments that provoke positive responses from those around them (they like people and they're likable).
- They are both social and independent (they get along well with others but aren't needy).
- They are optimistic and confident in their abilities.
- They cope with stressors and problems well.
- They tend to be internally, not externally motivated.
- They are easygoing.
- They are good at self-regulation (can monitor and control own emotional states and behaviors).
- They access positive people and opportunities.
- They gain strength from facing challenges, rather than being weakened by them.

Family Characteristics:
- Stable, cohesive families with strong emotional bonds and resources.
- Responsive, predictable, and firm parenting.
- Interesting and stimulating environments and experiences.

Community Characteristics:
- Adequate resources, both human and material.

---

and be a positive force for her children. Precious shows resilience by moving ahead with her life and making significant strides forward, but, like Jenny in *Forrest Gump*, her history exacts a cost.

Note that both Matilda and Precious "escape" into a smaller imaginary reality as one means of coping with their lives. This approach appears in nonfictional accounts of survivors as well. The following is a quote from Tyler Perry,[13] who was a victim of sexual and physical abuse: "I could go to this park (in my mind) that my mother and my aunt had taken me to. . . . I'm there in this park running and playing, and it was such a good day," Perry said to oprah.com. "So, every time somebody was doing something to me that was horrible, that was awful, I could go to this park in my mind until it was over."

What Matilda, Precious, and Tyler Perry demonstrate might be described as the ability to manage strong feelings and impulses, to help them cope in a healthy way.

ARE SOME PEOPLE JUST BORN RESILIENT?

Science, philosophy, literature, and almost all other human endeavors constantly wrestle with a set of questions involving what we used to call "fate." Are we born with a set of unalterable traits, or do we change throughout our lives? Some explanations take a middle course—While changes can be made, it is easier to make changes in people while they are very young: "Just as the twig is bent, the tree is inclined."[14] In the past we've also tended to believe that if something is biologically based, it is unchangeable. For example, there are a number of people trying to understand how resilience may be encoded in our genes.[15] Psychological aspects of a person, such as the ability to tolerate frustration, tended to be viewed as more subject to our control. This stark division, with biological meaning "fixed" and psychological meaning "changeable" is starting to blur. It turns out that your brain and even the expression of your genetic code (how your genes impact you in reality) can change over time in response to life experiences. There are at least two ways this can happen.

Neuroplasticity

Everyone builds neurological connections throughout childhood, and your neurological structure changes throughout your life. As we mentioned in chapter 4, we call this adaptive characteristic of our brain neuroplasticity. Of course there are limitations. Very rarely, a child will be found who has little (e.g., Danielle in chapter 4) or no human interaction during the early years of life.[16,17] These children can have tremendous difficulties learning language and "normal" human behavior. Barring such significant and apparently permanent insults specific to critical periods in development, however, our brains are rather amazing in their ability to adapt. We are also beginning to understand that this adaptability lasts much longer than we thought.

Recently, a fair amount of attention has been given to the idea of toxic stress, which is based on the idea that negative things that happen when you are very young can have lifelong biological effects.[18] On the positive side, there are advantages in the young brain that make young children responsive to intervention. For example, speech recognition and language acquisition gains in children who are deaf appear to be greater when cochlear implants occur before age 5, which is attributed to the young brain's greater ability to adapt.[19] Promising positive neural alterations due to interventions with young maltreated children have likewise been found.[20]

While it may be easier to change the brain in young children, it does not mean all hope is lost once this period is past. Advances in neuroimaging have helped us understand that the major structural changes we thought concluded in the teen years actually continue well into the 20s (Figure 9.1).[21,22] Various interventions like

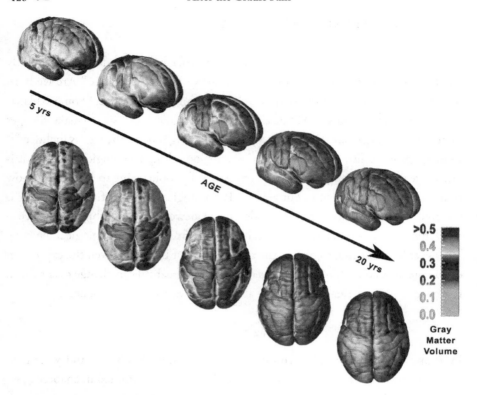

5 yrs

AGE

20 yrs

>0.5
0.4
0.3
0.2
0.1
0.0

Gray
Matter
Volume

FIGURE 9.1 Continuing Brain Development Through Adolescence

self-regulation training or meditation are increasingly understood to interact with the actual structure of your brain,[23] and intervention may have benefits even into our elder years.[24] When you think about it, this is really a quite hopeful perspective on the idea of overcoming past trauma or developing resiliency.

Epigenetics

Many of you may recall being in science class and seeing the twisting double helix shape of our DNA. Depending on when you went through high school, you may have been exposed to the idea that simple combinations of genes "caused" you to be who you are, or at least what you look like. Genes (or more commonly combinations of an array of genes) do control many things, like whether or not you are likely to get a range of genetically caused disorders like Fragile X syndrome. For many other things, however, it turns out though that the world around you and your experiences can sort of "turn genes on or off."[25] Genes combine to influence our behavior, and the expression of these "instructions" can be enabled or suppressed by what happens to you.[26] This may well impact resilience.[15] Research related to maltreatment suggests that this process works in relation to how later behaviors develop after trauma as well.[27-29] We aren't yet sure what all the practical implications of these "epigenetic" changes are or how reversible they may be. New research on honeybees suggests that at least some genetically proscribed castes in bee society can reverse.[30] We realize that we are not bees, but these kinds of findings lend hope that, we may discover that insults to our genetic expression may be plastic and reversible.

Some Stress Is Good

We alluded to toxic stress earlier[18,31]—the idea that if children get stressed too much when they are young, certain genes and neurological processes might function differently. But stress is not always bad. Turns out we need some level of stress in our lives[32] to teach us to respond and encourage growth. It's kind of like the temperature of porridge in the Goldilocks story being just right—you don't want too much, nor too little stress. The right amount of stress provides challenge and assists development. Scientists sometimes refer to having too much stress as having a high "allostatic load," which can alter not only behavior but also health outcomes.[33,34] This idea of a tipping point in how much stress is useful is not specific to neurobiological or social sciences, but is present in business and other areas, as illustrated in Figure 9.2.[35]

Where is that tipping point exactly? You may have heard about the Adverse Child Experiences Study (ACES), as it has gotten a lot of press. The original authors asked 10 questions (see Box 9.2) of a large number of adults (many in their 50s or older) seeking healthcare and they found that the more childhood adversities respondents said they experienced, the worse their health as an adult

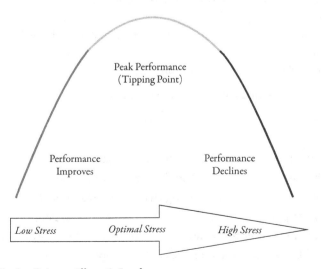

FIGURE 9.2 Tipping Point or Allostatic Load

BOX 9.2
ACES QUESTIONS

Prior to your 18th birthday (give yourself one point for each yes):

1. Did a parent or other adult in the household often or very often . . . Swear at you, insult you, put you down, or humiliate you? or Act in a way that made you afraid that you might be physically hurt?
2. Did a parent or other adult in the household often or very often . . . Push, grab, slap, or throw something at you? or Ever hit you so hard that you had marks or were injured?
3. Did an adult or person at least 5 years older than you ever . . . Touch or fondle you or have you touch their body in a sexual way? or Attempt or actually have oral, anal, or vaginal intercourse with you?
4. Did you often or very often feel that . . . No one in your family loved you or thought you were important or special? or Your family didn't look out for each other, feel close to each other, or support each other?
5. Did you often or very often feel that . . . You didn't have enough to eat, had to wear dirty clothes, and had no one to protect you? or Your parents were too drunk or high to take care of you or take you to the doctor if you needed it?
6. Was a biological parent ever lost to you through divorce, abandonment, or other reason?
7. Was your mother or stepmother . . . Often or very often pushed, grabbed, slapped, or had something thrown at her? or Sometimes, often, or very often kicked, bitten, hit with a fist, or hit with something hard? or Ever repeatedly hit over at least a few minutes or threatened with a gun or knife?
8. Did you live with anyone who was a problem drinker or alcoholic or who used street drugs?
9. Was a household member depressed or mentally ill, or did a household member attempt suicide?
10. Did a household member go to prison?

(Your ACES score is the total number of "yes" answers.)

---

was.[36] We call this totaling of risk factors "cumulative adversity," which is not radically different from notions of toxic stress or high allostatic load. These ideas are consistent with research suggesting that with chronic maltreatment comes an increased risk of poor outcomes.[37-39] As you might guess, people tend to be more resilient when they suffer fewer, less severe, and less chronic problems. So feel free to get your "ACE score," but remember that people are different and risk is not predestination.

CAN WE CREATE OR PROMOTE RESILIENCE?

The answer appears to be "yes," at least sometimes, with the right timing and intensity of service and support—even neurochemical changes attributed to maltreatment have been altered with intervention.[40] As simple as it sounds, research indicates that just being there and providing support for people during times of stress can have strong effects in increasing resilience.[41] On the other hand, we have a lot to learn about who can benefit from lower-level interventions like increasing social support or meditation skills training and who will need more intensive treatment approaches. For example, forms of mentoring combined with social skill training have shown promise to improve outcomes for maltreated children in foster care.[42] Other individuals will need much more intensive and structured intervention. There are evidence-based trauma-informed interventions that appear to have strong positive results for many young people—at least in the area of mental health and social behaviors.[43] Very often finding an effective treatment or intervention is a question of "fit"—some interventions may work better for some people than for others or at one age and not another. This is no different from many medical treatments. Anyone with medical issues like allergies, or high blood pressure, or worrisome cholesterol is likely to be familiar with the "try different things until something works" routine.

That being said, two of the most common approaches to intervene in maltreatment to promote positive child outcomes include parenting interventions and child-focused trauma intervention. Some of these we have alluded to in other chapters, and we mention them only briefly here.

Parenting Interventions

A number of interventions that were originally designed to help families to better handle disruptive children have been "repurposed" as child abuse interventions. Stronger relationships, better understanding of normative child behavior, and clear rules with appropriate (nonviolent) disciplinary approaches tend to make children better behaved and parents less stressed. Among the parenting interventions with the strongest evidence base are The Incredible Years, Parent Child Interaction Therapy, and Triple P.[44,45] All are fairly brief (a few months' duration). Emerging research does suggest promise in reducing rates of child abuse, though whether this works only for primary prevention or recurrence with child welfare–involved families or both is as yet unclear.[46–48] We are also beginning to explore whether or not these types of intervention directly impact a young child's response to stress. If they do, then we might actually be promoting positive coping abilities. A description of some of this work can be found at the following website[49]: http://www.acf.hhs.gov/programs/opre/research/ project/early-head-start-university-partnership-grants-buffering-children-from.

Interventions for Children

Unlike the way in which antibiotics eliminate the actual cause of bacterial infections, we cannot "unabuse" someone. Beyond stopping the abuse *per se*, individual treatment of victims of child abuse or neglect is really the treatment of problems and issues *caused by* child abuse like depression, anxiety, sleep disturbances, disruptive behavior, and many other problems.[50] Current approaches to helping victims of child abuse could be seen as attempts to foster resilience because they provide children with adaptive cognitive and behavioral skills.[51] For example, let's look at the common elements of various interventions within a broad category of treatments termed cognitive-behavior therapy (CBT). These interventions are among the most strongly evidence-based of child welfare–relevant interventions and is among the most widely used.[51,52] Cognitive-behavioral therapy focuses on three things—what you think, what you feel, and how you behave. A survivor of child sexual abuse like Precious might mistakenly perceive themselves as "damaged" or unworthy of other's positive regard. Cognitive-behavioral therapy would work on these "cognitive distortions" to help Precious understand that the abuse was not her fault and reveals nothing about who she is. Cognitive-behavioral therapy does this in part by teaching someone to practice new thoughts and notice when negative ideas begin to appear so they can be replaced with positive ones. Notice that we say practice thoughts not feelings. An interesting aspect of what we have learned about how our brains work is that as thoughts change, feelings tend to follow rather than the other way around. Recall that in the Harry Potter series the most powerful protective spell can only be conjured by focusing on one's most positive memory, and not just a feeling state.

There are a range of other interventions well supported by research that are tied to principles of CBT but are tailored to persons who have experienced trauma such as trauma-focused CBT (TF-CBT) or "attachment and biobehavioral catch-up" (ABC). If you are interested in exploring interventions used in the area of child maltreatment, there are a number of excellent websites you can use, including the California Evidence-Based Clearinghouse for Child Welfare (www.cebc4cw.org), the National Repository for Evidence-Based Programs and Practices (http://www. nrepp.samhsa.gov/), and the National Child Traumatic Stress Network (http:// www.nctsn.org/resources/audiences/parents-caregivers/treatments-that-work).

One last note regarding the use of what we call psychotropic drugs is warranted. Psychiatric medications can be helpful and are arguably necessary for some people, but the evidence shows they may work no better than other forms of psychotherapy for many common behavioral issues and also that they tend to work better when accompanied by other forms of psychotherapy.[53] It may help to think of it this way—sometimes neurochemical reactions in our brain require turning off or on or detuning or amplifying so that we are relieved of symptoms that may get in the way of learning positive thoughts and behaviors. An antidepressant, for example, is designed to make you feel better by interacting with chemicals in your brain. It does not address what is causing the depression, but it may allow you to start engaging in exercise, social activities, cognitive reframing, or other actions that can address the core issues. Currently, there is great concern that we are overmedicating children—particularly those who have been abused or neglected and are involved with child welfare.[53-55] Why are we worried? Some medications have significant side effects if used for too long or at certain developmental periods and, for many less severe childhood disorders, they do not seem to provide a level of benefit superior to other approaches that with less risk.[56-58]

PROMOTING POSITIVE OUTCOMES

Working with maltreating families or maltreated children to build resilience and improve longer-term outcomes is challenging, complicated, and yet still promising. Some maltreated individuals will and do find their own path to effective coping and positive life outcomes. In our view, while we do not always know how effective broad population level efforts are, there is nothing wrong with improving access to positive social supports, extracurricular activities, and opportunities for success for all children. Hopefully this will also benefit children who have experienced maltreatment. Further, we do have tools for helping those children and families who need something more, but access is not always easy. As we have noted many times, poverty and maltreatment are often closely related and poverty appears to impact access to effective intervention.[59] It is important that we have sufficient numbers of trained providers as well as adequate insurance coverage to meet the need for effective treatments.[60-62] Not only would providing better care probably save money but also it is the correct moral response to the needs of traumatized children.

10

Child Protection

A BROKEN SYSTEM? AN EVIL SYSTEM? A SYSTEM AT ALL?

RUMPELSTILTSKIN (see Figure 10.1) is a very old fairy tale.[1] In this story, the titular magical character appears to act out of self-interest, seeking some form of trade that impossibly disadvantages the other party. In at least one version, Rumpelstiltskin manipulates a young woman into agreeing to give her child to him in exchange for getting her out of a bad situation with a selfish king who thinks she can spin straw into gold. We never really find out why an elderly, mythical being would want a newborn child.

There is a certain similarity between Rumpelstiltskin's story and how many people seem to view child protective services (CPS). Child protective services workers are sometimes viewed as powerful (even evil) troublemaking beings who pop into the lives of families with the goal of taking children away at will.

In chapter 2 we covered "just the facts" about how the modern CPS system works. Here we deal with perceptions, misperceptions, controversies, and attempts at reform. As we have learned, our formal approach to child protection in the United States is less than 50 years old. That is not cause for excusing existing problems nor any assurance that if we just "give it time" things will all work out. We do believe that movement forward requires an accurate assessment of where we are. After all, one would not want to plan the first colony on the moon based on the idea it is made of cheese. In this chapter we wrestle with

FIGURE 10.1 Rumplestiltskin

questions like, Is CPS somehow villainous or at least hopelessly self-interested like Rumpelstiltskin? Why doesn't CPS prevent child abuse? Are reforms working or useless? Is there even a system to reform? We probably do not answer all these questions for you, but we endeavor to provide the information you need to decide for yourself.

CHILD PROTECTION WORKERS: HEROES OR VILLAINS?

Animal rescue organizations are somewhat similar to CPS in that they respond to calls of possible neglect or abuse of animals who, like children, cannot protect themselves. Television shows like *Animal Cops* invite us to view these professionals as heroic, rallying the public to support animal protection efforts and prevent abuse.[2] The job is depicted as rewarding and important, even when the animal cops extract animals from private property or remove them from protesting owners. There are few similar popular media images of CPS. It is not uncommon to see (or read) that child protection is a hated entity.[3]

Child welfare workers are routinely used as convenient bad guys in films.[4] Take "Ms. Grunion," a character in the recent children's film *Mr. Peabody*, for example. She is described on the "Mr. Peabody and Sherman Wiki" as "a dastardly social worker that is attempting to get Sherman taken away from Mr. Peabody. However, she does not actually care about Sherman's well-being, she actually wants to ruin Sherman's and Mr. Peabody's lives and make them miserable."[5] Ms. Grunion's character is obsessed with the desire to take away a child from his adoptive father, Rumpelstiltskin-like.

Recall from chapter 2 that the process of removing a child from their family is not easy and it violates the core system goal of keeping families together. Does that mean that CPS is always a positive force in family's lives or that all CPS worker's decisions are correct? No. but there is little reason to believe this is based on systemic ill intent or widespread hidden biases (like Ms. Grunion's supposed desire to ruin lives and obvious distaste for the fact that Mr. Peabody is a dog). The reality is that CPS decisions are often difficult and made under time limits with multiple families on a worker's caseload:

> I've got 30 days to put it together—do I close this? . . . it has to do with how you assess the situation—actually the questions you ask, the information you get, the responses you get. . . .So you weigh all those things but you're going by your gut feelings, your skills, experiences, I don't know what else—I don't have any magic, I can tell you that.[6(p95)]

Interestingly, there is a book that came out in 2004 that reported on a study of 30 "animal cops."[7] The contents suggest that although they may be held in more positive regard by the public than CPS, animal protection workers also face challenges. Animal protection workers tell similar stories of struggling with the right use of authority and making correct decisions in stressful situations.[8]

What Do Parents Think?

The short answer is, it depends whom you ask and when. Research suggests that perceptions of CPS by families vary according to the quality of the relationship with the worker and whether or not their child enters foster care. Families who perceive their workers to be caring, capable, genuine, and helpful report more satisfaction with their encounter with CPS (Box 10.1).[9-15] One mother remarked, "They're asking me how I need help and listening to me."[13(p817)] Other studies have found that families

---

BOX 10.1

CLIENT SATISFACTION WITH CPS SERVICES IN WASHINGTON STATE

- 70% of clients felt "my social worker was mostly there to help, not just to say what was wrong."
- 77% of clients felt respected.
- 66% were "satisfied with my contact with CPS."
- 76% were "satisfied" or "very satisfied" with the investigation.
- 61% reported that their family was doing better after the investigation.
- 9% reported that their family was doing worse after the investigation.

(English et al., 2002).[10]

---

are more satisfied when CPS provides more services.[13,14,16] In particular, when CPS workers can attend to the immediate (often material needs) of a family, the family's perception is more positive.[14,17] Families also appreciate workers who understand their cultural and social context.[18] This all makes intuitive sense, and these factors are consistent with the reasons people report liking other service providers, like their family doctor.[19]

The actual figures for how much clients like or dislike CPS workers might surprise you. Over the past several decades, various researchers[10,20–22] have found that most (about 60%–80%) of CPS clients see their worker positively and believe that their family is safer after receiving services. By way of comparison, these satisfaction ratings are only slightly lower than figures reported for people who voluntarily seek mental health services.[23,24] Of course, even if only 20% of CPS involved families are dissatisfied, this means that about 400,000 people per year might have negative stories to tell. Across studies, most negative comments fall into the following categories: being ineligible for or getting fewer services than desired, receiving insufficient information, having a child placed into care, or perceiving the worker as improperly exerting power.[10,11,12,14] So is CPS beloved by all? No. But available data certainly suggest a different picture of CPS than that portrayed by Ms. Grunion.

Some worry, however, that as negative media portrayals (fictional and not) of CPS become the norm, this may harm the morale of workers[5,25–27] and unduly influence public opinion. A recent study including California, England, Finland, and Norway found that less than 40% of the public had high levels of confidence in child welfare.[28] If the public generally perceives CPS in a negative light, it's possible that this complicates the ability to engage those families reported.

Child Protective Services Worker Morale and Retention

In the authors' experience and as revealed in first-person accounts and qualitative studies, people who decide to work in child protection generally do so because they want to help children. Turnover, however, is quite high. The job can be frustrating, stressful, and sad. Appropriate education and training are among the factors that enhance recruitment and retention of qualified CPS workers.[29] As we pointed out in chapter 2, the variation in preparation and degree expectations for CPS is often not in line with the challenges faced. Organizational factors like high caseloads and court decision timelines may also add to the likelihood of excessive stress and burnout,[6,11,30] as illustrated in a quote from a study of CPS in Canada:

> There was a sense of "I cannot keep doing this. I cannot meet the response times that's necessary." ... [I]t's the constant—it's like a wheel. And it just goes and it goes and it goes, and there's no stopping it.[30(p388)]

While we learned that families are more satisfied with CPS when they receive more services, services are not always easy to obtain.[6,31] Shdaimah captures this issue rather well in the title of a 2009 article, "CPS is Not a Housing Agency; Housing is a CPS Problem."[32] Imagine the frustration of a CPS worker trying to help a very poor family with significant housing needs who sees the following notice:

> The St. Louis Housing Authority (SLHA) Section 8 Housing Choice Voucher waiting list is currently closed. It was last open in July 2014, and prior to that in December 2007. There is no notice of when this waiting list will reopen.[33]

It seems unlikely that a person who feels undertrained and overwhelmed with caseloads or suffering from secondary trauma[34] will perform at the "top of their game." Imagine being a doctor and having no pharmacies available to fulfill your prescriptions. It is perhaps not surprising the CPS worker recruitment and retention is a major concern.[29-31]

INTRUSIVENESS AND BIAS IN CHILD PROTECTIVE SERVICES?

Returning to Ms. Grunion's character for a moment, she appears to have a particular bias against a dog being a parent. One of the recurring criticisms of CPS revolves around perceptions of possible bias or undue surveillance. We discussed this in relation to poverty in chapter 4 and were unable to find evidence that this exists at a practically important level. Now we explore the issues of race as well as ongoing intrusion in the lives of reported families.

What About Race?

Black families are about twice as likely to be reported to CPS as are white families.[35] This is a serious concern. It is, however, important that we correctly identify the cause. For example, belief that this form of racial disproportionality was caused by racial bias within CPS led to a great deal of money spent and many policies enacted to improve the training of child welfare professionals to be culturally sensitive.[36] It is, of course, a good thing to be culturally sensitive. On the other hand, there are two fundamental reasons why making child protection workers culturally sensitive cannot fix disproportionate reporting.

One, that we have already talked about and will not spend too much time on here, is the simple fact that CPS does not generate its own reports. The CPS workers are mandated reporters, but as we pointed out in chapter 4, they do not try to find cases, they respond to other people's calls (like the fire department). While racial bias among mandated (or non-mandated) reporters could exist outside CPS, early work found very small and inconsistent effects[37] and recent work finds no evidence for this.[38]

Our second reason brings us back to poverty. In the United States, black children are about three times more likely to live in poverty than white children,[39] and similar or greater disparities exist for American Indian and Alaskan Native children.[40] Poor children of color are also much more likely to live in areas of concentrated poverty.[39,40] Children living in areas of extreme disadvantage face a range of educational and health disparities that increase the need for a range of health and social services.[41] While some research indicates that close proximity to certain social services may be protective against maltreatment,[42] such services are often harder to access in severely disadvantaged communities.[43–45] We made the case in chapter 4 that while most poor families do not maltreat their children, poverty increases the risk of maltreatment. Black children are much more likely to live in families and communities that are severely disadvantaged. It is quite plausible that the racial disproportionality in child welfare (at least at the reporting level) is primarily driven by economic inequities in the United States that place undue strain on families which triggers reports by others that are hoping CPS can help.[46,47] In studies where both family and community poverty are controlled, low-income black children are not more likely to be reported than similarly poor white children.[48]

Not Just Black and White?

So far, the vast majority of research, opinion, and press on disproportionality has focused on differences in CPS participation between black and white children. This is, in part, because our data on other racial and ethnic groups has limitations. For example, in chapter 2 we learned that tribal governments can set up independent child protection systems. These systems do not always cross-report to state agencies,[49] so their numbers are not correct in national reports. There are other problems due to aggregation of data on populations into single groups like "Asian." This can cause misleading conclusions. Overall, Asian Americans have lower rates of maltreatment (officially reported or otherwise estimated) than other groups.[50] Certain ethnic groups within this category (e.g., Vietnamese and Cambodian families), however, are overrepresented compared to their proportion in the population.[50] Immigrant status may also matter but is not captured in CPS data. For example, despite high poverty within many Hispanic/Latino communities, there is a phenomenon often called the "Hispanic Paradox." Due to poverty, we would expect higher Hispanic rates of maltreatment, poor health, and other similar outcomes compared to whites, but that is not what the data show.[38,50] It looks like this effect, however, is limited to more recent immigrants and decays for subsequent US-born generations.[51-53] Is there racial/ethnic disproportionality in CPS for other groups? It's hard to study with currently available data.

Bias Against Families After Contact with Child Protective Services?

There is a common notion that it is hard to overcome a first impression. Similarly, some advocates and scholars have suggested that once a family is identified by CPS, they continue to be followed and are at higher risk of being re-reported. Recently this idea was used to suggest that a child served by CPS might be watched for the rest of their lives for a variety of reasons—possibly causing intergenerational reports if they become parents.[54] In the age of "big data," perhaps it is easy for some people to consider (and even worry about) it being possible for CPS to follow children forever and flag them as risks for possible later intervention. The data, however, don't support this idea.

Studies of CPS families and recurrence (within a few months or years of the first report) have found a very small increased risk right away that decreases rapidly once contact ends.[55,56] A recent study found no evidence that persons with a CPS history who became parents were more likely to be reported by a mandated reporter, and found they were very unlikely to be reported by social services.[57] While *substantiated* perpetrators can be added to central registries that are maintained for many years for employment checks, this is not true for the child subjects of reports. Many states actually destroy records on children and nonperpetrator adults within a few years of a report.[58] CPS rarely has the capacity for easy long-term tracking of cases. Given that studies find a rapid decay in risk of re-report for served cases within just a few months of initial services, long-term or intergenerational surveillance by CPS seems very unlikely. Additionally, of course, we hit the same old issue—CPS does not create it's own reports.

AFTER A REPORT: IS CHILD PROTECTIVE SERVICES DECISION-MAKING RACIST?

Even if CPS biases do not impact initial reports, is it possible there could be bias in later decisions? Several recent books and some press coverage have flatly asserted that CPS makes racist decisions that lead to later system overrepresentation—particularly in foster care. Examples of arguments on both sides of this issue can be found online on the Child Welfare Information Gateway.[59] We do our best to briefly summarize the empirical evidence.

Concluding an Investigation

Recall from chapter 2 that a traditional investigation involves a CPS worker deciding whether or not to substantiate a case. The vast majority of children who enter foster care due to maltreatment do so only after a report has been substantiated. Studies have found inconsistent and very small effects at this stage—typically limited to certain regions or particular workers in a study.[60-62] Comparing children of similar incomes, a recent large study found lower-income black children had lower (not higher) substantiation rates than lower-income white children.[53] The best available recent evidence suggests that there is no practically large effect of racial bias at this stage.

Foster Care Placement

It is hard to escape the centrality of foster care in the public discourse about racial disproportionality in child welfare. This has been the topic of heated exchanges that have at times spilled over into child protection policy.[63-65] There are at least two issues that complicate understanding this issue—poverty and who decides.

We have already talked about the intersection of poverty and race in the United States and the association of poverty with problems that can severely impair parenting like mental illness or substance abuse. An early large-scale study found that racial differences in placement went away once these other related issues were controlled.[66] Sounds straightforward, but what if a poor family also lives in a disadvantaged neighborhood with limited access to services? It is possible that the overlap of poverty and associated problems, race, and lack of access to services makes it much harder for a family whose children are at risk of placement to achieve progress on case goals to keep the child(ren) safe. This could lead to disproportionate placement even though it has nothing to do with CPS bias in decisions.[44] Some are testing this theory by improving community services in low-income areas to help address disparities in placement.[67]

Another complicating factor is that placement into care is not solely a CPS decision. Recall that within a few days of a child being taken into care, it is a family or juvenile court judge that decides to uphold the decision. As we mentioned in chapter 2, we actually don't have a lot of data on judicial decision-making and foster care placement.[68] The CPS worker does make a recommendation to the court, but how often that recommendation is altered according to legal counsel, expert testimony, or the judge's discretion is not known.

Race and Child Protective Services in Historical Context

It is hard to find current empirical data that suggest that widespread bias within today's CPS system is a significant driver of current disproportionality. Could there be other reasons for both disproportionality and the persistent view of CPS as a racist institution? We think so, and for this we turn to history.[69]

Historically, placement into orphanages and foster care was sometimes rooted in extremely destructive and clearly racist (and/or classist or religious or ideological) philosophies.[65,69–71] We have already mentioned examples like the orphan trains and Indian Boarding Schools. There were, however, other examples of practices in which children were grossly unequally treated by race. For example, in the 1800s, several private organizations that arose out of concern for how children were treated in almshouses, simply refused to help Black children.[65] Could the current CPS system be somehow still carrying forward these behaviors perhaps through some type of unconscious bias?[72] Possibly, but, as we pointed out earlier, the empirical data on bias in the modern system has found mixed or very small associations with decision-making.

Are there other ways racism could be operating? Quite possibly. Let's revisit what was happening in the decades just prior to the advent of the modern CPS system. In the 1950s Black children did start to enter care at higher rates. One legal scholar suggests that this was due to government spending shifting from in-home services to foster care.[72] But to divest there has to be an investment. Quite sadly, it is hard to find evidence that the government was ever doing much to support Black communities in the first half of the 20th century. Most histories of Black communities in the United States prior to 1960 describe a very grassroots-level social service system that was supported through churches, clubs, activist organizations, and philanthropy—not the federal, state, or even local government.[73,74] There were however significant government policy shifts outside social services that are salient to the question.

During the first half of the 20th century there was a northward migration of Black populations and increasing segregation by race and class.[75] The federal government at worst actively supported and at best turned a blind eye toward racist approaches to zoning, loans, and freeway construction that helped establish and maintain concentrated areas of poverty.[76] This did not go unnoticed. Martin Luther King Jr. said this about the increasing racialization of poverty in the late 1960s:

> When the Constitution was written, a strange formula to determine taxes and representation declared that the Negro was sixty percent of a person. Today another curious formula seems to declare that he is fifty percent of a person. Of the good things in life, the Negro has approximately one half those of whites. Of the bad things of life, he has twice those of whites. Thus half of all Negroes live in substandard housing. And Negroes have half the income of whites . . . their segregated schools receive substantially less money per student than the white schools.[77]

This is not all "past history." Black and other children of color remain at vastly greater risk of living in concentrated poverty.[39,40] As stated earlier, for many families this also means increased risk of a variety of untoward outcomes that make it difficult to parent and decreased access to preventive services.[42-43]

How Do We Fix Disproportionality?

Is there strong evidence that bias within current child protection practices is causing disproportionality? No. Does that mean racism never exists in CPS? No, but it's not sufficient to be the main cause of disproportionality. We think the situation was rather eloquently summed up in a 2015 article by Leroy Pelton, a researcher who did work on poverty and maltreatment for decades:

> Such disproportionalities in poverty can be linked historically to racism, but from outside the system. Of course, any racial prejudice affecting any decisions whatsoever being made within the child welfare system must be directly addressed, but even its eradication within the system will not substantially reduce racial disproportionalities within that system. If racial disproportionalities within the child welfare system trouble us, we must recognize their roots in poverty, and address poverty and its material deficits as best we can within the system itself, as well as outside of it.[47(p34)]

We also still see instances in which policies like the Indian Child Welfare Act, designed to right some of the past wrongs for this population, are still ignored.[78] Clearly policies and services designed to prevent unnecessary or inappropriate placements need to be fully funded, effective, and equitably applied.

NEW DIRECTIONS IN CHILD PROTECTIVE SERVICES: PROMISING AND COST-EFFECTIVE?

Many of the criticisms of CPS seem to imply some type of financial incentive or at least insufficient competition to prevent waste. First, there is no reason public child welfare agencies or staff would feel compelled to bring children into care—quite the opposite is true. Since the 1980s the federal and state legislation controlling CPS practice requires that they not remove children unless there is no other alternative. There are actually sanctions based on federal reviews related to whether or not agencies are taking sufficient care to avoid foster care placement (see https://www.childwelfare.gov/topics/management/reform/child-and-family-services-reviews/). There are some financial incentives for adoption, but these go to the adoptive families, not the public child welfare agency. Some state costs associated with foster care are reimbursed by the federal government, but state and local governments still pay about forty percent of the costs of foster care[79]. While there may not be an incentive to take children into foster care, some argue that public agencies lack the incentive to improve outcomes like permanency. This, of course, is not the same as deriving financial gain from placement.

Privatizing Child Protection

In an effort to save money and supposedly improve outcomes, many states (and some other countries) have started contracting out child protective services to private agencies.[80–82] This is most common with foster care and adoptions and less common with "front-end" functions like initial investigations. This is not a return to the primacy of independent nonprofit agencies over 100 years ago we talked about in chapter 1. Privatization today means that nonprofit and for-profit agencies "bid" for government funds to do child protection work.

There are some clear problems with the idea of the market economy working to create a more effective CPS. You are likely to choose to buy one car among many because you think it is a better product at a better price. In child protection, however, the family cannot shop for services and the child, who is the main consumer, has no "purchasing power" at all. The client or consumer is actually the government.[80,82–83] The mechanism to effect improvements is dependent on the "performance-based contract" between the private agencies that are successful in obtaining the funds and the state providing the funds.[80,82] The idea is that either agencies receive some incentive for better outcomes or poor performing agencies are unable to get their contracts renewed. In some cases the competitive process itself leads to larger agencies eventually merging with smaller agencies or causing them to close because larger agencies can provide the services at lower cost.[80,82] In places where there are few agencies to choose from, the government may find it difficult to end contracts based on poor performance because they must still have access to a sufficient number of homes.[80-84] The "invisible hand of the market" is essentially removed from the equation.

There is, sadly and surprisingly, relatively little outcome research on CPS privatization, even though it has been going on for about 20 years. Most available reports provide guidance to states based on "lessons learned" but do not speak to its effectiveness per se. Those that have examined costs and outcomes typically find that the expected cost savings to the state does not occur.[80,82,84-85] While some states are happy with their movement toward privatization, Nebraska's experience was generally recognized as a terrible failure that increased costs and hurt children.[84] Privatization of foster care agencies was also a key issue in the recent scandal regarding Native American children in South Dakota.[78] A 2015 article in *Mother Jones* linked privatized foster care to the death of a young girl, Alexandra Hill.[86] A reporter reviewing several cases of tragic outcomes related to California's privatization of foster care captures the potential problem rather well:

> The flow of money to private foster care—now about $400 million a year—introduced a powerful incentive for some to spend as little as possible and pack homes with as many children as they could."[85]

What is important to note, that privatization (unless there is corruption as appears to be true in the South Dakota case) is NOT an incentive for the government to take children into care. The private agency does not pay CPS to remove more children. The potential profit (for the private agency) lies in winning the state government contract by being able to foster a large a number of children at the lowest possible cost per child.

Differential Response

Another reform designed to improve outcomes was mentioned in chapter 2—the advent of "differential" or "alternative" response systems. We don't review what it does here but we talk about whether it works. Data on early adopters suggested that younger children and cases including physical or sexual abuse were typically assigned to a traditional investigation while others were more frequently assigned to the assessment track—as intended.[87] Over time, however, it's not clear that higher-risk cases are always correctly screened into the investigative track[88] and, like so many other things we have talked about, the state criteria for screening varies.

So is the traditional system or this alternative system better? You may already be getting used to the fact that we are often going to say, "it depends." Several early "success stories" were really more about improved family satisfaction than outcomes.[89] Additionally, the testing of early models included additional resources provided by non-CPS charitable groups to address things like immediate family material needs.[90,91] This as one might guess, is not true for most of these approaches and was not sustainable past the pilot years for those that did have extra funds initially.[90] Over time some studies suggest families fare a little, but not a lot, better; some studies suggest no difference; and in at least one study children were less safe.[88–90] There is no strong evidence that this approach provides a big improvement in terms of costs and outcomes[89,92]—though people do seem to like it.[14,92]

WHY DOESN'T CHILD PROTECTIVE SERVICES PREVENT CHILD ABUSE?

The two reforms above were basically trying to do more with less or at least no additional financial investment. People often wonder why we see so many stories of abused children who still get hurt despite the existence of or even the direct involvement of CPS. After all, isn't CPS charged with protecting those children? The first answer is that CPS has no truly preventative role—it is called, ambulance-like, only after maltreatment occurs. A second answer seems to be that even when we are shocked by tragedy we are unwilling to invest in the kinds of changes that would have been preventive.

Jill Lepore recently wrote an excellent article about the Baby Doe case in Boston[93] that highlights how such cases drive public outrage, lawsuits, and continuing criticism without really addressing underlying issues. Here is an excerpt highlighting the ongoing nature of the crisis:

> It (public child welfare agency) was renamed the Department of Children and Families in 2008, under the Act Protecting Children in the Care of the Commonwealth, an omnibus reform that also created the Office of the Child Advocate, in response to the case of an eleven-year-old girl who was brought to an emergency room in a coma, having been severely beaten; one doctor said that her injuries were so grave it was as if she'd been in a high-speed car

accident. Social workers had earlier investigated charges of abuse but had determined that the injuries were self-inflicted. The reform law came with virtually no new funding. (About the only mention of money, in the legislation itself, is this: "The department may pay a sum not to exceed $1,100 for the funeral and burial of a child in its care.") It was passed in the midst of both a global financial collapse and an opiate epidemic. From the time that the D.C.F. got its name until 2014, its budget was cut every year; adjusted for inflation, more than a hundred and thirty million dollars was slashed. . . . Programs for the poor are poor programs. And they are made poorer when they fail, and when they are needed most.

It is ironic that even in such a dramatic case, the end result addresses only the most tragic of outcomes—being able to pay for the funeral.

Can We Divert Child Protective Services Money to Support Prevention?

Frustration with such cases and so-called reforms has led some advocates to call for vastly reducing or abolishing the whole CPS system. The expected financial savings could then be invested in other programs otherwise employed to help communities to better care for their children.[94,95] The basic idea is simple—"fix" the community to prevent child abuse instead of responding to it. We are actually in favor of the concept of community support generally. Certainly healthy communities are an important part of child rearing. The overriding problem is the cost-savings argument. It simply doesn't add up.

Recall from chapter 2 that we spend roughly $30 billion dollars a year on child welfare, and the biggest expenditure is foster care. Recent Texas figures estimate that less than 6 cents on the dollar are spent on preventive services with intact families, a number consistent with national estimates.[79,96] The proportion of the CPS budget that could be saved by cutting their "discretionary" functions is very small—probably no more than about 2 billion dollars a year, or $6 per US citizen. You just can't vastly improve every community in the United States at a cost of $6 per person.

We could divert more money if we radically reduced foster care, but this would take money to do correctly. Why? Let's take another lesson from history. In the late 1950s we began a massive shift toward deinstitutionalization of the mentally ill. No one would argue that placement in a mental institution was the ideal treatment setting for most psychiatric patients, but the lack of planning and development (and funding) of community supports led to disaster for many patients, who ended up homeless or worse.[97] To reduce foster care we would either have to invest a lot more to support families or perhaps increase adoptions. There is no indication from past history that we have been particularly good at adopting or caring for children who cannot be cared for by their own families without outside support. While adoptions have increased in recent years, even policy initiatives with financial supports for potential adoptive parents have not led to the dramatic increase in adoptions anticipated.[98,99] We are not arguing that children should remain in foster care, but it would take a substantial investment of funds to radically downsize the system in a way that promotes the well-being of children that currently need this level of care.

Should We Turn Child Protective Services Functions Over to Law Enforcement?

Another cost-savings option suggested is to move the CPS investigative function to the police.[100] The idea is that they are used to evidentiary processes and already have to be involved in foster care placement. The same problems occur here. First, the costs associated with CPS investigations currently is a very small fraction of the CPS budget.[101] Second, in most cases, there does not appear to be a desire on the part of law enforcement to take on this additional role.[102] This has been tried. In states where investigations are primarily the domain of police, there are specialized units created and CPS still functions to provide services and provide out-of-home care.[103] Some research on the use of police for child abuse investigation has found similar complaints of inadequate training, high caseloads, and difficulty collaborating with other professionals.[104] What little work we could find suggests that this approach spawns a new CPS within police departments, which may not be any less expensive or efficient.

IS THE CHILD PROTECTIVE SYSTEM BROKEN?

At this point it may sound like we are suggesting that all reforms are doomed to failure and the current CPS system is as good as it gets. We are not, but we would point out two things: First, changes need to be made with clearly articulated goals and reasonable means of achieving those goals (including funding). Second, reforms to date tend to view CPS as a broken thing to be fixed. Something cannot really be broken if it was never whole. You can't "fix" a bridge that was never completed. You need to complete it.

Here we expand a bit on a point we have made before.[101] Consider this example. Its late, you wake up, and you smell smoke. You race around the house and discover that there is a fire burning out of control. In the United States you call 9-1-1 immediately. You have some expectations of what will happen next.

- First, there will be a fire station with adequate staff and resources to respond quickly.
- When they arrive, the firefighters will know exactly what a fire is and will have the tools, skills, and water to put out or at least control the fire.
- If someone is hurt, an ambulance will come.
- If an ambulance comes, the paramedics will know how to do emergency procedures and get that person to a hospital.
- The hospital is open and staffed by competent physicians who have time to see the patient.
- Treatment is provided by hospitals, including needed follow-up.
- Insurance companies, neighbors, and charities will be available to help with the aftermath.

This is an emergency response *system*. We pay for it willingly and depend on it. Let's compare this to what happens when you call CPS.

- We learned in chapter 2 that about 40% of the time, CPS will not send anyone. Imagine calling 9-1-1 and having the person politely ask you to wait until most of the house is consumed in flames and then call back.
- If someone from CPS does respond, the preparation of that person is going to vary a lot based on state standards. Imagine having a fire fighter that may or may not know how to properly assess the extent of the fire and safety needs of your family.
- What about the crisis (fire) itself? Child protective services is really a case management response in most cases. Workers try to connect families to resources from other agencies. Imagine a fire fighter showing up without the fire truck because they share them across stations. You will have to wait until they find a truck with water to respond.
- If the situation is bad enough, someone may need immediate care. Foster care might be called our "hospital." A foster family per se is not a treatment. So our "hospital" is really just a building from a treatment perspective. The availability of well-trained and supported foster parents (unlike medical personnel in an ER) will vary a lot.[104] Other services a child in foster care needs will have to come from somewhere else.

Viewed this way, CPS hardly seems like a system like 9-1-1. It's like we started to build something 50 years ago without ever really thinking about all the pieces needed to create a functional and effective response. Maybe we should think about finishing what we started.

NEXT STEPS

Before we move to offering more detailed ideas for improving our prevention of and response to maltreatment in the final chapter, we leave you with a few thoughts about the potential for finishing a functional CPS system. There are some bright spots. The fact you are reading this book suggests progress toward awareness of maltreatment as a significant social and public health problem that we have a responsibility to address. Technology and increasing awareness of effective practices (which we review in the next chapter) are increasing our ability to identify needs earlier, to better collaborate among agencies, to more effectively report on outcomes under differing service and policy conditions, and to provide better responses to the needs of families and children. So we have more and better tools available to build something that works than we did 50 years ago.

On the negative side, we see no way to make this a cost-neutral effort. If we want something better, we must invest with compassion, have clear measurable goals, and rigorously evaluate what is put into place so that we do not reinvent wheels or cause harm. We must be proactive rather than reactive to costs, public misperceptions, or tragedy. It's a large task, but we are optimistic.

11

A Fairy Tale Ending? What You Can Do

and What We Can Do Together

FAIRY TALES, at least the modern versions, typically conclude with happy endings. While authors write the endings to fairy tales, writing the end of this story is really your job. If you are new to the subject, it is our hope that you have become more interested in and aware of the complicated issue of child abuse and neglect. If you are an advocate or researcher already, we hope you will find that we have done justice to what is known and perhaps even pointed out some avenues for inquiry and action. In all cases, it is our hope you are thinking about what can be done to prevent maltreatment and improve our response to it. We are concluding our part of the story by talking about possibilities or choices (Figure 11.1). These should be thought of as a menu of options—some have strong evidence behind them, while others are promising ideas or issues we need to start thinking more seriously about.

MOVING FORWARD

The possibilities that follow range from very small and personal to grand policy. Several of the smaller action items are also recommended in the *Building Community Building Hope Prevention Resource Guide.*[1] We have roughly divided these options for action into four separate sections: within your family, within your community, as a professional, and, finally, within the realm of policy and advocacy.

FIGURE 11.1 Choices

WHAT YOU CAN DO WITHIN YOUR FAMILY

The battle against child maltreatment includes a home front in the literal sense. While most of us don't engage in actions that would be considered abusive or neglectful, all parents and caregivers are fallible. Parenting, even under the most benevolent circumstances, is not an easy job. Most of the suggestions in this section are not "anti-maltreatment" tactics per se—they're general ways of attending to issues that are likely to help you parent well. They are also good skills to model for others. Modeling increases the effectiveness of behavior training within structured parenting programs,[2,3] and it may be that this applies to transmission of behaviors to the community as well.[4] In other words, working on being a better parent may have a "ripple effect."

Take Care of Yourself

As we discussed earlier in the book, stress (at least too much of it) is bad for you. It is worth reducing stress in your life as much as you can while enhancing positive coping skills to deal with those stressors that are unavoidable. How is this related to parenting? Deeply stressed people don't always act as they normally would or have the energy to parent.[5] Some studies indicate that high levels of stress among parents may impact their children's behavior, even if their parenting practices are not directly impaired.[6,7] Further, building the capacity for healthy family functioning may help buffer some of the impact of external stressors on child behaviors and youth development.[8,9] In other words, the negative impact of stress in your life may increase the level of stress and disruption in your child's life, but the good news is that positive coping skills and supports spill over in a positive way. Some of these coping strategies are very simple and just common sense—like getting sufficient exercise, which is recommended by the Mayo Clinic[10] as one of the best means to manage stress.

How do you tell when you are overly stressed? It is easy to notice when a particular stressful event "freaks us out," but sometimes stress can creep up on you. There is a nice resource on stress that may be of some help[11] available at http://www.helpguide.org/articles/stress/stress-symptoms-causes-and-effects.htm. If the stress in your life reaches a point that you begin to use unhealthy coping mechanisms or are struggling to cope at all, then it's time to seek help. Not sure how? Fortunately, there's a nationwide number (2-1-1—just those three digits) you can call and someone will help you contact mental health or social service agencies. The service is also available online (http://www.211us.org/).

Enjoy Your Children

Your relationship with your children is among the best predictors of positive outcomes, both for your children and for you.[12] There is no way we know to guarantee that your child will always be happy or make good choices, but doing fun things together will make the journey more enjoyable. Play has important benefits for developing positive relationships with your child[13] and most parenting courses spend time on play activities. We can get very busy between work and home and children's activities. In a recent *New York Times* article on overscheduling kids, the experts pointed out that it is not the number of activities that are the problem but rather whether the children are enjoying then and you are able to create a time together that is fun for both of you.[14]

It is also important to remember that having fun does not require having a lot of money. When we googled "free activities for families" a number of sites popped up with suggestions in the community and activities to do at home. There are also any number of children's books that are engaging for both parent and child—some even provide great positive parenting advice. Several of our favorites are on the list compiled by McGuire[15] on scholastic.com—although we note the list does leave out the classic *Everybody Poops* by Gomi.

Build Up the Social Support in Your Life

The idea of the importance of social support in our lives has been around for a long time.[16] Having your own informal "support group" can make parenting a lot easier and less worrisome.[17] Sometimes this gets overemphasized as a need for first-time parents rather than parents at any stage of family life. We are social animals and are not meant to tackle problems like raising a child alone.

Talk to Your Child About Being Safe

When children have been asked about their own well-being, security and safety rank high on their list, and children generally report this is the parent's job.[18] Again, there is nothing we can recommend that is an absolute guarantee that your child will remain safe, but there are things parents can do. As we mentioned earlier, most formal programs designed to keep children safe from harm dwell on "stranger danger"—though we are aware of at least one parenting program that covers an adult's role in raising safe kids in the home as well as in the community.[19] Having a general rule that your family doesn't have secrets, that your child has a right not to be touched in uncomfortable ways, and that they have the right to feel safe are all important ideas.[20] Make sure that they know this applies to everyone they know within and outside the family. Be ready and open to them talking to you. If there is a concern, supporting them and following through on the information is key.

Of course, even though few children are harmed by strangers, there are standard safety rules all children should know such as never to take gifts from strangers and never to go anywhere with them. Children should memorize their own phone number and address as early as possible. You can also help your child identify safe people and places in your neighborhood where they can go if you are not available. The National Crime Prevention Council has some more detailed advice in this area (http://www.ncpc.org/topics/violent-crime-and-personal-safety/strangers).

Not a Parent?

Nonparents can play a useful role in preventing abuse or neglect as a member of an extended family by being an extra support for those relatives who are parents. Research indicates that extended family support can help buffer stresses that negatively impact parenting.[21,22] Research also indicates, however, that support of the caregiver should not include condoning or ignoring problematic or maltreating behaviors.[23] You may be one of the people with the best opportunity to support children in your extended family when things get tough for them.[24] Nonparents can also engage in any of the activities in the following sections.

WHAT YOU CAN DO IN YOUR COMMUNITY

There are many ways you can be personally involved in the lives of children who are at high risk for or who have been maltreated. These can range from preventive programs like Big Brothers/Big Sisters, to more direct roles with maltreated children, like becoming a foster parent.

Foster Parenting

Foster parents provide housing and support to children who can no longer stay in their homes. Foster parenting isn't well reimbursed and is challenging, but is also rewarding.[25] Several kinds of foster homes exist, including kinship care, nonrelative care, and families specially trained to deal with children with special needs. So-called "Fost-Adopt" homes are for families that are hoping to adopt. Children may be placed in such families when it is very likely that the child will be freed for adoption. A nice overview of the process of becoming a foster parent can be found on this site: http://www.adoptuskids.org/for-families/how-to-foster.

Court Appointed Special Advocates and Guardians ad Litem

These are adults who help represent children in the foster care and family court systems. Depending on how the legal system works in your state, you may be able to volunteer as a CASA (court appointed special advocate) or a GAL (guardian ad litem). Some states use these terms to mean the same thing. Often, however, a GAL is a volunteer attorney for the child. Generally, a CASA has more frequent contact with the child then a GAL and serves in an almost mentor-like role, but also reports information about the child and represents the child's opinion to the judge when court hearings on a case occur.[26] A good introduction to this can be found here: http://www.casaforchildren.org/site/c.mtJSJ7MPIsE/b.5301309/k.9D58/Volunteering.htm.

Volunteering

You may already be involved as a volunteer in an organization that serves children like Big Brothers/Big Sisters, schools, scouting, or other local organizations. There are numerous volunteer roles that provide the opportunity to support a family or child. There are many suggestions, tip sheets, and even a calendar that lists one thing you can do each day to build a supportive community in the *Building Community, Building Hope*[1] resource mentioned earlier.

Be a Good Sentinel

Most states want people to report if they have a have at least a "reasonable suspicion" of child abuse or neglect, which is more than a hunch but less than thinking it is likely. If a child directly discloses maltreatment to you, be reassuring and let the child know that you believe him, that he did the right thing telling you, and that you will call someone to help. It is beyond the scope of this book to provide training

---

BOX 11.1

CHILD ABUSE AND NEGLECT BEHAVIORAL "RED FLAGS"

- Withdrawal from friends or usual activities
- Changes in behavior—such as aggression, anger, hostility, or hyperactivity—or changes in school performance
- Depression, anxiety, or a sudden loss of self-confidence
- An apparent lack of supervision
- Frequent absences from school or reluctance to ride the school bus
- Reluctance to leave school activities, as if he or she doesn't want to go home
- Attempts at running away
- Rebellious or defiant behavior
- Attempts at suicide

(http://www.mayoclinic.org/diseases-conditions/child-abuse/basics/symptoms/con-20033789)

---

in reporting itself, but some common red flags for older children are provided in Box 11.1.

You will have to use your own judgment in deciding if making a child abuse hotline call is necessary. If you need help, Childhelp has a national hotline to assist persons with how this process works (1-800-4-A-Child). They can help guide you to your state or local child abuse hotline so you can make the report or you can Google the name of your state and the words "Child Abuse Hotline" and the correct number should pop up.

An emerging practice is the use of bystander training (which in the past has been restricted to prevention of sexual or domestic violence) to promote positive parenting.[27] Research on the effectiveness of this approach is just developing. The idea is that it might be possible to train the general public on ways in which to effectively intervene when witnessing harsh parenting before it rises to the level of a maltreatment concern.

Be an Advocate at Your Workplace or Social Organization

Find out whether your organization has a policy for recognizing and reporting child abuse or neglect. The local county or state child protective services (CPS) agency probably has a free "road show" talk available about child maltreatment policies and reporting. Maybe you can post the child abuse hotline number on your website or put up a poster in your organization's building.[28] The Centers for Disease Control and Prevention (CDC) has an excellent booklet, specific to child sexual abuse, on how agencies can do a better job recognizing and responding to this type of maltreatment available at (http://www.cdc.gov/ViolencePrevention/pdf/ PreventingChildSexualAbuse-a.pdf)

Maybe your organization can be designated as a safe place. You may have seen the yellow signs with "SAFE PLACE" written in black on fire stations and other businesses. This means that an organization has volunteered to provide a safe place for a child or teen in crisis to wait while someone calls the locally designated response agency that will then help the child or teen (http://nationalsafeplace.org/mobile/ how-safe-place-works/).

WHAT YOU CAN DO AS A PROFESSIONAL

Some readers may work in fields where they routinely encounter child abuse and neglect, even though they do not work for CPS (e.g., healthcare providers, emergency response personnel, teachers). Here are a few suggestions on ways you can improve your response.

Inventory Your Own Knowledge

As mentioned in an earlier chapter, there is tremendous variation in how much training professionals receive about child abuse and neglect. For example, while a pediatric subspecialty in child maltreatment does exist,[29] most healthcare providers receive perhaps a lecture or two in school at most. If, after inventorying your knowledge, you feel there are gaps in regard to understanding your professional response, then we encourage you to seek out training. There are often trainings and presentations available at professional conferences or webinars sponsored by organizations like the CDC. In many cases, such trainings also allow you to fulfill continuing education requirements. You can also look up your state's policy for mandatory reporting at the Child Welfare Information Gateway online[30] or go to your own state's social services website.

If you work in a family support agency or provide mental health services, be sure you or someone on your staff is trained in the most effective approaches for working with trauma and child welfare–involved families.[31-34] We realize that sometimes keeping up on the research evidence is difficult, but there are excellent resources we have mentioned before, like the California Evidence-Based Clearinghouse for Child Welfare (http://www.cebc4cw.org/) or the National Child Traumatic Stress Network (http://www.nctsn.org/), that provide up-to-date information about best practices and contact information to get more information or training.

Know Local Resources

Beyond the hotline number, it is a good thing to have a listing of resources you can provide to families for needs that your agency cannot meet. Often times the state social services websites or regional councils on child abuse and neglect have links to information about a range of services available. Professionals can also call the 2-1-1 number we mentioned earlier. Ideally, you or someone in your organization should go one step further and call (or even visit) the potential service providers. If you understand the eligibility requirements and how the process of requesting services works, you can make a more effective referral that improves the likelihood a person gets connected to services.[35,36] Sending someone to a service they do not qualify for can be frustrating.

Volunteer

As a professional you might also consider becoming involved in local organizations. This does not have to be a direct service role. For example, many agencies have governing boards that assist them in fundraising and provide suggestions for policy and program improvement. Most metropolitan areas also have some form of council dedicated to issues of child maltreatment or strengthening families that welcome professionals in their membership who may help with legislative advocacy or community events. We googled "community councils on child abuse and neglect" and instantly found contacts for several such groups.

CHANGING PROGRAMMING, POLICY, AND LAW

For readers who are activists, policy makers, researchers, or those who just want to think more at the "big picture" level, we now move on to more formal program and policy options. We start with some universal prevention approaches and move toward intervention.

Primary/Universal Prevention

Universal prevention approaches are designed to impact society as a whole (or at least a large part of it), not just children or families experiencing maltreatment.

Poverty Reduction

We hope we have made the case that poverty places a tremendous strain on families and is a leading risk factor for maltreatment. One option for prevention would be to invest in developing capacities of individuals and communities to eliminate poverty. It is a big job, but it is not outside the realm of possibility.[37] We do seem to be moving the needle in some areas, including beginning to "spread out" geographically concentrated poverty.[38] We are also beginning to learn more about what types of socioeconomic intervention might reduce abuse and neglect.[39–41] Evidence suggests the socioeconomic impact of other interventions might have positive collateral effects. For example, research is emerging on the effectiveness of individualized development accounts,[42,43] two-generation educational approaches that seek to improve parental education levels and employment while providing child care and child education,[44,45] or raising the minimum wage or increases to the earned income tax credit.[46,47] Of course, it is important that we do this in a purposive way and invest in rigorous assessment so we learn what works for whom.

Changing Attitudes and Providing Information

We could learn from some of our international neighbors (e.g., most Scandinavian countries, Australia, etc.) and work on improving people's understanding of positive parenting. Recall in chapter 3 that Scandinavian countries have made pretty strong gains in changing norms about corporal punishment. One means of large-scale communication is through public service announcements (PSAs), which can take the form of everything from roadside billboards warning you to use your seatbelt to brief television spots warning you of the hazards of drug use. Of course, it is hard to gauge the promise of PSAs as part of child maltreatment prevention efforts, because most of the research on PSAs has focused on changes in attitudes rather than changes in behaviors.[48,49] When they have been used in child maltreatment, these campaigns were combined with other program elements making it difficult to disentangle the effect of the announcements themselves.[50] On the other hand, there is some evidence of promise in the effect of PSAs on the reduction of physical abuse.[51]

We have many more means of using technology that we could make better use of to get information to those in need. While the Internet is a great resource, sometimes it can be hard to locate the website you need for a given issue. In Canada there is a *Parents Matter* website that has gone a long way toward fixing this. No matter what age(s) your child(ren) might be or whether you are seeking resources for parenting or child care or health, this site provides numerous links all at one central location: http://www.parentsmatter.ca/index.cfm?fuseaction=Page. ViewPage&PageID=618. There are also an increasing number of apps aimed at supporting parents. For example, "Total Baby" is designed to be a resource for parents of newborns and "SitORSquat" helps you find that elusive public bathroom when your child needs one. There are even apps specific to child abuse for the public (e.g., "child abuse information") and for forensic decision-making about child injury designed for child protection and medical personnel "Child Protector." We do not yet have evidence on the effect of these tools, but it seems worth trying to understand whether such approaches can help prevent maltreatment.

Home Visitation Programs for Parents of Young Children

In recent years, a range of home visitation interventions for working with families of infants and toddlers (0–3 years old) has been developed (e.g., Early Head Start, Parents as Teachers, nurse home visitation). Many people see these programs as a key part of child maltreatment prevention.[24,52] A home visitor makes periodic visits to the family (usually over many months) and helps with advice, information, referrals, and basic parenting support. These programs do appear to help increase the time between births and reduce child injuries, and might help mothers to get more formal education and improve parenting behavior and attitudes. Some studies indicate that there are benefits to child cognitive and socioemotional development.[53,54] Some research indicates that longer-term programs that are more intensive and incorporate health and other issues show promising downstream effects on youth and young adult behavior.[55] It isn't clear, however, that home visiting can prevent child maltreatment per se.

Recent research and systematic reviews of prior work show limited, nonexistent, or inconsistent effects of home visiting on child abuse rates.[54,56] Most existing home visitation programs are also plagued by high dropout rates for a variety of reasons, including parents being overwhelmed with other responsibilities, having unstable living conditions, or returning to work, or the quality of the relationship with the home visitor.[56–58] We are not at all against home visiting programs. They are a valuable piece of the puzzle in supporting young families, but we caution readers not to view the current models as a "silver bullet" for combating child maltreatment.

Alternative Early Childhood Parenting Supports

There may be other ways of delivering parenting information that can fill in gaps in access or acceptability of traditional home visitation. For example, research is underway to explore integration of parenting support with pediatric primary care.[59,60] Digital means of delivering parenting programs on the Internet or through apps is increasing, with early evidence suggesting successful uptake and some promising results.[23,61–63] It is too early to assess effectiveness in reducing child maltreatment, but the use of information technology does have the potential to improve the reach of positive parenting programs at a relatively low cost.

Families with Preschool-Aged or Older Children

In the United States, we have tended to focus much of the public attention on parenting of very young children (under age 4). While this is a critical period of development, the skills one learns to effectively parent an infant may not be the same skills needed in the transition to school or the teenage years. Some advocates have suggested we embrace a "Nordic" model, where family support services are made available across the life span, free of charge, to all. On the other hand, this approach has not been without financial challenges, and such systems still wrestle with a child-centric approach as compared to limiting intrusion into the family.[64,65] Universal parenting support for older children (ages 4 through 12) was tested once in North Carolina with a program called Triple P.[50] While there were some promising findings, the state cut funding to the program shortly after the conclusion of the study. Online approaches to positive parenting of older children are also being explored,[63] but it is too early to gauge the effectiveness of this approach.

Systemic Issues and Intervention

At various points in this book we have raised systemic issues related to communication and functioning within CPS and between CPS and other systems. There are several options to address this issue.

Complete the Child Protection System

As pointed out in chapter 10, we do not have a "finished" child protection system with uniform training or adequate caseload expectations or sufficient resources to respond to families in need before things reach toxic levels. Even when the state deems it necessary to place children into foster care, we have neglected to provide sufficient training and support for foster caregivers and sufficient access to effective child-level services that can promote their educational, health, and mental health well-being. Since the 1980s, we would argue, reforms have been reactive to specific cases, limited to specific decision points only, and often focused on cost savings. This latter goal is perplexing to us, given our willingness to spend billions of dollars on the poor outcomes related to ineffective prevention and intervention.[66] What would the outcomes for children and families be like if we had a completed, functioning CPS system? It seems worth trying to answer this question, but this will take proactive and systematic planning and evaluation. There are various models—from trauma-informed systems to integration of evidence-based practices with child protection in this country and others—being proposed and tested that offer promising alternatives to the incomplete, patchwork system we have now.[34,52,67,68]

Training and Collaboration for Domestic Violence

Another way child protection could move forward (and is doing so in some places) is in providing better training about domestic violence and improved collaboration with domestic violence professionals. We do not review here the many approaches discussed at the end of chapter 7, but if the reader is particularly interested in this area we encourage them to revisit that section.

Reducing Barriers to Accessing Material Resources

We mentioned poverty reduction, but there is an intermediate step that does not alter income itself but rather deals with day-to-day material needs of poor families, including those known to CPS.[69] As we mentioned in chapter 4, Maslow helped us understand that people have a set of basic needs that must be met before they can move on to prioritizing relationships and other achievements. Many CPS-involved families struggle in the bottom layer of his pyramid with immediate needs related to housing or food. Many other families are struggling with the second layer, trying to acquire the resources needed to be healthy, employed, and safe. We are just beginning to understand and test approaches to addressing basic material needs like housing, utility assistance, or food.[39,70] Perhaps if professionals involved in the lives of vulnerable children and families can assist with such material needs,[71] this might allow families to move beyond the crisis levels of Maslow's hierarchy so that they can put positive parenting practices into action.

Establish Cross-Site/Cross-Sector Data

Let's say a parent takes their child to the emergency room (ER) twice for somewhat suspicious injuries. If they take the child to the same ER, doctors or nurses are much more likely to be concerned the second time and explore the possibility of maltreatment. That may not happen if the parent goes to two different ERs. While healthcare systems have all moved to electronic medical records (EMRs), the systems are not always linked. Making sure that EMRs speak to each other would be very helpful in making sure that hospitals had all the information they need to identify and report maltreatment.[72,73]

Linking electronic data across systems can have implications for prevention as well. A recent study showed that among the (very few) newborns with a very high number of risk factors on their birth records (e.g., no prenatal care, maternal substance abuse, etc.) 89.5% had a CPS report in their first 5 years of life.[74] If families could be identified by a set of risk factors at birth, a family support agency (not necessarily CPS) could offer *strictly voluntary* preventative services before the call is ever made. Setting up systems to allow simple cross-checking is increasingly cheaper as advances in technology are made, and this is being done in some states to better understand how to target prevention and intervention.[75-78]

For some readers this idea may seem a bit scary. What about privacy concerns?[79] Is it morally OK to be looking over family's shoulders like that? This is an emerging and critical debate we need to have as a society. Data isn't just *family* data, it is also *child* data. If we decide it is the state's responsibility to protect children from serious harm, then we must wrestle with the state's right to information that makes this easier. We also have to remember such approaches identify risk, *not* predestination. Policies guiding the use of such information need to be designed to that services offered based on risk were voluntary, preventive, and acceptable when offered.

Computerized systems that link information across multiple sources (albeit not focused on families or maltreatment) are becoming widespread. Twenty years ago if you applied for a loan you might have spent hours or days collecting all the paperwork required, but not today. There is a data system behind that. There is a huge linked data system behind games like *Pokemon Go*. It seems quite unlikely that we will reverse the course of developing such linked systems now that they are here. Despite the recent attention to international hacking, there are ways to secure data so that only the right individuals may access only what is needed.[80] It seems reasonable to explore this as a tool for prevention and improving coordination of care once intervention is required.

Improving and Expanding Treatment

This section focuses on care following maltreatment.

Evidence-Based Care for Children

We discussed several evidence-based approaches for supporting children and websites that can be accessed for more information in our chapter on resilience. Knowing what to do, however, is not the same as knowing how or where to do it or having the necessary political will to fund it. Recently, much attention had been given to creating trauma-informed systems to provide better assessments and access to quality care.[81] Trauma-informed systems are organizations or groups of organizations that are alert to and have the capacity to intervene with people who have had traumatic experiences. Interventions either take place within a system (e.g., child welfare or schools, etc.) or are part of a prearranged network of agencies that work with the lead organization to provide treatment. Agencies and states have recently begun to implement such systems, but we don't know yet if this improves access to quality intervention.[81-83]

Another barrier has been the expense of implementing many of the well-researched intervention packages. To help address this, there is a developing movement toward understanding what "common elements" work in programs. In other words, it might be possible to train providers on techniques that crosscut various evidence-based interventions rather than having to pay for the training and implementation of any one program.[84]

Evidence-Based Parenting Programs for Child Welfare–Involved Families

We have mentioned various parenting programs throughout this book. While there are increasing efforts to test existing parenting intervention with child welfare–involved families,[85-88] these programs are also generally quite expensive to implement. The "common elements" approach mentioned earlier is also being tried with parenting interventions.[89] More work is needed on the relative cost-effectiveness of different approaches and whether such programs are effective alone or in combination with other services.

Expand Adult Mental Health and Substance Abuse Programs

Keeping kids safe is also about keeping parents well. The association of parental mental health and substance abuse problems and maltreatment are well known.[90,91] This does not mean these issues are the root "cause" of maltreating behaviors, but once present, they obviously impair parenting. In our work with various agencies and programs over the years, the lack of availability and long waiting periods for adult mental health and substance abuse services are always on the top of the list of barriers for case managers. It is beyond the scope of this book to review available evidence-based approaches to various mental health and substance abuse problems. A good resource to learn more about evidence-based practices in this area is the website maintained by the Substance Abuse and Mental Health Services Administration (http://www. samhsa.gov/ebp-web-guide). Not to be repetitive, but removing barriers to quality services that adults need to parent their children is not without cost but is arguably a necessity.

Expand Best Practices and Innovative Programming

Since the authors are both researchers, this is going to sound a bit self-serving, but we do really believe that applied policy and program research is important to advancing prevention and intervention efforts. Why? You may have noticed that throughout this book we have had to use words like "we don't know," "promising," "emerging," and "we don't have good data on this" quite a lot. Data helps us know how big a problem is, whether it is changing over time, and where those changes are or are not taking place. Research also helps us understand what (one intervention or combinations of approaches) works for whom and in what context. When large-scale implementation of programs happens before those programs are adequately tested, bad, or at least expensive, things occur. Several well-known social interventions, such as D.A.R.E. (Drug and Alcohol Resistance Education) or Scared Straight–style programs, have been found to either have no meaningful positive effects (DARE[92]) or to have net negative effects (Scared Straight[93]). If you have school-aged children, it's likely your school still uses D.A.R.E. (http://www.dare.org/starting-a-dare-program/). So while research costs money, it can also save money in the long run.

Complex problems can be solved when we combine multiple perspectives (economic, health, mental health, social work, public health, engineering, etc.), rigorous testing, and cost analyses. This is why a person like Bill Gates funnels so much money into "Grand Challenges" research—he realizes that tackling tough issues requires bringing funding and the best thinking available on the topic together (http://gcgh. grandchallenges.org/about). The United States lacks a strong funding base to pursue many of the pressing questions in prevention and intervention related to child maltreatment. Right now, the National Institutes of Health are spending about 31 million dollars a year in child maltreatment research,[94] about the same amount of money as Cubs fans pay for concessions each year at Wrigley Field.[95] This is not a matter of waging a values war in terms of research dollars—we are not advocating that funds be shifted away from research on issues like cancer treatment or brain development. Nor are we against the consumption of hotdogs at a baseball game. The fact remains, however, that the relative lack of spending on child maltreatment research is indefensible, given the moral and economic costs of the problem. Multiplying the amount spent on child abuse research by a factor of 10 would have an unnoticeable effect on research spending but could pay real dividends for children.

COMPETING VALUES AND CHOICES AHEAD

As we write this, we worry that ending our book with a long list of possible intervention and policy options for the future may feel a bit anticlimactic. On the other hand, it seems irresponsible to generate interest in addressing the problem of child maltreatment without suggesting some possibilities for where to go from here. We have talked a lot about money, but we also realize that choices about next steps are not value free.

In American folk tales and folk heroes the idea of the "self-made man" is common.[96] For some, the idea that letting people figure stuff out for themselves, often phrased as "pulling yourself up by your own bootstraps," seems like the "American way."[97] From a child advocacy point of view, the "self-made man/bootstrap" model makes no sense. Children cannot choose their families or whether they will grow up in a devastated area of Detroit or in Beverly Hills. Children, by definition, require the care and support of others and have little control over their environments.

So on one hand you could look at child protection as a family (i.e., adult) issue. Adults should experience the consequences of their own actions. This is a bit like thinking about parents like the grasshopper in the Aesop's Fable, *The Ant and the Grasshopper.*[98] The grasshopper has fun and avoids the hard work of preparing for winter only to learn his lesson as he watches the ants prosper while he freezes and starves to death. Of course, the grasshopper does not have children. Would it still be a moral tale if the ants had let the grasshopper's young baby die because of his failure? Arguably without intervention (which may mean supporting a parent that does not fit the ideal of a "deserving" party), a child growing up in extreme poverty and experiencing trauma is a recipe for intergenerational disadvantage.[99,100]

Another deeply held value that we have mentioned repeatedly in this book is the idea of family autonomy and privacy. As McMullen[101] writes, we tend to adhere to this because we believe this strengthens families and parents will act in the best interest of their children. Some have made strong arguments that parental rights should only be limited when a child's rights to have their basic needs met are at risk,[102] while others (within and outside the United States) argue more forcefully for expanded rights for children that take into account their well-being.[65,103,104] Theoretically, a child's rights perspective expands preventive approaches, because it "removes" from consideration judgment of the reasons why the parent is not providing good care. The focus is on the child's outcomes. Wrestling with this tension between child rights and the privacy and supremacy of the family is partly illustrated by the quote from a recent presidential candidate in Box 11.2.

BOX 11.2
ONE WOMAN'S VIEWPOINT

"My views were shaped by what I had observed as a volunteer for legal services representing children in foster care and by my experiences at the Child Study Center in Yale–New Haven Hospital. I advised doctors as they tried to ascertain whether a child should be put into the child welfare system. I come from a strong family and believe in a parent's presumptive right to raise his or her child as he or she sees fit. But at the Yale–New Haven Hospital I saw children whose parents beat and burned them; who left them alone for days in squalid apartments; who failed and refused to seek necessary medical care. The truth was that certain parents abdicated their rights as parents."

H. Clinton. (2003). *Living History.* New York: Simon & Schuster, p. 50.

WRITING THE NEXT CHAPTER

At the end of chapter 1, we said we hoped this book would make a difference. By that we mean that we hope that you and others will become engaged in this issue. We realize different readers will have different values that may guide how they become engaged. Nor do we expect all readers to engage across all levels of potential actions. We hope we have provided a wide enough array of possibilities for action that you may find at least one or two that you can get behind. We also do not pretend that the ideas presented in this final chapter are an exhaustive list—in fact we hope that you and others will continue to develop better and more effective means of preventing and intervening after maltreatment.

It has been about 150 years since Mary Ellen's story began. Imagine that another 50 years have passed. Someone is reading about child abuse and neglect. Will it be an enormous social and public health problem that few people can comfortably discuss or will this be a historical account of an issue that is largely resolved? There is a modern "fairy tale" (and movie) called *Inkheart*[105] in which an author's writings come to life when read by certain people with a specific gift. We invite you to write the next chapter and hope that you can work with others to bring to life a story we can all be proud of.

WANT TO READ, WATCH, OR LISTEN MORE?

Note, this listing includes only books and Internet material that can be accessed without a university-level library account. Inclusion here does not indicate a ranking or preference but rather the ease of access, mention in our book, and readability. There are 10 sections:

- **Songs, Movies, and Folk Tales (a few sites for finding more)**
- **Fictional Novels**
- **Survivor Stories**
- **Child and Animal Protection Worker Accounts**
- **Child Maltreatment, Family Violence, and Society and Violence**
- **Child Welfare Policy**
- **Child Maltreatment Fatalities**
- **Child Maltreatment, Culture, and Race**
- **Children, Families, and Reform**
- **Facts and Statistics**

SONGS, MOVIES, AND FOLK TALES
Songs and Movies

Adams, E., Adams, S., Gilmer, M., Gordon, S., Heller, J., Koski, G., . . . Robinson, T. (2011, June). The hits keep coming: 30 songs inspired by domestic violence. *A.V. Club*. http://www.avclub.com/article/the-hits-keep-coming-30-songs-inspired-by-domestic-57741

List of songs about child abuse. https://en.wikipedia.org/wiki/List_of_songs_about_child_abuse

Films about child abuse https://en.wikipedia.org/wiki/Category:Films_about_child_abuse

Fairy Tales and Legends

http://www.native-languages.org/child-abuse.htm

Greenspan, J. (2013, Sept). The dark side of the Grimm fairy tales. *History.com*. http://www.history.com/news/the-dark-side-of-the-grimm-fairy-tales

http://www.surlalunefairytales.com

http://www.pitt.edu/~dash/grimmtales.html

FICTIONAL NOVELS

We tried to identify works that highlight the various forms of maltreatment from historical and contemporary views. All but the Rowling (2013) novels are referenced in this book as well.

Dahl, R. (1988). *Matilda*. Jonathon Cape. (emotional abuse and resilience)

King, S. (2011) *Carrie*. Anchor. (horror—emotional abuse)

Kline, C. (2013). *Orphan train*. William Morrow. (Note that this is historical fiction but gives an interesting and pretty accurate review of maltreatment and the orphan train period)

Roth, V. (2011). *Divergent*. Katherine Teagen Books. (physical abuse of one of main characters)

Rowling, J. K. (1998). *Harry Potter and the Sorcerers Stone*. Scholastic. (neglect and emotional abuse)

Rowling, J. K. (2013). *Casual vacancy*. Back Bay books. (fiction for adults; same author as Harry Potter—good illustration of child neglect)

Sapphire. (1997). *Push: A novel*. Vintage. (physical, sexual, and emotional abuse)

SURVIVOR STORIES

There are many books detailing true personal accounts of survivors. We list four here, one on Mary Ellen due to historical significance, another perhaps the best-known modern account, a third because it is currently a top seller, and the final because it is an excellent illustration of a multi-problem family that includes various kinds of maltreatment toward different siblings. It is also the subject of a recently released film. Going to any online book sales and typing these in will lead you to others.

Shelman, E., & Lazoritz, S. (2000). *Out of the darkness: The true story of Mary Ellen*. Dolphin Moon. (This is written in a historical fiction style but is factual.) Companion nonfiction work is *Case #1: The Mary Ellen Wilson files*, by the same authors.

Pelzer, D. (1995). *A child called "It": One child's courage to survive*. HCI.

Randis, K. (2013). *Spilled milk*. Self-published.

Wells, J. (2005). *The glass castle*. Charles Scribner Sons. (especially since it just came out in the theaters as a film)

CHILD AND ANIMAL PROTECTION WORKER ACCOUNTS

To our knowledge there are only two books related personal accounts of child protective services work, so both are included here. We also include the book referenced about animal protection workers as an interesting comparison.

Arluke, A. (2004). *Brute force: Animal police and the challenge of cruelty*. Purdue University Press.

Norman, E. (2009). *No one would believe It: Experiences of a child abuse investigator*. Author.

Parent, M. (1998). *Turning stones: A caseworker's story*. Ballantine Books.

CHILD MALTREATMENT, FAMILY VIOLENCE, AND SOCIETY AND VIOLENCE

Most of these works are referenced in this book. We added a few additional works specific to domestic violence.

Brockliss, L., & Montgomery, H. (Eds.). (2010). *Childhood and violence: In the western tradition*. Oxbow Books.

Davies, J., & Lyon, E. (2015). *Domestic violence advocacy: Complex lives/difficult choices* (2nd ed.). Sage.

Donnelly, M., & Straus, M. (Eds.). (2013). *Corporal punishment of children in theoretical perspective*. Yale University Press.

Finkelhor, D. (2008). *Childhood victimization*. Oxford University Press.

Finkelhor, D. (2010). *Sexually victimized children*. Simon and Schuster.

Pinker, S. (2011). *The better angels of our nature: The decline of violence in history and its causes*. Penguin UK.

Reardon, K., & Noblet, C. (2009). *Childhood denied: Ending the nightmare of child abuse and neglect*. Sage.

Renzetti, C. M., & Miley, C. H. (2014). *Violence in gay and lesbian domestic partnerships*. Routledge.

Seto, M. (2008). *Pedophilia and sexual offending against children*. American Psychological Association.

Strauss, M. (2001). *Beating the devil out of them*. Transaction Publishers.

Wallace, H., & Robeson, C. (2013). *Family violence: Legal, medical and social perspectives* (7th ed.). Routledge.

CHILD WELFARE POLICY

These works range from more historical perspectives to current thoughts on the child protection system.

Commission to Eliminate Child Abuse and Neglect Fatalities. (2016). *Within our reach*. https://eliminatechildabusefatalities.sites.usa.gov/files/2016/03/CECANF-final-report.pdf

Costin, L., Karger, H., & Stoesz, D. (1996). *The politics of child abuse in America*. Oxford University Press.

Fletcher, M., Singel, W., & Fort, K. (2009). *Facing the future: The Indian Child Welfare Act at 30*. Michigan State University Press.

Gilbert, N., Parton, N., & Skivenes, M. (2011). *Child protection systems: International trends and orientations*. Oxford University Press.

Jagannathan, R., & Camasso, M. (2013). *Protecting children in the age of outrage*. Oxford University Press.

Korbin, J., & Krugman, R. (Eds). (2014). *Handbook of child maltreatment*. Springer.

Lindsey, D. (2004). *The welfare of children*. Oxford University Press.

Mathews, B., & Bross, D. C. (2015). *Mandatory reporting laws and the identification of severe child abuse and neglect* (Vol. 4). Springer.

Pecora, P. J., Whittaker, J. K., Maluccio, A. N., & Barth, R. P., DePanfilis, D., & Plotnick, R. D. (2009). *The child welfare challenge: Policy, practice, and research*. Aldine Transaction.

CHILD MALTREATMENT FATALITIES

We do not go into a lot of detail on this topic in our book, but realize readers might be particularly interested, given the media coverage. We do caution that the accounts described in Miller and Burch in particular are quite graphic.

Commission to Eliminate Child Abuse and Neglect Fatalities. (2016). *Within our reach*. https://eliminatechildabusefatalities.sites.usa.gov/files/2016/03/CECANF-final-report.pdf

Gelles, R. (1997) *The book of David: How preserving families can cost children's lives*. Basic Books.

Lepore, J. (2016, February). Baby Doe: A political history of tragedy. *The New Yorker*.

Miller, C., & Burch, A. (2014, March). *Innocents lost: Preserving families but losing children*. http://media.miamiherald.com/static/media/projects/2014/innocents-lost/database/

CHILD MALTREATMENT, CULTURE, AND RACE

Bartholet, E., Wulczyn, F., Barth, R., & Lederman, C. (2011, June). *Race and child welfare*. Chapin Hall Issue in Brief. http://www.chapinhall.org/sites/default/files/publications/07_13_11_Race_Child_Welfare_IB.pdf

Cultural competence: Child abuse and neglect. (Several resources available on page, all 2010 or earlier.) https://www.childwelfare.gov/topics/systemwide/cultural/can/

Dorgan, B. L., Shenandoah, J., Bigfoot, D., Broderick, E., Brown, E., Davidson, V., . . . Zimmerman, M. (2014, November). *Ending violence so American Indian Alaska Native children can thrive*. Attorney General's Advisory Committee. US Department of Justice. https://www.justice.gov/sites/default/files/defendingchildhood/pages/attachments/2014/11/18/finalaianreport.pdf

Fong, R., Dettlaff, A., James, J., & Rodriguez, C. (Eds). *Addressing racial disproportionality and disparities in human services: Multisystemic approaches* (pp. 41–69). Columbia University Press.

Gray, K. (2011, March). What's really behind black child-abuse stats. *The Root*. http://www.theroot.com/articles/culture/2011/03/black_childabuse_statistics_report_debunks_bias_assumptions/

Hemenway, E. (n.d.). *Indian children forced to assimilate at white boarding schools*. National Park Service. http://www.nps.gov/articles/the-warrior-children.htm

Poverty, not bias, explains racial/ethnic differences in child abuse. (2014, September). http://wolterskluwer.com/company/newsroom/news/health/2014/09/poverty-not-bias-explains-racial-ethnic-differences-in-child-abuse.html

Roberts, D. (2003) *Shattered bonds: The color of child welfare*. Basic Civitas Books.

CHILDREN, FAMILIES, AND REFORM

Biglan, A. (2015). *The nurture effect: How science of human behavior can improve o͞ world*. New Harbinger Publications.

Blacklock, N., & Phillips, R. (Eds.). Reshaping the child protection response to ͟o͞ ͟olence through collaborative working. *Domestic violence and protecting children: ͟ ͟inking and approaches*. Jessica Kingsley.

Freymond, N., & Cameron, G. (Eds.). (2006). *Towards positive systems of child and family welfare: International comparisons of child protection, family service and community caring systems*. University of Toronto Press.

Osher, D. (2014). Colorado makes child abuse data website public (cdhsdatamatters.org). *The Denver Post*. http://www.denverpost.com/2014/04/17/colorado-makes-child-abuse-data-website-public/ (Included here as an example of making administrative data accessible for policy and program evaluation.)

Reynolds, A. J., Rolnick, A. J., & Temple, J. A. (2015). *Health and education in early childhood*. Cambridge University Press.

Sherraden, M. (2005). *Inclusion in the American Dream: Assets, poverty, and public policy*. Oxford University Press.

US DHHS, Administration for Children and Families & Friends National Center for Community-Based Child Abuse Prevention. (2016). *Building community, building hope*. https://www.childwelfare.gov/pubPDFs/guide.pdf

FACTS AND STATISTICS

Child Welfare Gateway. State statutes search. https://www.childwelfare.gov/topics/systemwide/laws-policies/state/

DeVooght, K., Fletcher, M., & Cooper, H. (2014, September). *Federal, state and local spending to address child abuse and neglect in SFY 2012*. Publication #2014-47. Child trends. http://www.childtrends.org/wp-content/uploads/2014/09/2014-47ChildWelfareSpending2012.pdf

Kids Count. Data on child and family well-being in the United States by state. http://datacenter.kidscount.org/

National Center for Children in Poverty. (2014). *Child poverty*. http://www.nccp.org/topics/childpoverty.html

National Intimate Partner and Sexual Violence Survey. https://www.cdc.gov/violenceprevention/nisvs/

World Health Organization. (2006). *Preventing child maltreatment: A guide to taking action and generating evidence*. http://apps.who.int/iris/bitstream/10665/43499/1/9241594365_eng.pdf

US DHHS. (2017). *Child maltreatment 2015*. https://www.acf.hhs.gov/sites/default/files/cb/cm2015.pdf

REFERENCES

INTRODUCTION

1. Jefferson, T. (1789). Thomas Jefferson to Richard Price. https://www.loc.gov/exhibits/jefferson/60.html

2. United Nations International Children's Emergency Fund. (1989). *Convention on the rights of the child.* http://digitalcommons.ilr.cornell.edu/cgi/viewcontent.cgi?article=1007&context=child

3. Devaney, J., & Spratt, T. (2009). Child abuse as a complex and wicked problem: Reflecting on policy developments in the United Kingdom in working with children and families with multiple problems. *Children and Youth Services Review, 31,* 635–641.

4. Kiger, P., & Spoon, M. (2011, January). Top 10 NASA inventions. *HowStuffWorks.com.* http://science.howstuffworks.com/innovation/inventions/top-5-nasa-inventions.htm

5. King Jr, M. L. (2010). *Stride toward freedom: The Montgomery story* (Vol. 1). Beacon Press.

6. Berrick, J., Needell, B., Barth, R. & Jonson-Reid, M. (1998). *The tender years: Toward developmentally sensitive child welfare services for very young children.* NY: Oxford University Press.

7. Mallon, G. P., & Hess, P. M. (2014). *Child Welfare for the Twenty-first Century: A Handbook of Practices, Policies, & Programs.* Columbia University Press.

8. Reardon, K. & Noblet, C. (2009). *Childhood denied: Ending the nightmare of child abuse and neglect.* Thousand Oaks, CA: Sage.

9. Roberts, D. E. (2002). *Shattered bonds: The color of child welfare.* Basic Books.

10. Schofield, G., & Ward, E. (2011). *Understanding and working with parents of children in long-term foster care.* Jessica Kingsley Publishers.

11. Dubowitz, H., & DePanfilis, D. (Eds.). (2000). *Handbook for children protection practice.* Thousand Oaks, CA: Sage.

12. Korbin, J. E., & Krugman, R. D. (Eds.). (2014). *Handbook of child maltreatment*. New York, NY: Springer.

13. Pelzer, D. (1995). *A child called "It"* (reissue ed.). *Deerfield Beach,* FL: HCI Publishing.

14. Pinker, S. (2011). *The better angels of our nature: Why violence has declined* (Vol. 75). New York: Viking.

15. CDC (2014). *Steps to create safe, stable, nurturing relationships and environments.* https:// www.cdc.gov/violenceprevention/pdf/essentials_for_childhood_framework.pdf

CHAPTER I

1. Opie, I., & Opie, P. (1997). *The Oxford dictionary of nursery rhymes* (2nd ed.). New York, NY: Oxford University Press.

2. Brockliss, L., & Montgomery, H. (Eds.). (2010). *Childhood and violence: In the western tradition.* Oxford, UK: Oxbow Books.

3. US Department of Labor. (2015). *2014 Findings on the worst forms of child labor.* Washington, DC: USGPO. http://www.dol.gov/ilab/reports/child-labor/findings/2014TDA/ 2014TDA.pdf

4. Muller, A. (2010). Children and physical cruelty: The Lockean and Rousseauvian Revolution. (pp. 129–134). In L. Brockliss & H. Montgomery (Eds.), *Childhood and violence in the western tradition.* Oxford, UK: Oxbow Books.

5. Bremner, R. (1971). *Children and youth in America. Volume II: 1866–1932.* Cambridge, MA: Harvard University Press.

6. Shelman, E., & Lazoritz, S. (1999). *Out of the darkness: The true story of Mary Ellen.* New York, NY: Dolphin Moon.

7. Shelman, E., & Lazoritz, S. (2012). *Case #1: The Mary Ellen Wilson files.* New York, NY: Dolphin Moon.

8. Preston, S., & Haines, M. (1991). The social and medical context of child mortality in the late nineteenth century. In *The fatal years: Child mortality in late nineteenth-century* (pp. 3–48). Princeton, NJ: Princeton University Press. http://www.nber.org/chapters/c11541

9. United Neighborhood Houses. (n.d.). *NYC settlement house history.* http://www.unhny. org/about/history

10. Franklin, D. (1986). Mary Richmond and Jane Addams: From moral certainty to rational inquiry in social work practice. *Social Service Review, 60,* 504–525.

11. Schlereth, T. (1991). *Victorian America: Transformations in everyday life.* New York, NY: Harper Perennial.

12. Tacon, P. (1982). Carlinhos: The hard gloss of city polish. *UNICEF News, 111,* 4–6.

13. Sudworth, J. (2016, April). *Counting the cost of China's left-behind children.* BBC News. http://www.bbc.com/news/world-asia-china-35994481

14. Kline, C. (2013). *Orphan train.* New York, NY: William Morrow Paperbacks.

15. Laplanche, J. (1987). *New foundations for psychoanalysis* (D. Macey, Trans.). Oxford, UK: Basil Blackwell.

16. Masson, J. (2003). *The assault on truth: Freud's suppression of the seduction theory.* New York, NY: Ballantine Books.

17. CHILDREN'S Bureau. (1913). *White House Conference.* http://www.pcya.org/ SiteCollectionDocuments/History%20of%20US%20Children%27s%20Policy%20 %28Yarrow%29.pdf

18. Pelton, L. (1978). Child abuse and neglect: The myth of classlessness. *American Journal of Orthopsychiatry, 48,* 608–617.

19. Pelton, L. (1994). *The role of material factors in child abuse and neglect.* New York, NY: Guilford.

20. Pelton, L. (2015). The continuing role of material factors in child maltreatment and placement. *Child Abuse and Neglect, 41,* 30–39.

21. Hindman, H. (2002). *Child labor: An American history.* New York, NY: M. E. Sharpe.

22. Trattner, W. (1984). *From poor law to welfare state: A history of social welfare in America* (3rd ed.). New York, NY: The Free Press.

23. Ludmerer, K. (2010). Commentary: Understanding the Flexner Report. *Academic Medicine, 85,* 193–196.

24. Winsten, P. (n.d.). *A century of service.* Alliance for Strong Families. http://alliance1.org/centennial/book/introduction

25. Bradbury, D. E. (1956). *Four decades of action for children.* Children's Bureau, USGPO. https://www.ssa.gov/history/pdf/child1.pdf

26. Risman, B. (2010). *Families as they really are.* New York, NY: Norton.

27. Costin, L., Karger, H., & Stoesz, D. (1996). *The politics of child abuse in America.* New York, NY: Oxford University Press.

28. Kempe, C., Silverman, F., Steele, B., Droegemueller, W, & Silver, H. (1962). The battered-child syndrome. *JAMA, 181,* 17–24.

29. Salzberg, S. (2015, February). Anti-vaccine movement causes worst measles epidemic in 20 years. *Forbes.* http://www.forbes.com/sites/stevensalzberg/2015/02/01/anti-vaccine-movement-causes-worst-measles-epidemic-in-20-years/#31c903a17ef9

30. Cohen, E., & Falco, M. (2011, January). Retracted autism study an "elaborate fraud," British journal finds. *Health.* http://www.cnn.com/2011/HEALTH/01/05/autism.vaccines/index.html

31. Bronfenbrenner, U. (1974). Developmental research, public policy, and the ecology of childhood. *Child Development, 45,* 1–5.

32. Belsky, J. (1984). The determinants of parenting: A process model. *Child Development, 55,* 83–96.

CHAPTER 2

1. Wikipedia. (2017, January). *Sleeping beauty* (1959 film). https://en.wikipedia.org/wiki/Sleeping_Beauty_(1959_film)

2. US DHHS, Children's Bureau. (2017). *Child maltreatment 2015.* Washington, DC: Author. http://www.acf.hhs.gov/programs/cb/resource/child-maltreatment-2015

3. Greenspan, J. (2013, September). The dark side of the Grimm fairy tales. *History.com.* http://www.history.com/news/the-dark-side-of-the-grimm-fairy-tales

4. Parent, M. (1998). *Turning stones: A caseworker's story.* New York, NY: Ballantine Books.

5. Child Abuse Protection and Treatment Act (1974), PL 93–247.

6. Indian Child Welfare Act (1978), PL 95–608.

7. Adoption Assistance and Child Welfare Act (1980), PL 96–272.

8. Adoption and Safe Families Act (1997), PL105–89.

9. Child Welfare Information Gateway. (2016). *Major federal legislation concerned with child protection, child welfare, and adoption.* Washington, DC: US Department of Health and Human Services, Children's Bureau.

10. Pecora, P., Whittaker, J., Maluccio, A., Barth, R., & DePanfilis, D. (2010). *The child welfare challenge: Policy practice and research*. Piscataway, NJ: Transaction Publishers.

11. US DHHS. (1981), *Study findings: National study of the incidence and severity of child abuse and neglect*. DHHS publication number OHDS 81-30325. Washington, DC: USGPO.

12. Peddle, N., Wang, C., Edwards, M., Gaudiosi, J., Yuan, Y., & Fluke, J. (2003, April). *The evolution of a national reporting system on child maltreatment: 25 years of progress*. Presentation at the 14th National Conference on Child Abuse and Neglect. https://www.acf.hhs.gov/sites/default/files/cb/nccan14_workshop_42.pdf

13. US DHHS, Children's Bureau (2002). *Child maltreatment 2000*. Washington, DC: Author.

14. Finkelhor, D. (2008). *Childhood victimization*. New York, NY: Oxford University Press.

15. Sedlak, A., Mettenburg, J., Basena, M., Petta, I., McPherson, K., Greene, A., & Li, S. (2010). *Fourth National Incidence Study of Child Abuse and Neglect (NIS–4): Report to Congress*. Washington, DC: US Department of Health and Human Services, Administration for Children and Families.

16. Gilbert, R., Fluke, J., O'Donnell, M., Gonzalez-Izquierdo, A, Brownell, M., Gulliver, P., . . . Sidebotham, P. (2012). Child maltreatment: Variation in trends and policies in six developed countries. *Lancet, 379*, 758–772.

17. Child Welfare Information Gateway. (2015). Mandatory reporters of child abuse and neglect. *State Statutes*. Children's Bureau. https://www.childwelfare.gov/topics/systemwide/laws-policies/statutes/manda/

18. Walsh, W. A., & Jones, L. M. (2016). A statewide study of the public's knowledge of child abuse reporting laws. *Journal of Public Child Welfare, 10*, 561–579.

19. DeVooght, K., Child Trends, & Blazey, D. (2012). *Family foster care reimbursement rates in the US*. Annie E. Casey Foundation. http://www.childtrends.org/wp-content/uploads/2013/04/Foster-Care-Payment-Rate-Report.pdf

20. Whitaker, T. (2012). Professional social workers in the child welfare workforce: Findings from NASW. *Journal of Family Strengths, 12*, 1–13.

21. Holosko, M., & Faith, E. (2015). Educating BSW and MSW social workers to practice in child welfare services. In J. Wodarski, M. Holosko, & M. Feit (Eds.), *Evidence-informed practice and assessment in child welfare*. New York, NY: Springer.

22. Norman, E. (2009). *No one would believe it: Experiences of a child abuse investigator*. Author.

23. Mandell, D., Stalker, C., de Zeeuw Wright, M., Frensch, K., & Harvey, C. (2013). Sinking, swimming and sailing: Experiences of job satisfaction and emotional exhaustion in child welfare employees. *Child and Family Social Work, 18*, 383–393.

24. Narey, M. (2014). Making the education of social workers consistently effective: Report of Sir Martin Narey's independent review of the education of children's social workers. http://dera.ioe.ac.uk/19338/1/Social_worker_education_report.pdf

25. McFadden, P., Campbell, A., & Taylor, B. (2014). Resilience and burnout in child protection social work: Individual and organisational themes from a systematic literature review. *British Journal of Social Work, 45*, 1546–1563.

26. Cross, T., Finkelhor, D., & Ormrod, R. (2005). Police involvement in child protective services investigations: Literature review and secondary data analysis. *Child Maltreatment, 10*, 224–244.

27. Beal, S., Wingrove, T., & Weisz, V. (2014). Judicial case management in predicting length of stay in foster care. *Children and Youth Services Review, 44*, 16–19.

28. Ellett, A., & Steib, S. (2005). Child welfare and the courts: A statewide study with implications for professional development, practice, and change. *Research on Social Work Practice, 15,* 339–352.

29. Russell, J., Miller, N., & Nash, M. (2015). Judicial issues in child maltreatment. In J. Korbin & R. Krugman (Eds.), *Handbook of child maltreatment.* New York, NY: Springer Press.

30. Graham, L. (2009). Reparations, self-determination and the seventh generation. In M. Fletcher, W. Singel, & K. Fort (Eds.), *Facing the future: The Indian Child Welfare Act at 30.* East Lansing: Michigan State University Press.

31. Hemenway, E. (n.d.). *Indian children forced to assimilate at white boarding schools.* National Park Service. http://www.nps.gov/articles/the-warrior-children.htm

32. Margolis, E. (2004). Looking at discipline, looking at labour: photographic representations of Indian boarding schools. *Visual Studies, 19*(1), 72–96.

33. Curcio, A. A. (2006). Civil claims for uncivilized acts: Filing suit against the government for American Indian boarding school abuses. *Hastings Race & Poverty LJ, 4,* 4–130.

34. Indian Child Welfare Act of 1978 (25 U.S.C. §§ 1901-63)

35. Bureau of Indian Affairs. (2016). *Guidelines for implementing the Indian Child Welfare Act.* Office of the Assistant Secretary—Indian Affairs.https://www.indianaffairs.gov/cs/groups/public/documents/text/idc2-056831.pdf

36. Fletcher, M., Singel, W., & Fort, K. (Eds.). (2009). *Facing the future: The Indian Child Welfare Act at 30.* East Lansing: Michigan State University Press.

37. Sullivan, L. (2011, October). Native foster care: Lost children, shattered families. *All Things Considered.* National Public Radio. http://www.npr.org/2011/10/25/141672992/native-foster-care-lost-children-shattered-families

38. Child Welfare Information Gateway. (2016, February). Definitions of child abuse and neglect. *State Statutes.* Children's Bureau. https://www.childwelfare.gov/topics/systemwide/laws-policies/state/?CWIGFunctionsaction=statestatutes:main.getResults

39. Schwartz, K., Metz, J., Feldman, K., Sidbury, R., & Lindberg, D. (2014). Cutaneous findings mistaken for physical abuse: Present but not pervasive. *Pediatric Dermatology, 31,* 146–155.

40. Shusterman, G., Fluke, J., Hollinshead, D., & Yuan, Y. (2005). Alternative responses to child maltreatment: Findings from NCANDS. *Protecting Children, 20,* 32–42.

41. Child Welfare Information Gateway. (2014). *Differential response to reports of child abuse and neglect.* Washington, DC: US Department of Health and Human Services, Children's Bureau.

42. Fausset, R. (2014, September). South Carolina child welfare agency faced scrutiny before 5 siblings deaths. *New York Times.* http://www.nytimes.com/2014/09/13/us/scrutiny-of-south-carolina-agency-began-before-the-killing-of-5-siblings.html?_r=0

43. Lepore, J. (2016, February). Baby Doe: A political history of tragedy. *New Yorker.*

44. Hussey, J., Marshal, J., English, D., Knight, E., Lau, A., Dubowitz, H., & Kotch, J. (2005). Defining maltreatment according to substantiation: Distinction without a difference? *Child Abuse and Neglect, 29,* 479–492.

45. Kohl, P., Jonson-Reid, M., & Drake, B. (2009). Time to leave substantiation behind. *Child Maltreatment, 14,* 17–26.

46. Leiter, J., Myers, K., & Zingraff, M. (1994). Substantiated and unsubstantiated cases of child maltreatment: Do their consequences differ? *Social Work Research, 18,* 67–82.

47. Drake, B. (1996). Unraveling "unsubstantiated." *Child Maltreatment, 1,* 261–271.

48. FBI. (2012). Crime in the United States. *Uniform Crime Reports*. https://www.fbi.gov/about-us/cjis/ucr/crime-in-the-u.s/2012/crime-in-the-u.s.-2012/offenses-known-to-law-enforcement/clearances

49. Missouri's Children's Division. (2015). *Children's Division annual report: Fiscal year 2015*. http://dss.mo.gov/re/pdf/cs/2015-missouri-childrens-division-annual-report.pdf

50. Jonson-Reid, M., & Barth, R. (2000). From maltreatment report to juvenile incarceration: The role of child welfare services. *Child Abuse and Neglect, 24*, 505–520.

51. Berrick, J., Needell, B., Barth, R., & Jonson-Reid, M. (1998). *The tender years: Toward developmentally sensitive child welfare services for very young children*. New York, NY: Oxford University Press.

52. Webster, D., Armijo, M., Lee, S., Dawson, W., Magruder, J., Exel, M., . . . & Pixton, E. (May 2015). First entries into foster care by reason for removal. *California Child Welfare Indicators Project Reports*, UC Berkeley Center for Social Services Research. http://www.kidsdata.org/topic/16/fostercare-entries-reason/pie#fmt=13&loc=2&tf=86&ch=35,36,37,38&pdist=89

53. Jonson-Reid, M. (2003). Foster care and future risk of maltreatment. *Children and Youth Services Review, 25*, 271–294.

54. Child Welfare Information Gateway. (2016). *Foster care statistics 2014*. Washington, DC: US Department of Health and Human Services, Children's Bureau. https://www.childwelfare.gov/pubPDFs/foster.pdf

55. Raghavan, R., & Alexandrova, A. (2015). Toward a theory of child well-being. *Social Indicators Research, 121*, 887–902.

56. Jonson-Reid, M., & Drake, B. (2016). Child well-being: Where is it in our data systems? *Journal of Public Child Welfare, 10*, 457–465.

57. Children's Bureau, Administration for Children and Families, US Department of Health and Human Services. (n.d.). *Child Family Service Review Report and Results of the Child and Family Services Reviews*. https://library.childwelfare.gov/cwig/ws/cwmd/docs/cb_web/SearchForm

58. Commission to Eliminate Child Abuse and Neglect Fatalities. (2016). *Within our reach: A national strategy to eliminate child abuse and neglect fatalities*. Washington, DC: Government Printing Office.

59. The Protect Our Kids Act (2012), PL112–275.

60. Child Welfare 360. (2012, Spring). *Secondary trauma and the child welfare workforce*. Center for Advanced Studies in Child Welfare. http://www.nctsn.org/sites/default/files/assets/pdfs/CW360_2012.pdf

61. Burbank, A., & Achen, P. (2015, August). Child protection workers face danger, criticism. *USA Today*. http://www.usatoday.com/story/news/nation/2015/08/13/child-protection-workers-face-danger-criticism/31592077/

62. DeVooght, K., Fletcher, M., & Cooper, H. (2014, September). *Federal, state and local spending to address child abuse and neglect in SFY 2012*. Publication #2014-47. Child Trends. http://www.childtrends.org/wp-content/uploads/2014/09/2014-47ChildWelfareSpending2012.pdf

63. Fang, X., Brown, D., Florence, C., & Mercy, J. (2012). The economic burden of child maltreatment in the United States and implications for prevention. *Child Abuse and Neglect, 36*, 156–165.

64. Chantrall, C. (2017, February). *Total government spending in the United States. Federal, state, and local: Fiscal year 2017*. http://www.usgovernmentspending.com/breakdown

65. Jagannathan, R., & Camasso, M. (2013). *Protecting children in the age of outrage*. New York, NY: Oxford University Press.

CHAPTER 3

1. Kennell, N., Leyser, H., Brockliss, L., Muller, A., Humphries, J., Ellis, H., & Cretney, S. (2010). Physical cruelty and socialization (p. 107). In L. Brockliss & H. Montgomery (Eds.), *Childhood and violence: In the western tradition*. Oxford, UK: Oxbow Books.

2. Shannon, G. (1981). The survival of the child: Abuse in folktales. *Children's Literature in Education, 12,* 34–38.

3. US DHHS, Children's Bureau. (2016). *Child maltreatment 2014*. Washington, DC: Author. http://www.acf.hhs.gov/programs/cb/resource/child-maltreatment-2014

4. Sedlak, A., Mettenburg, J., Basena, M., Petta, I., McPherson, K., Greene, A., & Li, S. (2010). *Fourth National Incidence Study of Child Abuse and Neglect (NIS–4): Report to Congress*. Washington, DC: US Department of Health and Human Services, Administration for Children and Families.

5. Finkelhor, D., & Jones, L. (2006). Why have child maltreatment and child victimization declined? *Journal of Social Issues, 62,* 685–716.

6. Pinker, S. (2011). *The better angels of our nature: The decline of violence in history and its causes*. London, UK: Penguin Books.

7. Millett, L., Lanier, P., & Drake, B. (2011). Are economic trends associated with child maltreatment? Preliminary results from the recent recession using state level data. *Children and Youth Services Review, 33,* 1280–1287.

8. Finkelhor, D., Saito, K., & Jones, L. (2016). *Updated trends in child maltreatment, 2014*. Durham, NH: Crimes Against Children Research Center.

9. Bowman, S., Aitken, M., Robbins, J., & Baker, S. (2012). Trends in US pediatric drowning hospitalizations, 1993–2008. *Pediatrics, 129,* 275–281.

10. Menard, S., Weiss, A., Franzese, R., & Covey, H. (2014). Types of adolescent exposure to violence as predictors of adult intimate partner violence. *Child Abuse and Neglect, 38,* 627–639.

11. Widom, C. (1989). The cycle of violence. *Science, 244,* 160–166.

12. Caspi, A., McClay, J., Moffitt, T. E., Mill, J., Martin, J., Craig, I. W., . . . Poulton, R. (2002). Role of genotype in the cycle of violence in maltreated children. *Science, 297,* 851–854.

13. Ben David, V., Jonson-Reid, M., Drake, B., & Kohl, P. (2015). The association between childhood maltreatment experiences and the onset of maltreatment perpetration in young adulthood controlling for proximal and distal risk factors. *Child Abuse and Neglect, 46,* 132–141.

14. Widom, C., & Wilson, H. (2015). Intergenerational transmission of violence (pp. 27–45). In J. Lindert & I. Levav (Eds.), *Violence and Mental Health*. Dordrecht, Netherlands: Springer.

15. Shelman, E., & Lazoritz, S. (2003). *Out of the darkness: The story of Mary Ellen Wilson*. Dolphin Moon Pub.

16. Tucker, M., & Rodriguez, C. (2014). Family dysfunction and social isolation as moderators between stress and child physical abuse risk. *Journal of Family Violence, 29,* 175–186.

17. Barr, R., Rivara, F., Barr, M., Cummings, P., Taylor, J., Lengua, L., & Meredith-Benitz, E. (2009). Effectiveness of educational materials designed to change knowledge and behaviors regarding crying and shaken-baby syndrome in mothers of newborns: A randomized, controlled trial. *Pediatrics, 123,* 972–980.

18. Corbin, B. (2015, November). Take a break don't shake. *Prezi*. https://prezi.com/z_ucxj2cd-sww/take-a-break-dont-shake/

19. Dopke, C., & Milner, J. (2000). Impact of child noncompliance on stress appraisals, attributions, and disciplinary choices in mothers at high and low risk for child physical abuse. *Child Abuse and Neglect, 24,* 493–504.

20. Conger, R. (1976). Social control and social learning models of delinquency: A synthesis. *Criminology, 14,* 17–40.

21. Sampson, R., Raudenbush, S., & Earls, F. (1997). Neighborhoods and violent crime: A multilevel study of collective efficacy. *Science, 277,* 918–924.

22. Fraser, M. (2004). Intervention research in social work: Recent advances and continuing challenges. *Research on Social Work Practice, 14,* 210–222.

23. Black, D., Heyman, R., & Slep, A. (2001). Risk factors for child physical abuse. *Aggression and Violent Behavior, 6,* 121–188.

24. Chaffin, M., Kelleher, K., & Hollenberg, J. (1996). Onset of physical abuse and neglect: Psychiatric, substance abuse, and social risk factors from prospective community data. *Child Abuse and Neglect, 20,* 191–203.

25. Child Welfare Information Gateway. (2004, February). *Risk and protective factors for child abuse and neglect*. https://www.childwelfare.gov/pubPDFs/riskprotectivefactors.pdf

26. Drake, B., & Pandey, S. (1996). Understanding the relationship between neighborhood poverty and specific types of child maltreatment. *Child Abuse and Neglect, 20,* 1003–1018.

27. Mayo Clinic Staff. (n.d.). Temper tantrums in toddlers: How to keep the peace. *Infant and toddler health*. http://www.mayoclinic.org/healthy-lifestyle/infant-and-toddler-health/in-depth/tantrum/art-20047845

28. Russell, M. (2011, December). Move over Tiger Mom, it's "Wolf Dad"—Chinese father is media sensation at home for his tough discipline. *Newser*. http://www.newser.com/story/135385/move-over-tiger-mom-its-wolf-dad.html

29. Winfield, N. (2015, February). Pope says it is OK to spank kids, so long as their dignity is kept. *Seattle Times*. http://www.seattletimes.com/news/pope-says-its-ok-to-spank-kids-if-their-dignity-is-kept/

30. Enton, H. (2014). Americans' opinions on spanking vary by party, race, region and religion. *FiveThirtyEight*. http://fivethirtyeight.com/datalab/americans-opinions-on-spanking-vary-by-party-race-region-and-religion

31. Zolotor, A., Theodore, A., Runyan, D., Chang, J., & Laskey, A. (2011). Corporal punishment and physical abuse: Population-based trends for three-to-11-year-old children in the United States. *Child Abuse Review, 20,* 57–66.

32. Child Welfare Information Gateway. (n.d.). *State statutes*. https://www.childwelfare.gov/systemwide/laws_policies/statutes/define.cfm

33. Wright, N. (2014, September). Updated: Exclusive details on Adrian Peterson indictment charges. *CBS Houston*. http://houston.cbslocal.com/2014/09/12/exclusive-details-on-adrian-peterson-indictment-charges/

34. ESPN.com News Services. (2014, September). Peterson faced accusation in 2013. Author. http://espn.go.com/nfl/story/_/id/11534340/adrian-peterson-minnesota-vikings-faced-previous-child-abuse-accusation

35. Bloom, M. (2014, November). Adrian Peterson's suspension: What you need to know. *MPR News*. http://www.mprnews.org/story/2014/11/18/adrian-peterson

36. Vensel, M., & Kaszuba, M. (2014, October). Next for Adrian Peterson: Getting through the courts. *Star Tribune*. http://www.startribune.com/peterson-likely-to-miss-season-future-with-team-in-doubt/275400961/

37. Dwyer, K. (2014, September). Charles Barkley on Adrian Peterson: "Every black parent in the South" whips their children. *Yahoo Sports*. http://sports.yahoo.com/blogs/nba-ball-dont-lie/charles-barkley-on-adrian-peterson---every-black-parent-in-the-south--whips-their-children-202259157.html

38. Hanstock, B. (2014, September). Watch Cris Carter's emotional comments about child abuse. *SB Nation*. http://www.sbnation.com/lookit/2014/9/14/6147347/cris-carter-espn-comments-about-child-abuse

39. Straus, M. (2001). *Beating the devil out of them: Corporal punishment in American families and its effects on children*. Piscataway, NJ: Transaction Publishers.

40. Coleman, D., Dodge, K., & Campbell, S. (2010). Where and how to draw the line between reasonable corporal punishment and abuse. *Law and Contemporary Problems, 73*, 107–166.

41. Ferguson, C. (2013). Spanking, corporal punishment and negative long-term outcomes: A meta-analytic review of longitudinal studies. *Clinical Psychology Review, 33*, 196–208.

42. Knutson, J., DeGarmo, D., Koeppl, G., & Reid, J. (2005). Care neglect, supervisory neglect, and harsh parenting in the development of children's aggression: A replication and extension. *Child Maltreatment, 10*, 92–107.

43. Westbrook, T., Harden, B., Holmes, A., Meisch, A., & Whittaker, J. (2013). Physical discipline use and child behavior problems in low-income, high-risk African American families. *Early Education and Development, 24*, 923–945.

44. Finkelhor, D. (2008). *Childhood victimization*. New York, NY: Oxford University Press.

45. Ateah, C., & Durrant, J. (2005). Maternal use of physical punishment in response to child misbehavior: Implications for child abuse prevention. *Child Abuse and Neglect, 29*, 169–185.

46. Edmonds, M. (2008, June). How anger works. *HowStuffWorks.com*. http://science.howstuffworks.com/life/inside-the-mind/emotions/anger.htm

47. Lyman, J., McGwin, G., Malone, D., Taylor, A., Brissie, R., Davis, G., & Rue, L. (2003). Epidemiology of child homicide in Jefferson County, Alabama. *Child Abuse and Neglect, 27*, 1063–1073.

48. Kajese, T., Nguyen, L., Pham, G., Pham, V., Melhorn, K., & Kallail, K. (2011). Characteristics of child abuse homicides in the state of Kansas from 1994 to 2007. *Child Abuse and Neglect, 35*, 147–154.

49. Pearl, M., & Pearl, D. (1994/2015). *To train up a child*. Pleasantville, TN: No Greater Joy Ministries.

50. Bayer, A. (2013, November). Another couple found guilty of murder for parenting by "To train up a child." *Examiner.com*. http://www.examiner.com/article/another-couple-found-guilty-of-murder-for-parenting-by-to-train-up-a-child

51. CNN.com (2013, November). Controversial parenting book linked to the deaths of several children. http://ac360.blogs.cnn.com/2013/11/25/controversial-parenting-book-linked-to-the-deaths-of-several-children/

52. American Academy of Pediatrics. (1998). Guidance on effective discipline. *Pediatrics, 101*, 726.

53. Lee, S., Grogan-Kaylor, A., & Berger, L. (2014). Parental spanking of 1-year-old children and subsequent child protective services involvement. *Child Abuse and Neglect, 38,* 875–883.

54. Petska, H., & Sheets, L. (2014). Sentinel injuries: Subtle findings of physical abuse. *Pediatric Clinics of North America, 61,* 923–935.

55. Mersch, J. (2015, July). Shaken baby syndrome (Abusive head trauma). *Medicinenet.* http://www.medicinenet.com/shaken_baby_syndrome_abusive_head_trauma/article.htm

56. Ohlheiser, A. (2015, April). Woman called "mom of the year" after beating a young man out of Baltimore riots. *Washington Post.* http://www.washingtonpost.com/news/local/wp/2015/04/28/woman-called-mom-of-the-year-after-beating-a-young-man-out-of-baltimore-riots/

57. Cope, K. (2010). The age of discipline: The relevance of age to the reasonableness of corporal punishment. *Law and Contemporary Problems, 73,* 167–188.

58. Pollard-Sacks, D. (2002). Banning corporal punishment: A constitutional analysis. *American University Law Review, 52,* 447.

59. Durrant, J. (1999). Evaluating the success of Sweden's corporal punishment ban. *Child Abuse and Neglect, 23,* 435–448.

60. Renteln, A. (2010). Corporal punishment and the cultural defense. *Law and Contemporary Problems, 73,* 253–279.

61. Taylor, C., Hamvas, L., & Paris, R. (2011). Perceived instrumentality and normativeness of corporal punishment use among black mothers. *Family Relations, 60,* 60–72.

62. Tajima, E., & Harachi, T. (2010). Parenting beliefs and physical discipline practices among Southeast Asian immigrants: Parenting in the context of cultural adaptation to the United States. *Journal of Cross-Cultural Psychology, 41,* 212–235.

63. Poole, M., Seal, D., & Taylor, C. (2014). A systematic review of universal campaigns targeting child physical abuse prevention. *Health Education Research, 29,* 388–432.

64. Biglan, A. (2015). *The nurture effect. How science of human behavior can improve our lives and our world.* Oakland, CA: New Harbinger Publications.

CHAPTER 4

1. Greenspan, J. (2013, September). The dark side of the Grimm fairy tales. *History.com.* http://www.history.com/news/the-dark-side-of-the-grimm-fairy-tales

2. Scott, S. P. (Ed.). (n.d.). *The Visigothic code: (Forum judicum).* The Library of Iberian Resources Online. http://libro.uca.edu/vcode/vg4-4.htm

3. Pelton, L. (2015). The continuing role of material factors in child maltreatment and placement. *Child Abuse and Neglect, 41,* 30–39.

4. Drake, B., & Pandey, S. (1996). Understanding the relationship between neighborhood poverty and child maltreatment. *Child Abuse and Neglect, 20,* 1003–1018.

5. Jonson-Reid, M., Drake, B., & Zhou, P. (2013). Neglect subtypes, race, and poverty: Individual, family, and service characteristics. *Child Maltreatment, 18,* 30–41.

6. Nikulina, V., Widom, C., & Czaja, S. (2011). The role of childhood neglect and childhood poverty in predicting mental health, academic achievement and crime in adulthood. *American Journal of Community Psychology, 48*(3-4), 309–321.

7. Sedlak, A., Mettenburg, J., Basena, M., Petta, I., McPherson, K., Greene, A., & Li, S. (2010). *Fourth National Incidence Study of Child Abuse and Neglect (NIS–4): Report to Congress.*

Washington, DC: US Department of Health and Human Services, Administration for Children and Families.

8. Slack, K., Holl, J., McDaniel, M., Yoo, J., & Bolger, K. (2004). Understanding the risks of child neglect: An exploration of poverty and parenting characteristics. *Child Maltreatment, 9,* 395–408.

9. Jones, M. (2008). White House conferences on children. *Encyclopedia of children and childhood in history and society.* http://www.faqs.org/childhood/Wh-Z-and-other-topics/White-House-Conferences-on-Children.html

10. Siek, S. (2012). King's final message: Poverty is a civil rights issue. *CNN News.* http://inamerica.blogs.cnn.com/2012/01/16/kings-final-message-poverty-is-a-civil-rights-battle/

11. Current Population Survey. (2016, September). *Historical poverty tables: People and families—1959 to 2015.* https://www.census.gov/data/tables/time-series/demo/income-poverty/historical-poverty-people.html

12. Jonson-Reid, M., Drake, B., & Kohl, P. (2009). Is the overrepresentation of the poor in child welfare caseloads due to bias or need? *Children and Youth Services Review, 31,* 422–427.

13. Drake, B., & Jonson-Reid, M. (2014). Poverty and child maltreatment. In J. Korbin & H. Krugman (Eds.), *Handbook of child maltreatment* (pp. 131–148). Netherlands: Springer.

14. Herrenkohl, T., & Herrenkohl, R. (2007). Examining the overlap and prediction of multiple forms of child maltreatment, stressors, and socioeconomic status: A longitudinal analysis of youth outcomes. *Journal of Family Violence, 22,* 553–562.

15. McGuinness, T., & Schneider, K. (2007). Poverty, child maltreatment and foster care. *Journal of the American Psychiatric Nurses Association, 13,* 296–303

16. Biglan, A. (2015). *The nurture effect: How science of human behavior can improve our lives and our world.* Oakland, CA: New Harbinger.

17. US DHHS, Office of the Assistant Secretary for Planning and Evaluation. (2015). *2015 poverty guidelines.* Washington DC: Author. http://aspe.hhs.gov/poverty/15poverty.cfm.

18. US Census Bureau. (2013). *American community survey.* https://www.census.gov/quickfacts/table/PST045213/00

19. Staff Writer. (2011). *Average utility costs per month: What's normal?* http://ohmyapt.apartmentratings.com/breaking-down-the-average-utility-costs-per-month-whats-normal.html

20. Warne, L., & Ostria, M. (2013, November). *How differences in the cost of living affect low income families.* Issue Brief 133. National Center for Policy Analysis. http://www.ncpa.org/pdfs/ib133.pdf

21. US Department of Agriculture. (2015, March). Child nutrition programs: Income eligibility guidelines. *Federal Register, 80.* http://www.fns.usda.gov/sites/default/files/NSLPFactSheet.pdf

22. Drake, B., & Rank, M. (2009). The racial divide among American children in poverty: Assessing the importance of neighborhoods. *Children and Youth Services Review, 31,* 1264–1271.

23. Conger, R., Wallace, L., Sun, Y., Simons, R., McLoyd, V., & Brody, G. (2002). Economic pressure in African American families: A replication and extension of the family stress model. *Developmental Psychology, 38,* 179.

24. Duva, J., & Metzger, S. (2010). Addressing poverty as a major risk factor in child neglect: Promising policy and practice. *Protecting Children, 25,* 63–74.

25. Fowler, P., Henry, D., Schoeny, M., Landsverk, J., Chavira, D., & Taylor, J. (2013). Inadequate housing among families under investigation for child abuse and neglect: Prevalence from a national probability sample. *American Journal of Community Psychology, 52*, 106–114.

26. Cambria, N. (2016, June). The crisis within: How toxic stress and trauma endanger our children. *St Louis Post Dispatch.* http://graphics.stltoday.com/apps/stress/

27. Newland, R., Crnic, K., Cox, M., & Mills-Koonce, W. (2013). The family model stress and maternal psychological symptoms: Mediated pathways from economic hardship to parenting. *Journal of Family Psychology, 27*, 96–105.

28. Coulton, C., Crampton, D., Irwin, M., Spilsbury, J., & Korbin, J. (2007). How neighborhoods influence child maltreatment: A review of the literature and alternative pathways. *Child Abuse and Neglect, 31*, 1117–1142.

29. Drake, B., Lee, S., & Jonson-Reid, M. (2009). Race and child maltreatment reporting: Are blacks over-represented? *Children and Youth Services Review, 31*, 309–316.

30. Marcotte, D. (2013). High school dropout and teen childbearing. *Economics of Education Review, 34*, 258–268.

31. Putnam-Hornstein, E., Cederbaum, J., King, B., Eastman, A., & Trickett, P. (2015). A population-level and longitudinal study of adolescent mothers and intergenerational maltreatment. *American Journal of Epidemiology, 181*, 496–503.

32. Reich, J. (2006). *Fixing families: Parents, power, and the child welfare system.* New York, NY: Routledge.

33. US DHHS, Children's Bureau. (2017). *Child maltreatment 2015.* Washington DC: Author. http://www.acf.hhs.gov/programs/cb/resource/child-maltreatment-2015

34. Finkelhor, D., Saito, K., & Jones, L. (2015). *Updated trends in child maltreatment, 2013.* Durham, NH: Crimes against Children Research Center.

35. Jonson-Reid, M., Drake, B., Chung, S., & Way, I. (2003). Cross-type recidivism among referrals to a state child welfare agency. *Child Abuse and Neglect, 27*, 889–917.

36. Child Welfare Information Gateway. (2016, February). *State statutes.* https://www.childwelfare.gov/topics/systemwide/laws-policies/state/?CWIGFunctionsaction=statestatutes:main.getResults

37. Hohman, M., Oliver, R., & Wright, W. (2004). Methamphetamine abuse and manufacture: The child welfare response. *Social Work, 49*(3), 373–381.

38. DeGregory, L. (2008, January). The girl in the window. *Tampa Bay Times.* http://www.tampabay.com/features/humaninterest/the-girl-in-the-window/750838

39. Gilbert, R., Widom, C. S., Browne, K., Fergusson, D., Webb, E., & Janson, S. (2009). Burden and consequences of child maltreatment in high-income countries. *Lancet, 373*, 68–81.

40. Vachon, D., Krueger, R., Rogosch, F., & Cicchetti, D. (2015). Assessment of the harmful psychiatric and behavioral effects of different forms of child maltreatment. *JAMA Psychiatry, 72*, 1135–1142.

41. Bremner, R. (1971). *Children and youth in America. Volume II: 1866–1932.* Cambridge, MA: Harvard University Press.

42. Maslow, A. (1943). A theory of human motivation. *Psychological Review, 50*, 370–396.

43. Smithells, R., & Newman, C. (1992). Recognition of thalidomide defects. *Journal of Medical Genetics, 29, 716–723.*

44. Blakemore, S. (2012). Imaging brain development: The adolescent brain. *Neuroimage, 61*, 397–406.

45. Hensch, T. (2016). The power of the infant brain. *Scientific American, 314*, 64–69.

46. Luby, J., Belden, A., Botteron, K., Marrus, N., Harms, M. P., Babb, C., . . . Barch, D. (2013). The effects of poverty on childhood brain development: The mediating effect of caregiving and stressful life events. *JAMA Pediatrics, 167*, 1135–1142.

47. Bailey, R., West, K., Jr., & Black, R. (2015). The epidemiology of global micronutrient deficiencies. *Annals of Nutrition and Metabolism, 66*(Suppl. 2), 22–33.

48. Iannotti, L., Jean Louis Dulience, S., Wolff, P., Cox, K., Lesorogol, C., & Kohl, P. (2016). Nutrition factors predict earlier acquisition of motor and language milestones among young children in Haiti. *Acta Paediatrica, 105*.

49. Garlinghouse, T., & Trowbridge, S. (2015). Child well-being in context. *U. Pa. JL and Soc. Change, 18*, 105–124.

50. Calheiros, M. M., Monteiro, M. B., Patrício, J. N., & Carmona, M. (2016). Defining child maltreatment among lay people and community professionals: Exploring consensus in ratings of severity. *Journal of Child and Family Studies, 25*, 2292–2305.

51. FindLaw. (2014). When can you leave a child home alone? *Findlaw.com.* http://family.findlaw.com/parental-rights-and-liability/when-can-you-leave-a-child-home-alone-.html

52. De Roo, A., Chounthirath, T., & Smith, G. (2013). Television-related injuries to children in the United States, 1990–2011. *Pediatrics, 132*, 267–274.

53. First People. (n.d.). The deserted children: A Gros ventre legend. *The legends.* http://www.firstpeople.us/FP-Html-Legends/TheDesertedChildren-GrosVentre.html

54. Bowlby, J. (1969). *Attachment and loss: Vol.1. Loss.* New York: Basic Books.

55. Wolff, M. S., & Ijzendoorn, M. H. (1997). Sensitivity and attachment: A meta-analysis on parental antecedents of infant attachment. *Child Development, 68*, 571–591.

56. Constantino, J., Chackes, L., Wartner, U., Gross, M., Brophy, S., Vitale, J., & Heath, A. (2006). Mental representations of attachment in identical female twins with and without conduct problems. *Child Psychiatry and Human Development, 37*, 65–72.

57. Laible, D., & Thompson, R. (2000). Mother-child discourse, attachment security, shared positive affect, and early conscience development. *Child Development, 71*, 1424–1440.

58. Kim, J., & Cicchetti, D. (2004). A longitudinal study of child maltreatment, mother–child relationship quality and maladjustment: The role of self-esteem and social competence. *Journal of Abnormal Child Psychology, 32*, 341–354.

59. Hildyard, K., & Wolfe, D. (2002). Child neglect: Developmental issues and outcomes. *Child Abuse and Neglect, 26*, 679–695.

60. Bright, C., & Jonson-Reid, M. (2008). Onset of juvenile court involvement: Exploring gender-specific associations with maltreatment and poverty. *Children and Youth Services Review, 30*, 914–927.

61. Chapple, C., Tyler, K., & Bersani, B. (2005). Child neglect and adolescent violence: Examining the effects of self-control and peer rejection. *Violence and Victims, 20*, 39–53.

62. Snyder, S., & Merritt, D. (2015). The influence of supervisory neglect on subtypes of emerging adult substance use after controlling for familial factors, relationship status, and individual traits. *Substance Abuse, 36*, 507–514.

63. Widom, C., Czaja, S., Wilson, H., Allwood, M., & Chauhan, P. (2013). Do the long-term consequences of neglect differ for children of different races and ethnic backgrounds?. *Child Maltreatment, 18*, 42–55.

64. Dubowitz, H. (2007). Understanding and addressing the "neglect of neglect": Digging into the molehill. *Child Abuse and Neglect, 31*, 603–606.

65. Pears, K., Kim, H., & Fisher, P. (2008). Psychosocial and cognitive functioning of children with specific profiles of maltreatment. *Child Abuse and Neglect, 32,* 958–971.

66. Vachon, D., Krueger, R., Rogosch, F., & Cicchetti, D. (2015). Assessment of the harmful psychiatric and behavioral effects of different forms of child maltreatment. *JAMA Psychiatry, 72,* 1135–1142.

67. Lee, S., Taylor, C., & Bellamy, J. (2012). Paternal depression and risk for child neglect in father-involved families of young children. *Child Abuse and Neglect, 36,* 461–469.

68. Cash, S., & Wilke, D. (2003). An ecological model of maternal substance abuse and child neglect: Issues, analyses, and recommendations. *American Journal of Orthopsychiatry, 73,* 392.

69. Scannapieco, M., & Connell-Carrick, K. (2005). Focus on the first years: Correlates of substantiation of child maltreatment for families with children 0 to 4. *Children and Youth Services Review, 27,* 1307–1323.

70. Hair, N., Hanson, J., Wolfe, B., & Pollak, S. (2015). Association of child poverty, brain development, and academic achievement. *JAMA Pediatrics, 169,* 822–829.

71. Luby, J. (2015). Poverty's most insidious damage: The developing brain. *JAMA Pediatrics, 169,* 810–811.

72. Jonson-Reid, M., Emery, C., Drake, B., & Stahlschmidt, M. (2010). Understanding chronically re-reported cases: Implications for services and research. *Child Maltreatment, 15,* 271–281.

73. California Evidence-Based Clearinghouse. (2016). *Safecare.* http://www.cebc4cw.org/program/safecare/

74. DePanfilis, D., & Dubowitz, H. (2005). Family Connections: A program for preventing child neglect. *Child Maltreatment, 10,* 108–123.

75. Yoshikawa, H., Aber, J., & Beardslee, W. (2012). The effects of poverty on the mental, emotional, and behavioral health of children and youth: implications for prevention. *American Psychologist, 67,* 272.

76. Cancian, M., Yang, M., & Slack, K. (2013). The effect of additional child support income on the risk of child maltreatment. *Social Service Review, 87,* 417–437.

CHAPTER 5

1. Windling, T. (2004). The path of needles and pins. *Journal of Mythic Arts.* http://www.endicott-studio.com/articleslist/the-path-of-needles-and-pinsby-terri-windling.html

2. Greenspan, J. (2013, September). The dark side of the Grimm Fairy Tales. *History.com.* http://www.history.com/news/the-dark-side-of-the-grimm-fairy-tales

3. Mintz, S. (2012, July). Placing childhood sexual abuse in historical perspective. *The Immanent Frame.* http://blogs.ssrc.org/tif/2012/07/13/placing-childhood-sexual-abuse-in-historical-perspective/

4. Walsh, K., Berthelsen, D., & Nicholson, J. M. (2014). Sexual abuse prevention education. In S. Garvis & D. Pendergast (Eds.), *Health and wellbeing in childhood.* Australia: Cambridge University Press.

5. Finer, L, & Philbin, J. (2013). Sexual initiation, contraceptive use, and pregnancy among young adolescents. *Pediatrics, 131,* 886–891.

6. ANON. (2015). *Age of consent by state.* Marathon Studios Enterprises. https://www.age-of-consent.info/

7. The Lewin Group; Fishman, M., Gardiner, K., & Glosser, A. (2006, September). *Exploring community responses to statutory rape*. Washington, DC: Office of Assistant Secretary for Planning and Evaluation, US DHHS.

8. National Center for Youth Law. (2010). *When sexual intercourse with a minor must be reported as child abuse: California Law*. http://teenhealthlaw.org/wp-content/uploads/2015/10/Cal_sexual_abuse_reporting__6-10.pdf

9. Silva-de-Alwis, R. (2008, January). *Child marriage and the law: Legislative reform initiative series*. New York: United Nations Children's Fund. http://www.unicef.org/policyanalysis/files/Child_Marriage_and_the_Law(1).pdf

10. Stritof, S. (2016, February). *Teen marriage law trends*. http://marriage.about.com/cs/teen-marriage/a/teenus.htm

11. Child Welfare Information Gateway. (2016, February). *Definitions of child abuse and neglect*. State Statutes. https://www.childwelfare.gov/pubPDFs/define.pdf

12. Johnson, C. F. (2004). Child sexual abuse. *Lancet, 364,* 462–470.

13. Langeland, W., Smit, J., Merckelbach, H., de Vries, G., Hoogendoorn, A., & Draijer, N. (2015). Inconsistent retrospective self-reports of childhood sexual abuse and their correlates in the general population. *Social Psychiatry and Psychiatric Epidemiology, 50,* 603–612.

14. Snyder, H. (2000). *Sexual assault of young children as reported to law enforcement: Victim, incident and offender characteristics* (NCJ 182990). Washington, DC: US Department of Justice, Office of Justice Programs. Bureau of Justice Statistics. http://bjs.ojp.usdoj.gov/content/pub/pdf/saycrle.pdf

15. Finkelhor, D., Shattuck, A., Turner, H., & Hamby, S. (2014). The lifetime prevalence of child sexual abuse and sexual assault assessed in late adolescence. *Journal of Adolescent Health, 55,* 329–333.

16. Truman, J. (2011, September). *Criminal victimization, 2010*. Bureau of Justice Statistics Bulletin (CJ 235508). Washington DC: Bureau of Justice Statistics. http://www.bjs.gov/content/pub/pdf/cv10.pdf

17. Stoltenborgh, M., Bakermans-Kranenburg, M., Alink, L., & IJzendoorn, M. (2015). The prevalence of child maltreatment across the globe: Review of a series of meta-analyses. *Child Abuse Review, 24,* 37–50.

18. Sedlak, A., Mettenburg, J., Basena, M., Petta, I., McPherson, K., Greene, A., & Li, S. (2010). *Fourth National Incidence Study of Child Abuse and Neglect (NIS–4): Report to Congress*. Washington, DC: US Department of Health and Human Services, Administration for Children and Families.

19. US Department of Health and Human Services. (2017). *Child maltreatment 2015*. Administration for Children and Families. US Government Printing Office.

20. Kim, H., Wildeman, C., Jonson-Reid, M., & Drake, B. (2017). Lifetime prevalence of investigating child maltreatment among US children. *American Journal of Public Health*, e1–e7.

21. Pipe, M., Lamb, M., Orbach, Y., & Cederborg, A. (Eds.). (2007). *Child sexual abuse: Disclosure, delay, and denial*. Routledge.

22. Finkelhor, D. (2009). The prevention of childhood sexual abuse. *The Future of Children, 19,* 169–194.

23. Friedman, M., Marshal, M., Guadamuz, T., Wei, C., Wong, C., Saewyc, E., & Stall, R. (2011). A meta-analysis of disparities in childhood sexual abuse, parental physical abuse, and peer

victimization among sexual minority and sexual nonminority individuals. *American Journal of Public Health, 101,* 1481–1494.

24. Skarbek, D., Hahn, K., & Parrish, P. (2009). Stop sexual abuse in special education: An ecological model of prevention and intervention strategies for sexual abuse in special education. *Sexuality and Disability, 27,* 155–164.

25. Stalker, K., & McArthur, K. (2012). Child abuse, child protection and disabled children: A review of recent research. *Child Abuse Review, 21,* 24–40.

26. Jonson-Reid, M., & Hausmann-Stabile, C., Meneses, C., Linhorst, D., & Hanrahan, K. (2012). *Sexual abuse and assault among persons with developmental disabilities in Saint Louis County: Final report.* St. Louis, MO: Washington University, George Warren Brown School of Social Work.

27. Sterzing, P., Hong, J., Gartner, R., & Auslander, W. (2016). Child maltreatment and bullying victimization among a community-based sample of sexual minority youth: The meditating role of psychological distress. *Journal of Child and Adolescent Trauma, 9,* 283–293.

28. Hornor, G. (2010). Child sexual abuse: Consequences and implications. *Journal of Pediatric Health Care, 24,* 358–364.

29. Maniglio, R. (2015). Significance, nature, and direction of the association between child sexual abuse and conduct disorder: A systematic review. *Trauma, Violence, and Abuse, 16,* 241–257.

30. Trickett, P., Noll, J., & Putnam, F. (2011). The impact of sexual abuse on female development: Lessons from a multigenerational, longitudinal research study. *Development and Psychopathology, 23,* 453–476.

31. Pittenger, S., Huit, T., & Hansen, D. (2016). Applying ecological systems theory to sexual revictimization of youth: A review with implications for research and practice. *Aggression and Violent Behavior, 26,* 35–45.

32. Fergusson, D., McLeod, G., & Horwood, L. (2013). Childhood sexual abuse and adult developmental outcomes: Findings from a 30-year longitudinal study in New Zealand. *Child Abuse and Neglect, 37,* 664–674.

33. Danese, A., & Tan, M. (2014). Childhood maltreatment and obesity: Systematic review and meta-analysis. *Molecular Psychiatry, 19,* 544–554.

34. Duncan, A., Sartor, C., Jonson-Reid, M., Munn-Chernoff, M., Eschenbacher, M., Diemer, E., . . . Heath, A. (2015). Associations between body mass index, post-traumatic stress disorder, and child maltreatment in young women. *Child Abuse and Neglect, 45,* 154–162.

35. Widom, C., Czaja, S., Bentley, T., & Johnson, M. (2012). A prospective investigation of physical health outcomes in abused and neglected children: New findings from a 30-year follow-up. *American Journal of Public Health, 102,* 1135–1144.

36. Noll, J., Shenk, C., & Putnam, K. (2009). Childhood sexual abuse and adolescent pregnancy: A meta-analytic update. *Journal of Pediatric Psychology, 34,* 366–378.

37. Roberts, R., O'Connor, T., Dunn, J., Golding, J., & ALSPAC Study Team. (2004). The effects of child sexual abuse in later family life: Mental health, parenting and adjustment of offspring. *Child Abuse and Neglect, 28,* 525–545.

38. Oshima, K., Jonson-Reid, M., & Seay. K. (2014). The influence of childhood sexual abuse on adolescent outcomes: The roles of gender, poverty, and revictimization. *Journal of Child Sexual Abuse, 23,* 367–386.

39. Cohen, J., Deblinger, E., Mannarino, A., & Steer, R. (2004). A multisite, randomized controlled trial for children with sexual abuse–related PTSD symptoms. *Journal of the American Academy of Child and Adolescent Psychiatry, 43,* 393–402.

40. Jonzon, E., & Lindblad, F. (2006). Risk factors and protective factors in relation to subjective health among adult female victims of child sexual abuse. *Child Abuse and Neglect, 30,* 127–143.

41. Trask, E., Walsh, K., & DiLillo, D. (2011). Treatment effects for common outcomes of child sexual abuse: A current meta-analysis. *Aggression and Violent Behavior, 16,* 6–19.

42. Wiley, D. (2014, July). Pope Francis: "About 2%" of Catholic clergy paedophiles. Europe *BBC.com.* http://www.bbc.com/news/world-europe-28282050

43. American Psychiatric Association. (2013). Official Diagnostic Criteria for Pedophilic Disorder (DSM 5, 302.2, F65.4). *Diagnostic and statistical manual of mental disorders* (5th ed.). Washington, DC: Author.

44. Seto, M. (2008). *Pedophilia and sexual offending against children: Theory, assessment and intervention.* Washington, DC: American Psychological Association.

45. Seto, M., Babchishin, K., Pullman, L., & McPhail, I. (2015). The puzzle of intrafamilial child sexual abuse: A meta-analysis comparing intrafamilial and extrafamilial offenders with child victims. *Clinical Psychology Review, 39,* 42–57.

46. Ohlheiser, A. (2015, May). A timeline of the molestation allegations against Josh Duggar. *Washington Post.* http://www.washingtonpost.com/news/acts-of-faith/wp/2015/05/23/a-timeline-of-the-molestation-allegations-against-josh-duggar/

47. Pulliam, B. (2014, February). Conservative leader Bill Gothard on leave following abuse allegations. Religion News Service. *Washington Post.* https://www.washingtonpost.com/national/religion/conservative-leader-bill-gothard-on-leave-following-abuse-allegations/2014/02/28/51f1aac6-a0bb-11e3-878c-65222df220eb_story.html

48. Finkelhor, D., Ormrod, R., & Chaffin, M. (2009). Juveniles who commit sex offenses against minors. *Juvenile Justice Bulletin.* US Department of Justice. https://www.ncjrs.gov/pdf-files1/ojjdp/227763.pdf

49. Finkelhor, D. (2010). *Sexually victimized children.* New York: The Free Press.

50. Pérez-Fuentes, G., Olfson, M., Villegas, L., Morcillo, C., Wang, S., & Blanco, C. (2013). Prevalence and correlates of child sexual abuse: A national study. *Comprehensive Psychiatry, 54,* 16–27.

51. Daniels, L., Magness, G., Siegel-Magness, S., Winfrey, O., Heller, T., Perry, T., & Cortes, L. (Producers) & Daniels, L (Director). (2009). *Precious.* United States: Lionsgate.

52. Huckabee, M. (2015, May 22). Facebook post about the Duggar family. https://www.facebook.com/mikehuckabee/posts/10152994543137869

53. Godbout, N., Briere, J., Sabourin, S., & Lussier, Y. (2014). Child sexual abuse and subsequent relational and personal functioning: The role of parental support. *Child Abuse and Neglect, 38,* 317–325.

54. Bolen, R., Dessel, A., & Sutter, J. (2015). Parents will be parents: Conceptualizing and measuring nonoffending parent and other caregiver support following disclosure of sexual abuse. *Journal of Aggression, Maltreatment and Trauma, 24,* 41–67.

55. Fuller, G. (2016). Non-offending parents as secondary victims of child sexual assault. *Trends and Issues in Crime and Criminal Justice, 500,* 1.

56. Bolen, R., & Gergely, K. (2015). A meta-analytic review of the relationship between non-offending caregiver support and postdisclosure functioning in sexually abused children. *Trauma, Violence, and Abuse, 16,* 258–279.

57. Gibson, L. (2015). Erin's law: Preventing child sexual abuse through education. *Journal of Law and Education, 44,* 263–272.

58. Conte, J., Wolf, S., & Smith, T. (1989). What sexual offenders tell us about prevention strategies. *Child Abuse and Neglect, 13,* 293–301.

59. Elliott, M., Browne, K., & Kilcoyne, J. (1995). Child sexual abuse prevention: What offenders tell us. *Child Abuse and Neglect, 19,* 579–594.

60. Walsh, W., Cross, T., Jones, L., Simone, M., & Kolko, D. (2007). Which sexual abuse victims receive a forensic medical examination? The impact of Children's Advocacy Centers. *Child Abuse and Neglect, 31,* 1053–1068.

61. Adams, J., Starling, S., Frasier, L., Palusci, V., Shapiro, R., Finkel, M., & Botash, A. (2012). Diagnostic accuracy in child sexual abuse medical evaluation: Role of experience, training, and expert case review. *Child Abuse and Neglect, 36,* 383–392.

62. Collins, J. (2007). Lady Madonna, children at your feet: The criminal justice system's romanticization of the parent-child relationship. *Iowa Law Review, 93,* 131–184.

63. Stroud, D., Martens, S., & Barker, J. (2000). Criminal investigation of child sexual abuse: A comparison of cases referred to the prosecutor to those not referred. *Child Abuse and Neglect, 24,* 689–700.

64. Finkelhor, D., Cross, T., & Cantor, E. (2005). The justice system for juvenile victims a comprehensive model of case flow. *Trauma, Violence, and Abuse, 6,* 83–102.

65. Cross, T., Walsh, W., Simone, M., & Jones, L. (2003). Prosecution of child abuse: A meta-analysis of rates of criminal justice decisions. *Trauma, Violence, and Abuse, 4,* 323–340.

66. Walfield, S. (2015). When a cleared rape is not cleared a multilevel study of arrest and exceptional clearance. *Journal of Interpersonal Violence, 31,* 1767–1792.

67. Mejia, P., Cheyne, A., & Dorfman, L. (2012). News coverage of child sexual abuse and prevention, 2007–2009. *Journal of Child Sexual Abuse, 21,* 470–487.

68. Pipe, M., Lamb, M., Orbach, Y., & Cederborg, A. (2013). Seeking resolution in the disclosure wars: An overview. In M. Pipe, M. Lamb, Y. Orbach, & A. Cederborg (Eds.), *Child sexual abuse: Disclosure, delay, and denial* (pp. 1–10). Routledge, NY.

69. Jones, L., Cross, T., Walsh, W., & Simone, M. (2007). Do Children's Advocacy Centers improve families' experiences of child sexual abuse investigations? *Child Abuse and Neglect, 31,* 1069–1085.

70. Hill, A. (2012). Help for children after child sexual abuse: Using a qualitative approach to design and test therapeutic interventions that may include non-offending parents. *Qualitative Social Work, 11,* 362–378.

71. Cohen, J., Murray, L., & Mannarino, A. (2013). Trauma-focused cognitive behaviour therapy for child sexual abuse. In P. Graham & S. Reynolds (Eds.), *Cognitive Behaviour Therapy for Children and Families* (pp. 145–158). Cambridge: Cambridge University Press.

72. Elmquist, J., Shorey, R., Febres, J., Zapor, H., Klostermann, K., Schratter, A., & Stuart, G. L. (2015). A review of Children's Advocacy Centers'(CACs) response to cases of child maltreatment in the United States. *Aggression and Violent Behavior, 25,* 26–34.

73. Mrazek, P., & Kempe, C. (Eds.). (2014). *Sexually abused children and their families.* Netherlands: Elsevier.

74. Barbaree, H., & Marshall, W. (Eds.). (2008). *The juvenile sex offender*. New York, NY: Guilford Press.

75. Chaffin, M., Berliner, L., Block, R., Johnson, T., Friedrich, W., Louis, D., . . . Madden, C. (2008). Report of the ATSA task force on children with sexual behavior problems. *Child Maltreatment, 13,* 199.

76. Schwartz, B. (Ed.). (2011). *Handbook of sex offender treatment*. Kingston, NJ: Civic Research Institute.

77. Horn, J., Eisenberg, M., Nicholls, C. M., Mulder, J., Webster, S., Paskell, C., . . . Jago, N. (2015). Stop It Now! A pilot study into the limits and benefits of a free helpline preventing child sexual abuse. *Journal of Child Sexual Abuse, 24,* 853–872.

78. Beier, K., Ahlers, C., Goecker, D., Neutze, J., Mundt, I., Hupp, E., & Schaefer, G. (2009). Can pedophiles be reached for primary prevention of child sexual abuse? First results of the Berlin Prevention Project Dunkelfeld (PPD). *Journal of Forensic Psychiatry and Psychology, 20,* 851–867.

79. Topping, K., & Barron, I. (2009). School-based child sexual abuse prevention programs: A review of effectiveness. *Review of Educational Research, 79,* 431–463.

80. Kenny, M., Capri, V., Ryan, E., & Runyon, M. (2008). Child sexual abuse: From prevention to self-protection. *Child Abuse Review, 17,* 36–54.

81. Wurtele, S., & Kenny, M. (2010). Partnering with parents to prevent childhood sexual abuse. *Child Abuse Review, 19,* 130–152.

82. Wurtele, S. (2009). Preventing sexual abuse of children in the twenty-first century: Preparing for challenges and opportunities. *Journal of Child Sexual Abuse, 18,* 1–18.

CHAPTER 6

1. Leeb, R., Paulozzi, L., Melanson, C., Simon, T., & Arias, I. (2008). *Child maltreatment surveillance: Uniform definitions for public health and recommended data elements*, Version 1.0. Atlanta (GA): Centers for Disease Control and Prevention, National Center for Injury Prevention and Control.

2. Borowsky, I., Taliaferro, L., & McMorris, B. (2013). Suicidal thinking and behavior among youth involved in verbal and social bullying: Risk and protective factors. *Journal of Adolescent Health, 53,* S4–S12.

3. Monks, C., Smith, P., Naylor, P., Barter, C., Ireland, J., & Coyne, I. (2009). Bullying in different contexts: Commonalities, differences and the role of theory. *Aggression and Violent Behavior, 14,* 146–156.

4. Maslow, A. (1943). A theory of human motivation. *Psychological Review, 50,* 370–396.

5. Biglan, A. (2015). *The nurture effect: How science of human behavior can improve our lives and our world*. Oakland, CA: New Harbinger Publications.

6. Wolfe, D., & McIsaac, C. (2011). Distinguishing between poor/dysfunctional parenting and child emotional maltreatment. *Child Abuse and Neglect, 35,* 802–813.

7. Malimabe-Ramagoshi, R., Maree, J., Alexander, D., & Molepo, M. (2007). Child abuse in Setswana folktales. *Early Child Development and Care, 177,* 433–448.

8. American Humane Association. (2013). *Emotional abuse*. http://www.americanhumane.org/children/stop-child-abuse/fact-sheets/emotional-abuse.html?gclid=CLLNtIOD-MwCFQIcaQodPJkP9Q

9. *Carrie*. Directed by Brian De Palma. Based on story by Stephen King. United Artists, 1976.

10. Huffington Post and Esquire Network. (2014, December). These are the parents we all know from Little League sidelines. *Huffpost Sports. The Huffington Post*. http://www.huffington-post.com/2014/12/23/little-league-parents_n_6312916.html

11. Pappas. (2013, January). "Tiger Mom" study says both Amy Chua and her critics have a point. *Huffington Post*. http://www.huffingtonpost.com/2013/01/22/tiger-mom-study_n_2526522.html

12. Dewar, G. (2011–2012). Traditional Chinese parenting: What research says about Chinese kids and why they succeed. *Parenting Science*. http://www.parentingscience.com/chinese-parenting.html

13. Coleman, D., Dodge, K., & Campbell, S. (2010). Where and how to draw the line between reasonable corporal punishment and abuse. *Law and Contemporary Problems, 73,* 107–166.

14. Spak, K. (2012, May). Mom arrested after daughter's punishment: Shaved 12-year-old's head, made her wear diaper outside. *Newser*. http://Www.Newser.Com/Story/145702/Mom-Arrested-After-Daughters-Punishment.Html.

15. Templeton, D. (2014, November). Childhood trauma can cause trauma for life. *Pittsburgh Post-Gazette*. http://www.post-gazette.com/news/health/2014/11/11/Childhood-trauma-can-cause-trauma-for-life/stories/201410270173

16. Stoltenborgh, M., Bakermans-Kranenburg, M., Alink, L., & van IJzendoorn, M. (2012). The universality of childhood emotional abuse: A meta-analysis of worldwide prevalence. *Journal of Aggression, Maltreatment and Trauma, 21,* 870–890.

17. US Department of Health and Human Services. (2017). *Child maltreatment 2015*. Administration for Children and Families. https://www.acf.hhs.gov/sites/default/files/cb/cm2015.pdf

18. Hamarman, S., Pope, K., & Czaja, S. (2002). Emotional abuse in children: Variations in legal definitions and rates across the United States. *Child Maltreatment, 7,* 303–311.

19. Finkelhor, D., Hamby, S., Turner, H., & Ormrod, R. (2011). *The Juvenile Victimization Questionnaire: 2nd Revision (JVQ-R2)*. Durham, NH: Crimes Against Children Research Center.

20. Grassi-Oliveira, R., Cogo-Moreira, H., Salum, G. A., Brietzke, E., Viola, T., Manfro, G., . . . Arteche, A. (2014). Childhood Trauma Questionnaire (CTQ) in Brazilian samples of different age groups: findings from confirmatory factor analysis. *PloS One, 9,* e87118.

21. Sedlak, A., Gragg, F., Mettenburg, J., Ciarico, J., Winglee, M., Shapiro, G., . . . McPherson, K. (2010). *Fourth National Incidence Study of Child Abuse and Neglect (NIS–4) Technical Report I: Design and methods summary*. Prepared under contract to the US Department of Health and Human Services. Rockville, MD: Westat.

22. Iwaniec, D., Larkin, E., & Higgins, S. (2006). Research review: Risk and resilience in cases of emotional abuse. *Child and Family Social Work, 11,* 73–82.

23. Rice, K. (2013, June). *Key study: Attachment in infant monkeys*. http://www.integratedsocio-psychology.net/infant_monkeys-attachment.html

24. Naughton, A., Maguire, S., Mann, M., Lumb, R., Tempest, V., Gracias, S., & Kemp, A. (2013). Emotional, behavioral, and developmental features indicative of neglect or emotional abuse in preschool children: A systematic review. *JAMA Pediatrics, 167,* 769–775.

25. Kuo, J. Khoury, J., Metcalfe, R., Fitzpatrick, S., & Goodwill, A. (2015). An examination of the relationship between childhood emotional abuse and borderline personality disorder

features: The role of difficulties with emotion regulation. *Child Abuse and Neglect, 39,* 147–155.

26. Gratz, K., Latzman, R., Tull, M., Reynolds, E., & Lejuez, C. (2011). Exploring the association between emotional abuse and childhood borderline personality features: The moderating role of personality traits. *Behavior Therapy, 42,* 493–508.

27. Shapero, B., Black, S., Liu, R., Klugman, J., Bender, R., Abramson, L., & Alloy, L. B. (2014). Stressful life events and depression symptoms: The effect of childhood emotional abuse on stress reactivity. *Journal of Clinical Psychology, 70,* 209–223.

28. Bigras, N., Godbout, N., Hébert, M., Runtz, M., & Daspe, M. (2015). Identity and relatedness as mediators between child emotional abuse and adult couple adjustment in women. *Child Abuse and Neglect, 50,* 85–93.

29. English, D., Thompson, R., White, C., & Wilson, D. (2015). Why should child welfare pay more attention to emotional maltreatment? *Children and Youth Services Review, 50,* 53–63.

30. Alvarez-Alonso, M., Jurado-Barba, R., Martinez-Martin, N., Espin-Jaime, J., Bolaños-Porrero, C., Ordoñez-Franco, A., . . . Manzanares, J. (2016). Association between maltreatment and polydrug use among adolescents. *Child Abuse and Neglect, 51,* 379–389.

31. Child Welfare Information Gateway. (2016, February). *Definitions of child abuse and neglect.* Washington, DC: US Department of Health and Human Services, Children's Bureau. See also https://www.childwelfare.gov/topics/systemwide/laws-policies/state/

32. Jonson-Reid, M., Drake, B., Chung, S., & Way, I. (2003). Cross-type recidivism among referrals to a state child welfare agency. *Child Abuse and Neglect, 27,* 889–917.

33. Trickett, P., Kim, K., & Prindle, J. (2011). Variations in emotional abuse experiences among multiply maltreated young adolescents and relations with developmental outcomes. *Child Abuse and Neglect, 35,* 876–886.

34. Jaffee, S., & Maikovich-Fong, A. (2011). Effects of chronic maltreatment and maltreatment timing on children's behavior and cognitive abilities. *Journal of Child Psychology and Psychiatry, 52,* 184–194.

35. Jonson-Reid, M., Kohl, P., & Drake, B. (2012). Child and adult outcomes of chronic child maltreatment *Pediatrics, 129,* 839–845.

36. Thompson, K., Hannan, S., & Miron, L. (2014). Fight, flight, and freeze: Threat sensitivity and emotion dysregulation in survivors of chronic childhood maltreatment. *Personality and Individual Differences, 69,* 28–32.

37. Vachon, D., Krueger, R., Rogosch, F., & Cicchetti, D. (2015). Assessment of the harmful psychiatric and behavioral effects of different forms of child maltreatment. *JAMA Psychiatry, 72,* 1135–1142.

38. Morey, R., Haswell, C., Hooper, S., & De Bellis, M. (2016). Amygdala, hippocampus, and ventral medial prefrontal cortex volumes differ in maltreated youth with and without chronic posttraumatic stress disorder. *Neuropsychopharmacology, 41,* 791–801.

39. Spinazzola, J., Hodgdon, H., Liang, L., Ford, J., Layne, C., Pynoos, R., . . . Kisiel, C. (2014). Unseen wounds: The contribution of psychological maltreatment to child and adolescent mental health and risk outcomes. *Psychological Trauma: Theory, Research, Practice, and Policy, 6,* S1–S18.

40. Landry, S., Smith, K., Swank, P., & Guttentag, C. (2008). A responsive parenting intervention: The optimal timing across early childhood for impacting maternal behaviors and child outcomes. *Developmental Psychology, 44,* 1335.

41. Baker, A., Brassard, M., Schneiderman, M., Donnelly, L., & Bahl, A. (2011). How well do evidence-based universal parenting programs teach parents about psychological maltreatment? A program review. *Child Abuse and Neglect, 35,* 855–865.

42. Barlow, J., MacMillan, H., Macdonald, G., Bennett, C., & Larkin, S. (2013). Psychological interventions to prevent recurrence of emotional abuse of children by their parents. *Cochrane Library.* http://onlinelibrary.wiley.com/doi/10.1002/14651858.CD010725/pdf

43. Burchinal, M., Follmer, A., & Bryant, D. (1996). The relations of maternal social support and family structure with maternal responsiveness and child outcomes among African American families. *Developmental Psychology, 32,* 1073.

44. Green, B., Furrer, C., & McAllister, C. (2011). Does attachment style influence social support or the other way around? A longitudinal study of Early Head Start mothers. *Attachment and Human Development, 13,* 27–47.

CHAPTER 7

1. Jacobs, J. (1890). *English fairy tales.* London: David Nutt. http://www.surlalunefairytales.com/bluebeard/stories/mrfox.html

2. Lang, A. (1891). Bluebeard. *The blue fairy book* (5th ed., pp. 290–295). London and New York: Longmans, Green, and Company. Excerpt available online: http://www.pitt.edu/~dash/type0312.html

3. Adams, E., Adams, S., Gilmer, M., Gordon, S., Heller, J., Koski, G., . . . Robinson, T. (2011, June). The hits keep coming: 30 songs inspired by domestic violence. *A.V. Club.* http://www.avclub.com/article/the-hits-keep-coming-30-songs-inspired-by-domestic-57741

4. Rolling Stones. Under my thumb. Lyrics available online: http://www.azlyrics.com/lyrics/rollingstones/undermythumb.html

5. Centers for Disease Control and Prevention. (2014, February). *The National Intimate Partner and Sexual violence survey.* Detailed state tables. http://www.cdc.gov/violenceprevention/nisvs/state_tables.html.

6. UNICEF. (n.d.). *Behind closed doors: The impact of domestic violence on children.* https://www.unicef.org/protection/files/BehindClosedDoors.pdf

7. Tjaden, P., & Thoennes, N. (2000). *Full report of the prevalence, incidence, and consequences of violence against women: Findings from the National Violence Against Women Survey.* Washington, DC: US Department of Justice.

8. Mills, R., Kisely, S., Alati, R., Strathearn, L., & Najman, J. (2016). Self-reported and agency-notified child sexual abuse in a population-based birth cohort. *Journal of Psychiatric Research, 74,* 87–93.

9. Johnson, M. (2006). Conflict and control gender symmetry and asymmetry in domestic violence. *Violence Against Women, 12,* 1003–1018.

10. Swan, S., Gambone, L., Caldwell, J., Sullivan, T., & Snow, D. (2008). A review of research on women's use of violence with male intimate partners. *Violence and Victims, 23,* 301.

11. Breiding, M.J., Chen, J., & Black, M.C. (2014). *Intimate Partner Violence in the United States—2010.* Atlanta, GA: National Center for Injury Prevention and Control, Centers for Disease Control and Prevention.

12. Black, M., Basile, K., Breiding, M., Smith, S., Walters, M., Merrick, M., . . . Stevens, M. (2011). *The National Intimate Partner and Sexual Violence Survey (NISVS): 2010 summary report.*

Atlanta, GA: National Center for Injury Prevention and Control, Centers for Disease Control and Prevention.

13. Tsui, V., Cheung, M., & Leung, P. (2010). Help-seeking among male victims of partner abuse: Men's hard times. *Journal of Community Psychology, 38,* 769–780.

14. Muller, H., Desmarais, S., & Hamel, J. (2009). Do judicial responses to restraining order requests discriminate against male victims of domestic violence? *Journal of Family Violence, 24,* 625–637.

15. Renzetti, C., & Miley, C. (2007). *Violence in gay and lesbian domestic partnerships.* Binghamton, NY: Haworth Press.

16. Benson, S. (2014). Lesbian mother survivors of domestic abuse: A plea for legal clarity. *University of Illinois Law Review.* Slip Opinions 18. *2014,* 18–24http://papers.ssrn.com/sol3/papers.cfm?abstract_id=2552746

17. Wood, S., & Sommers, M. (2011). Consequences of intimate partner violence on child witnesses: A systematic review of the literature. *Journal of Child and Adolescent Psychiatric Nursing, 24,* 223–236.

18. Bauer, P., & Leventon, J. (2013). Memory for one-time experiences in the second year of life: Implications for the status of episodic memory. *Infancy, 18,* 755–781.

19. Howe, M. (2013). Memory development: Implications for adults recalling childhood experiences in the courtroom. *Nature Reviews Neuroscience, 14,* 869–876.

20. MacDonell, K. (2012). The combined and independent impact of witnessed intimate partner violence and child maltreatment. *Partner Abuse, 3,* 358–378.

21. Stark, E. (2007). *Coercive control.* http://www.nottinghamshire.pcc.police.uk/Document-Library/News-and-Events/Chance-for-Change/Professor-Evan-Stark-Chance-for-Change-Conference-Presentation.pdf

22. Herrenkohl, T., Sousa, C., Tajima, E., Herrenkohl, R., & Moylan, C. (2008). Intersection of child abuse and children's exposure to domestic violence. *Trauma, Violence, and Abuse, 9,* 84–99.

23. Gilbert, A., Bauer, N., Carroll, A., & Downs, S. (2013). Child exposure to parental violence and psychological distress associated with delayed milestones. *Pediatrics, 132,* e1577–e1583.

24. Graham-Bermann, S., & Perkins, S. (2010). Effects of early exposure and lifetime exposure to intimate partner violence (IPV) on child adjustment. *Violence and Victims, 25,* 427–439.

25. Levendosky, A., Bogat, G., & Martinez-Torteya, C. (2013). PTSD symptoms in young children exposed to intimate partner violence. *Violence Against Women, 19,* 187–201.

26. Yost, N., Bloom, S., McIntire, D., & Leveno, K. (2005). A prospective observational study of domestic violence during pregnancy. *Obstetrics and Gynecology, 106,* 61–65.

27. Johnson, J., Haider, F., Ellis, K., Hay, D., & Lindow, S. (2003). The prevalence of domestic violence in pregnant women. *BJOG: An International Journal of Obstetrics and Gynaecology, 110,* 272–275.

28. Bailey, B. (2010). Partner violence during pregnancy: Prevalence, effects, screening, and management. *International Journal of Women's Health, 2,* 183–197.

29. Jasinski, J. (2004). Pregnancy and domestic violence: A review of the literature. *Trauma, Violence, and Abuse, 5,* 47–64.

30. Gewirtz, A., & Medhanie, A. (2008). Proximity and risk in children's witnessing of intimate partner violence incidents. *Journal of Emotional Abuse, 8*(1–2), 67–82.

31. Family Violence Prevention Fund. (2010). *Realizing the promise of home visitation: Addressing domestic violence and child maltreatment; A guide for policy makers.* https://www.futureswith-outviolence.org/userfiles/file/Children_and_Families/Realizing%20the%20Promise%20of%20Home%20Visitation%202-10.pdf

32. Fusco, R. (2013). "It's hard enough to deal with all the abuse issues": Child welfare workers' experiences with intimate partner violence on their caseloads. *Children and Youth Services Review, 35,* 1946–1953.

33. Kohl, P., Barth, R., Hazen, A., & Landsverk, J. (2005). Child welfare as a gateway to domestic violence services. *Children and Youth Services Review, 27,* 1203–1221.

34. Kelleher, K., Gardner, W., Coben, J., Barth, R., Edleson, J., & Hazen, A. (2006). *Co-occurring intimate partner violence and child maltreatment: Local policies/practices and relationships to child placement, family services and residence. Final report* (Doc No 213503). https://www.ncjrs.gov/pdffiles1/nij/grants/213503.pdf

35. Hamby, S., Finkelhor, D., Turner, H., & Ormrod, R. (2010). The overlap of witnessing partner violence with child maltreatment and other victimizations in a nationally representative survey of youth. *Child Abuse and Neglect, 34,* 734–741.

36. Dong, M., Anda, R., Felitti, V., Dube, S., Williamson, D., Thompson, T., Loo, C., & Giles, W. (2004). The interrelatedness of multiple forms of childhood abuse, neglect, and household dysfunction. *Child Abuse and Neglect, 28,* 771–784.

37. Jones, L., Gross, E., & Becker, I. (2002). The characteristics of domestic violence victims in a child protective service caseload. *Families in Society, 83,* 405–415.

38. Lee, L., Kotch, J., & Cox, C. (2004). Child maltreatment in families experiencing domestic violence. *Violence and Victims, 19,* 573–591.

39. Millett, L., Seay, K., & Kohl, P. (2015). A national study of intimate partner violence risk among female caregivers involved in the child welfare system: The role of nativity, acculturation, and legal status. *Children and Youth Services Review, 48,* 60–69.

40. Antle, B., Barbee, A., Sullivan, D., Yankeelov, P., Johnson, L., & Cunningham, M. (2007). The relationship between domestic violence and child neglect. *Brief Treatment and Crisis Intervention, 7,* 364.

41. Sousa, C., Herrenkohl, T., Moylan, C., Tajima, E., Klika, J., Herrenkohl, R., & Russo, M. (2011). Longitudinal study on the effects of child abuse and children's exposure to domestic violence, parent-child attachments, and antisocial behavior in adolescence. *Journal of Interpersonal Violence, 26,* 111–136.

42. Graham-Bermann, S., Castor, L., Miller, L., & Howell, K. (2012). The impact of intimate partner violence and additional traumatic events on trauma symptoms and PTSD in preschool-aged children. *Journal of Traumatic Stress, 25,* 393–400.

43. English, D., Graham, J., Newton, R., Lewis, T., Thompson, R., Kotch, J., & Weisbart, C. (2009). At-risk and maltreated children exposed to intimate partner aggression/violence: What the conflict looks like and its relationship to child outcomes. *Child Maltreatment, 14,* 157–171.

44. McGuigan, W., & Pratt, C. (2001). The predictive impact of domestic violence on three types of child maltreatment. *Child Abuse and Neglect, 25,* 869–883.

45. Jouriles, E., McDonald, R., Smith Slep, A., Heyman, R., & Garrido, E. (2008). Child abuse in the context of domestic violence: Prevalence, explanations, and practice implications. *Violence and Victims, 23,* 221–235.

46. Gastaldo, E. (2014, November). Battered woman serving longer sentence than her abuser convicted for "allowing" ex to abuse their child. *Newser*. http://www.Newser.Com/Story/ 198558/Battered-Woman-Serving-Longer-Sentence-Than-Her-Abuser.Html

47. Bragg, L. (2003). *Child protection in families experiencing domestic violence*. Washington, DC: US DHHS. https://www.childwelfare.gov/pubPDFs/domesticviolence.pdf

48. Cox, C., Kotch, J., & Everson, M. (2003). A longitudinal study of modifying influences in the relationship between domestic violence and child maltreatment. *Journal of Family Violence, 18,* 5–17.

49. Holmes, M. (2013). Aggressive behavior of children exposed to intimate partner violence: An examination of maternal mental health, maternal warmth and child maltreatment. *Child Abuse and Neglect, 37,* 520–530.

50. Rumm, P., Cummings, P., Krauss, M., Bell, M., & Rivara, F. (2000). Identified spouse abuse as a risk factor for child abuse. *Child Abuse and Neglect, 24,* 1375–1381.

51. Renner, L. (2009). Intimate partner violence victimization and parenting stress: Assessing the mediating role of depressive symptoms. *Violence Against Women, 15,* 1380–1401.

52. Jewkes, R. (2002). Intimate partner violence: causes and prevention. *Lancet, 359,* 1423–1429.

53. Hazen, A., Connelly, C., Kelleher, K., Landsverk, J., & Barth, R. (2004). Intimate partner violence among female caregivers of children reported for child maltreatment. *Child Abuse and Neglect, 28,* 301–319.

54. Millett, L., Kohl, P. L., Jonson-Reid, M., Drake, B., & Petra, M. (2013). Child maltreatment victimization and subsequent perpetration of young adult intimate partner violence: An exploration of mediating factors. *Child Maltreatment, 18,* 71–84.

55. DeLisi, M., & Vaughn, M. G. (2012). Still psychopathic after all these years. In M. DeLisi & P. Conis (Eds.), *Violent offenders: Theory, research, policy, and practice* (pp. 95–108). Burlington, MA: Jones & Bartlett Learning.

56. Coid, J., Yang, M., Ullrich, S., Roberts, A., & Hare, R. (2009). Prevalence and correlates of psychopathic traits in the household population of Great Britain. *International Journal of Law and Psychiatry, 32,* 65–73.

57. Vaughn, M., DeLisi, M., Gunter, T., Fu, Q., Beaver, K., Perron, B., & Howard, M. (2011). The severe 5%: A latent class analysis of the externalizing behavior spectrum in the United States. *Journal of Criminal Justice, 39,* 75–80.

58. Black, T., Trocmé, N., Fallon, B., & MacLaurin, B. (2008). The Canadian child welfare system response to exposure to domestic violence investigations. *Child Abuse and Neglect, 32,* 393–404.

59. Edleson, J., Gassman-Pines, J., & Hill, M. (2006). Defining child exposure to domestic violence as neglect: Minnesota's difficult experience. *Social Work, 51,* 167–174.

60. Edleson, J., Mbilinyi, L., Beeman, S., & Hagemeister, A. (2003). How children are involved in adult domestic violence results from a four-city telephone survey. *Journal of Interpersonal Violence, 18,* 18–32.

61. Banner, A. (2014, December). "Failure to protect" laws punish victims of domestic violence. *Huffington Post*. http://www.huffingtonpost.com/adam-banner/do-failure-to-protect-law_ b_6237346.html

62. Center for Relationship Abuse Awareness. (2015). *Resources in California on child protective services*. http://stoprelationshipabuse.org/professional-resources/child-protective-services/

63. Jenney, A., Mishna, F., Alaggia, R., & Scott, K. (2014). Doing the right thing? (Re) considering risk assessment and safety planning in child protection work with domestic violence cases. *Children and Youth Services Review, 47,* 92–101.

64. Miller, C., & Burch, A. (2014, March). Innocents lost: Preserving families but losing children. *Miami Herald.* http://media.miamiherald.com/static/media/projects/2014/innocents-lost/database/

65. Alaggia, R., Gadalla, T., Shlonsky, A., Jenney, A., & Daciuk, J. (2015). Does differential response make a difference? Examining domestic violence cases in child protection services. *Child and Family Social Work, 20,* 83–95.

66. Child Welfare Information Gateway. (2014). *Domestic violence and the child welfare system.* Washington DC: US DHHS. https://www.childwelfare.gov/pubs/factsheets/domestic_violence.

67. Nowling, M. (2003). Protecting children who witness domestic violence: Is Nicholson v. Williams an adequate response? *Family Court Review, 41,* 507–526.

68. Kohl, P., Edleson, J, English, D., & Barth, R (2005). Domestic violence and pathways into child welfare services: Findings from the National Survey of Child and Adolescent Well-Being. *Children and Youth Services Review, 27,* 1167–1182.

69. Child Welfare Information Gateway (2016, February). *Definitions of child abuse and neglect.* State Statutes. https://www.childwelfare.gov/pubPDFs/define.pdf

70. Jonson-Reid, M., Edmond, T., Lauritsen, J., & Schneider, D. (2016). Violence prevention: Public health and policy. In A. Eyler, R. Brownson, J. Chriqui, & S. Russell (Eds.), *Prevention policy and public health* (pp. 229–248). New York, NY: Oxford University Press.

71. Hester, M. (2011). The three planet model: Towards an understanding of contradictions in approaches to women and children's safety in contexts of domestic violence. *British Journal of Social Work, 41,* 837–853.

72. Hughes, J., & Chau, S. (2013). Making complex decisions: Child protection workers' practices and interventions with families experiencing intimate partner violence. *Children and Youth Services Review, 35,* 611–617.

73. White, P. (2005). You may never see your child again: Adjusting the batterer's visitation rights to protect children from future abuse. *American University Journal of Gender, Social Policy and the Law, 13,* 327–352.

74. Mancini, J., Nelson, J., Bowen, G., & Martin, J. (2006). Preventing intimate partner violence: A community capacity approach. *Journal of Aggression, Maltreatment and Trauma, 13,* 203–227.

75. National Football League. (2014). *NFL personal conduct policy.* http://static.nfl.com/static/content/public/photo/2014/12/10/0ap3000000441637.pdf

76. MacMillan, H., Wathen, C., & Varcoe, C. (2013). Intimate partner violence in the family: Considerations for children's safety. *Child Abuse and Neglect, 37,* 1186–1191.

77. Alderson, S., Kelly, L., & Westmarland, N. (2015). Expanding understandings of success. Domestic violence perpetrator programmes, children and fathering. In N. Stanley & C. Humphreys (Eds.), *Domestic violence and protecting children: New thinking and approaches* (pp. 182–195). London: Jessica Kingsley.

78. Dubowitz, H., Feigelman, S., Lane, W., & Kim, J. (2009). Pediatric primary care to help prevent child maltreatment: The Safe Environment for Every Kid (SEEK) model. *Pediatrics, 123,* 858–864.

79. Greenbook Initiative. (2009, August). *Tools and resources.* http://thegreenbook.info/read. htm

80. Cross, T., Mathews, B., Tonmyr, L., Scott, D., & Ouimet, C. (2012). Child welfare policy and practice on children's exposure to domestic violence. *Child Abuse and Neglect, 36,* 210–216.

81. O'Malley, C., Li, L., Schroder, A., & McKeever, S. (n.d.). *Child exposure to domestic violence: An exploration of policy defining it as maltreatment.* St. Louis, MO: Center for Violence and Injury Prevention, Washington University. https://cvip.wustl.edu/outreach/ Documents/Child%20Exposure%20to%20Domestic%20Violence%20August%202014.pdf

82. Blacklock, N., & Phillips, R. (2015). Reshaping child protection response to domestic violence through collaborative working. In N. Stanley & C. Humphreys (Eds.), *Domestic violence and protecting children: New thinking and approaches* (pp. 196–213). London: Jessica Kingsley.

83. Ogbonnaya, I., & Kohl, P. (2016). Profiles of child-welfare-involved caregivers identified by caseworkers as having a domestic violence problem then and now. *Journal of Interpersonal Violence.* Advance online publication. http://jiv.sagepub.com/content/early/2016/02/24/ 0886260516632352.full

84. Taggart, S. (2009). *Child and family service review outcomes: Strategies to improve domestic violence responses in CFSR program improvement plans.* National Resource Center for Child Protective Services, the Family Violence Prevention Fund, and the National Council of Juvenile and Family Court Judges. http://nrccps.org/documents/2009/pdf/Strategies_To_ Improve_Domestic_Violence_Responses__in_CFSR_PIP.pdf

85. Turner, W., Broad, J., Drinkwater, J., Firth, A., Hester, M., Stanley, N., . . . Feder, G. (2015). Interventions to improve the response of professionals to children exposed to domestic violence and abuse: A systematic review. *Child Abuse Review.* Open access. http://onlinelibrary. wiley.com/doi/10.1002/car.2385/pdf.

86. Humphreys, C., & Absler, D. (2011). History repeating: Child protection responses to domestic violence. *Child and Family Social Work, 16,* 464–473.

CHAPTER 8

1. Finkelhor, D., Ormrod, R., Turner, H., & Hamby, S. (2005). The victimization of children and youth: A comprehensive, national survey. *Child Maltreatment, 10,* 5–25.

2. Sedlak, A., Mettenburg, J., Basena, M., Petta, I., McPherson, K., Greene, A., & Li, S. (2010). *Fourth National Incidence Study of Child Abuse and Neglect (NIS–4): Report to Congress.* Washington, DC: US Department of Health and Human Services, Administration for Children and Families.

3. Greenaway, K. (19th century). *Mother Goose; or, The old nursery rhymes.* London: Frederick Warner.

4. Lang, A. (1903). The boy who could keep a secret. *The crimson fairy book* (Lit2Go Edition). Retrieved June 29, 2016, from http://etc.usf.edu/lit2go/142/the-crimson-fairy-book/5121/ the-boy-who-could-keep-a-secret/

5. Giraldo, N. (1980). Hell is for Children [recorded by Pat Benatar]. On *Crimes of Passion.* Chrysalis. Lyrics available online: https://play.google.com/music/preview/Tpj5bqg wi5i627f2ffwer4sei3m?lyrics=1&utm_source=google&utm_medium=search&utm_ campaign=lyrics&pcampaignid=kp-songlyrics

6. Malloy, L., Lyon, T., & Quas, J. (2007). Filial dependency and recantation of child sexual abuse allegations. *Journal of the American Academy of Children and Adolescent Psychiatry, 46,* 162–170

7. McElvaney, R. (2015). Disclosure of child sexual abuse: Delays, non-disclosure and partial disclosure; what the research tells us and implications for practice. *Child Abuse Review, 24,* 159–169.

8. Rush, E., Lyon, T., Ahern, E., & Quas, J. (2014). Disclosure suspicion bias and abuse disclosure comparisons between sexual and physical abuse. *Child Maltreatment, 19,* 113–118.

9. Reder, P., Dunca, S., & Lucey, C. (2003). *Studies in the assessment of parenting.* UK: Brunner-Routledge.

10. Malloy, L., Brubacher, S., & Lamb, M. (2013). "Because she's one who listens": Children discuss disclosure recipients in forensic interviews. *Child Maltreatment, 18,* 245–251.

11. McElvaney, R., Greene, S., & Hogan, D. (2014). To tell or not to tell? Factors influencing young people's informal disclosures of child sexual abuse. *Journal of Interpersonal Violence, 29,* 928–947.

12. Montgomery County Commissioners and Office of Children and Youth. (2004). *Legally mandated reporting requirements of suspected child abuse and child neglect: Recommended medical protocol.* www.montcopa.org/DocumentCenter/View/3691

13. Keeshin, B., & Dubowitz, H. (2013). Childhood neglect: The role of the paediatrician. *Paediatrics and Child Health, 18,* e39.

14. US DHHS, Children's Bureau. (2017). *Child maltreatment 2015.* Washington, DC: Author. http://www.acf.hhs.gov/programs/cb/resource/child-maltreatment-2015

15. Brown, D., & Lamb, M. (2015). Can children be useful witnesses? It depends how they are questioned. *Child Development Perspectives, 9,* 250–255.

16. Lamb, M., Orbach, Y., Hershkowitz, I., Esplin, P., & Horowitz, D. (2007). A structured forensic interview protocol improves the quality and informativeness of investigative interviews with children: A review of research using the NICHD Investigative Interview Protocol. *Child Abuse and Neglect, 31,* 1201–1231.

17. Horner-Johnson, W., & Drum, C. (2006). Prevalence of maltreatment of people with intellectual disabilities: A review of recently published research. *Developmental Disabilities Research Reviews, 12,* 57–69.

18. Jonson-Reid, M., & Hausmann-Stabile, C., Meneses, C., Linhorst, D., & Hanrahan, K. (2012). *Sexual abuse and assault among persons with developmental disabilities in Saint Louis County: Final report.* St. Louis, MO: Washington University in St. Louis, George Warren Brown School of Social Work.

19. Skarbek, D., Hahn, K., & Parrish, P. (2009). Stop sexual abuse in special education: An ecological model of prevention and intervention strategies for sexual abuse in special education. *Sexuality and Disability, 27,* 155–164.

20. Stalker, K., & McArthur, K. (2012). Child abuse, child protection and disabled children: A review of recent research. *Child Abuse Review, 21,* 24–40.

21. Hibbard, R., & Desch, L.; Committee on Child Abuse and Neglect and Council on Children with Disabilities. (2007). Maltreatment of children with disabilities. *Pediatrics, 119,* 1018–1025.

22. Jones, L., Bellis, M., Wood, S., Hughes, K., McCoy, E., Eckley, L., . . . Officer, A. (2012). Prevalence and risk of violence against children with disabilities: A systematic review and meta-analysis of observational studies. *Lancet, 380,* 899–907.

23. Sullivan, M., & Knutson, J. (2000). Maltreatment and disability: A population-based epidemiological study. *Child Abuse and Neglect, 24,* 1257–1273.

24. Svensson, B., Eriksson, U. B., & Janson, S. (2013). Exploring risk for abuse of children with chronic conditions or disabilities–parent's perceptions of stressors and the role of professionals. *Child: Care, Health and Development, 39,* 887–893.

25. Stith, S., Liu, T., Davies, L., Boykin, E., Alder, M., Harris, J., . . . Dees, J. (2009). Risk factors in child maltreatment: A meta-analytic review of the literature. *Aggression and Violent Behavior, 14,* 13–29.

26. National Child Abuse and Neglect Data System. (n.d.). *Child files.* http://www.ndacan.cornell.edu/

27. McCarty, C. (2007). Exclusive: Couple arrested in extreme case of child abuse. *KLAS TV Las Vegas.* http://www.lasvegasnow.com/news/exclusive-couple-arrested-in-extreme-case-of-child-abuse

28. Laner, M., Benin, M., & Ventrone, N. (2001). Bystander attitudes toward victims of violence: Who's worth helping? *Deviant Behavior, 22,* 23–42.

29. Fledderjohann, J., & Johnson, D. (2012). What predicts the actions taken toward observed child neglect? The influence of community context and bystander characteristics. *Social Science Quarterly, 93,* 1030–1052.

30. Louwers, E., Korfage, I., Affourtit, M., De Koning, H., & Moll, H. (2012). Facilitators and barriers to screening for child abuse in the emergency department. *BMC Pediatrics, 12,* 167–173.

31. Tingberg, B., Bredlöv, B., & Ygge, B. (2008). Nurses' experience in clinical encounters with children experiencing abuse and their parents. *Journal of Clinical Nursing, 17,* 2718–2724.

32. Pietrantonio, A., Wright, E., Gibson, K., Alldred, T., Jacobson, D., & Niec, A. (2013). Mandatory reporting of child abuse and neglect: Crafting a positive process for health professionals and caregivers. *Child Abuse and Neglect, 37,* 102–109.

33. Black, M., & Ponirakis, A. (2000). Computer-administered interviews with children about maltreatment methodological, developmental, and ethical issues. *Journal of Interpersonal Violence, 15,* 682–695.

34. Edwards, V., Dube, S., Felitti, V., & Anda, R. (2007). It's ok to ask about past abuse. *American Psychologist, 62,* 327–328.

35. Runyan, D. (2000). The ethical, legal, and methodological implications of directly asking children about abuse. *Journal of Interpersonal Violence, 15,* 675–681.

36. Brooks-Gunn, J., Schneider, W., & Waldfogel, J. (2013). The Great Recession and the risk for child maltreatment. *Child Abuse and Neglect, 37,* 721–729.

37. Becker-Blease, K., & Freyd, J. (2006). Research participants telling the truth about their lives: The ethics of asking and not asking about abuse. *American Psychologist, 61,* 218.

38. Jaffe, A., DiLillo, D., Hoffman, L., Haikalis, M., & Dykstra, R. (2015). Does it hurt to ask? A meta-analysis of participant reactions to trauma research. *Clinical Psychology Review, 40,* 40–56.

39. Finkelhor, D., Vanderminden, J., Turner, H., Shattuck, A., & Hamby, S. (2014). Youth exposure to violence prevention programs in a national sample. *Child Abuse and Neglect, 38,* 677–686.

40. Miller, C., & Burch, A. (2014, March). Innocents lost: Preserving families but losing children. *Miami Herald.* http://media.miamiherald.com/static/media/projects/2014/innocents-lost/database/

41. Jonson-Reid, M., Kim, J., Citerman, B., Columbini, C., Essma, A., Fezzi, N., . . . Thomas, B. (2007). Maltreated children in schools: The interface of school social work and child welfare. *Children and Schools, 29,* 182–191.

42. Jones, R., Flaherty, E., Binns, H., Price, L., Slora, E., Abney, D., . . . Sege, R. (2008). Clinicians' description of factors influencing their reporting of suspected child abuse: Report of the Child Abuse Reporting Experience Study Research Group. *Pediatrics, 122,* 259–266.

43. Morris, J., Johnson, C., & Clasen, M. (1985). To report or not to report: Physicians' attitudes toward discipline and child abuse. *American Journal of Diseases of Children, 139,* 194–197.

44. Alvarez, K., Kenny, M., Donohue, B., & Carpin, K. (2004). Why are professionals failing to initiate mandated reports of child maltreatment, and are there any empirically based training programs to assist professionals in the reporting process? *Aggression and Violent Behavior, 9,* 563–578.

45. Walsh, W., & Jones, L. (2016). A statewide study of the public's knowledge of child abuse reporting laws. *Journal of Public Child Welfare, 10,* 561–579.

46. DeVooght, K., Fletcher, M., & Cooper, H. (2014). *Federal, state, and local spending to address child abuse and neglect in SFY 2012.* The Urban Institute. http://www.childtrends.org/wp-content/uploads/2014/09/SFY-2012-Report-for-Posting-July2015.pdf

47. Coohey, C., Johnson, K., Renner, L., & Easton, S. (2013). Actuarial risk assessment in child protective services: Construction methodology and performance criteria. *Children and Youth Services Review, 35,* 151–161.

48. Wekerle, C. (2013). Resilience in the context of child maltreatment: Connections to the practice of mandatory reporting. *Child Abuse and Neglect, 37,* 93–101.

49. Gladstone, J., Dumbrill, G., Leslie, B., Koster, A., Young, M., & Ismaila, A. (2012). Looking at engagement and outcome from the perspectives of child protection workers and parents. *Children and Youth Services Review, 34,* 112–118.

50. Pietrantonio, A., Wright, E., Gibson, K. N., Alldred, T., Jacobson, D., & Niec, A. (2013). Mandatory reporting of child abuse and neglect: Crafting a positive process for health professionals and caregivers. *Child Abuse and Neglect, 37,* 102–109.

51. Jecker, N. (1993). Privacy beliefs and the violent family: Extending the ethical argument for physician intervention. *JAMA, 269,* 776–780.

52. Dingwall, R., Eekelaar, J., & Murray, T. (2014). *The protection of children: State intervention and family life* (Vol. 16). New Orleans, Louisiana: Quid Pro Books.

53. Hahm, H., & Guterman, N. (2001). The emerging problem of physical child abuse in South Korea. *Child Maltreatment, 6,* 169–179.

54. Reading, R., Bissell, S., Goldhagen, J., Harwin, J., Masson, J., Moynihan, S., . . . Webb, E. (2009). Promotion of children's rights and prevention of child maltreatment. *Lancet, 373,* 332–343.

55. Worley, N., & Melton, G. (2013). Mandated reporting laws and child maltreatment: The evolution of a flawed policy response. In R. Krugman & J. Korbin (Eds.), *C. Henry*

Kempe: A 50 year legacy to the field of child abuse and neglect (pp. 103–118). Dordrecht: Springer Netherlands.

56. Hug, S., & Seymour, A. (1987). What's the matter here? [recorded by 10000 Maniacs]. On *In my tribe*. Lyrics, EMI Music Publishing, available online: http://www.metrolyrics.com/whats-the-matter-here-lyrics-10000-maniacs.html

57. Carroll, J. (2007). Alyssa lies. *On Waitin' in the Country*. Arista Nashville. Lyrics and background: http://www.songfacts.com/detail.php?id=7566

58. Hamby, S., Weber, M. C., Grych, J., & Banyard, V. (2016). What difference do bystanders make? The association of bystander involvement with victim outcomes in a community sample. *Psychology of Violence, 6,* 91.

59. DiLorenzo, P., White, C. R., Morales, A., Paul, A., & Shaw, S. (2013). Innovative cross-system and community approaches for the prevention of child maltreatment. *Child Welfare, 92,* 161.

60. Van Dijken, M., Stams, G., & de Winter, M. (2016). Can community-based interventions prevent child maltreatment? *Children and Youth Services Review, 61,* 149–158.

61. AlJasser, M., & Al-Khenaizan, S. (2008). Cutaneous mimickers of child abuse: A primer for pediatricians. *European Journal of Pediatrics, 167,* 1221.

62. Schwartz, K., Metz, J., Feldman, K., Sidbury, R., & Lindberg, D. (2014). Cutaneous findings mistaken for physical abuse: Present but not pervasive. *Pediatric Dermatology, 31,* 146–155.

63. Mansell, J. (2006). The underlying instability in statutory child protection: Understanding the system dynamics driving risk assurance levels. *Social Policy Journal of New Zealand, 28,* 97.

64. Trocmé, N., Tourigny, M., MacLaurin, B., & Fallon, B. (2003). Major findings from the Canadian incidence study of reported child abuse and neglect. *Child Abuse and Neglect, 27,* 1427–1439.

65. MacKay, T. (2014). False allegations of child abuse in contested family law cases: The implications for psychological practice. *Educational and Child Psychology, 31,* 85.

66. Lukens, R. (2007). Impact of mandatory reporting requirements on the child welfare system. *Rutgers Journal of Law and Public Policy, 5,* 177.

67. Drake, B., & Jonson-Reid, M. (2007). A response to Melton based on the best available data. *Child Abuse and Neglect, 31,* 343–360.

68. Kenny, M. (2015). Training in reporting of child maltreatment: Where we are and where we need to go. In B. Mathews & D. Bross (Eds.), *Mandatory reporting laws and the identification of severe child abuse and neglect* (pp. 327–346). Dordrecht, Netherlands: Springer.

69. Lyon, T., Malloy, L., Quas, J., & Talwar, V. (2008). Coaching, truth induction, and young maltreated children's false allegations and false denials. *Child Development, 79,* 914–929.

70. Jagannathan, R., & Camasso, M. (2013). *Protecting children in the age of outrage.* New York, NY: Oxford University Press.

71. Pecora, P., Whittaker, J., Maluccio, A., Barth, R., DePanfilis, D., & Plotnick, R. (2009). *The child welfare challenge: Policy, practice, and research.* Piscataway, NJ: Aldine Transaction.

72. Pelton, L. (2015). The continuing role of material factors in child maltreatment and placement. *Child Abuse and Neglect, 41,* 30–39.

CHAPTER 9

1. Färber, S., & Färber, M. (2015). Fairy tales and wonderful stories as a pedagogical proposal for the elaboration of losses. *European Psychiatry, 30,* 1642.

2.   Masten, A., Cutuli, J., Herbers, J., & Reed, M. (2009). Resilience in development. In S. Lopez & C Snyder (Eds.), *The Oxford handbook of positive psychology*. New York, New York: Oxford University Press.

3.   McGloin, J., & Widom, C. (2001). Resilience among abused and neglected children grown up. *Development and Psychopathology, 13*, 1021–1038.

4.   Rowling, J. K. (1997–2007). Harry Potter (series). Description available online: https://en.wikipedia.org/wiki/Harry_Potter

5.   Finerman, W., Tisch, S., & Starkey, S. (Producers) & Zemeckis, R. (Director) (1994). *Forrest Gump*. United States: Paramount Pictures.

6.   Hitchcock, A. (Producer & Director). (1960). *Psycho*. United States: Paramount Pictures.

7.   Cicchetti, D. (2013). Annual research review: Resilient functioning in maltreated children: Past, present, and future perspectives. *Journal of Child Psychology and Psychiatry, 54*, 402–422.

8.   Klika, J., & Herrenkohl, T. (2013). A review of developmental research on resilience in maltreated children. *Trauma, Violence, and Abuse, 14*, 222–234.

9.   McMillen, J. (1999). Better for it: How people benefit from adversity. *Social Work, 44*, 455–468.

10.   Zolkoski, S., & Bullock, L. (2012). Resilience in children and youth: A review. *Children and Youth Services Review, 34*, 2295–2303.

11.   Dahl, R. (1988). *Matilda*. London: Jonathan Cape.

12.   Daniels, L., Magness, G., Siegel-Magness, S., Winfrey, O., Heller, T., Perry, T., & Cortes, L. (Producers) & Daniels, L (Director). (2009). *Precious*. United States: Lionsgate.

13.   Scribner, H. (2014, August). 9 Inspiring people who overcame childhood adversity. *Deseret News*. http://national.deseretnews.com/article/2045/9-inspiring-people-who-overcame-childhood-adversity.html#z7h92B3GUwaZ2MVC.99

14.   Pope, A. (1963 reprint). *Epistles to several persons*. Florida: University of Miami Press (originally published 1731).

15.   Kim-Cohen, J., & Turkewitz, R. (2012). Resilience and measured gene–environment interactions. *Development and Psychopathology, 24*, 1297–1306.

16.   Curtiss, S. (2014). *Genie: a psycholinguistic study of a modern-day wild child*. New York, NY Academic Press.

17.   DeGregory, L. (2008, January). The girl in the window. *Tampa Bay Times*. http://www.tampabay.com/features/humaninterest/the-girl-in-the-window/750838

18.   Shonkoff, J., Garner, A., Siegel, B., Dobbins, M., Earls, M., McGuinn, L., ... Wood, D. (2012). The lifelong effects of early childhood adversity and toxic stress. *Pediatrics, 129*, e232–e246.

19.   Marco-Algarra, J., Martínez-Beneyto, P., Morant-Ventura, A., Platero-Zamarreño, A., Latorre-Monteagudo, E., & Pitarch-Ribas, I. (2009). Cortical neuroplasticity in children after early cochlear implantation. *Audiological Medicine, 7*, 40–46.

20.   Cicchetti, D., Rogosch, F., Toth, S., & Sturge-Apple, M. (2011). Normalizing the development of cortisol regulation in maltreated infants through preventive interventions. *Development and Psychopathology, 23*, 789–800.

21.   Gogtay, N., Giedd, J., Lusk, L., Hayashi, K., Greenstein, D., Vaituzis, A., . . . Rapoport, J. (2004). Dynamic mapping of human cortical development during childhood through

early adulthood. *Proceedings of the National Academy of Sciences of the United States of America, 101,* 8174–8179.

22. Johnson, S., Blum, R., & Giedd, J. (2009). Adolescent maturity and the brain: The promise and pitfalls of neuroscience research in adolescent health policy. *Journal of Adolescent Health, 45,* 216–221.

23. Davidson, R., & McEwen, B. (2012). Social influences on neuroplasticity: Stress and interventions to promote well-being. *Nature Neuroscience, 15,* 689–695.

24. Vance, D., & Wright, M. (2009). Positive and negative neuroplasticity: Implications for age-related cognitive declines. *Journal of Gerontological Nursing, 35,* 11–17.

25. Holliday, R. (2006). Epigenetics: A historical overview. *Epigenetics, 1,* 76–80.

26. Roth, T. (2012). Epigenetics of neurobiology and behavior during development and adulthood. *Developmental Psychobiology, 54,* 590–597.

27. Cicchetti, D., & Rogosch, F. (2012). Gene × environment interaction and resilience: Effects of child maltreatment and serotonin, corticotropin releasing hormone, dopamine, and oxytocin genes. *Development and Psychopathology, 24,* 411–427.

28. Jonson-Reid, M., Presnall, N., Drake, B., Fox, L., Bierut, L., Todd, R., Kane, P. B.A., Constantino, J. (2010). Joint effects of child maltreatment and inherited liability on antisocial development: An official records study. *Journal of American Academy of Child and Adolescent Psychiatry, 49,* 321–332.

29. Kim-Cohen, J., Caspi, A., Taylor, A., Williams, B., Newcombe, R., Craig, I. W., & Moffitt, T. E. (2006). MAOA, maltreatment, and gene–environment interaction predicting children's mental health: New evidence and a meta-analysis. *Molecular Psychiatry, 11,* 903–913.

30. Herb, B., Wolschin, F., Hansen, K., Aryee, M., Langmead, B., Irizarry, R., . . . Feinberg, A. (2012). Reversible switching between epigenetic states in honeybee behavioral subcastes. *Nature Neuroscience, 15,* 1371–1373.

31. Center on the Developing Child, Harvard University. (2015). *Key concepts: Toxic stress.* Available online: http://developingchild.harvard.edu/index.php/key_concepts/toxic_stress_response/

32. Lazarus, R. (1993). Coping theory and research: Past, present, and future. *Psychosomatic Medicine, 55,* 234–247.

33. Lanier, P., Jonson-Reid, M., Stahlschmidt, M., Drake, B., & Constantino, J. (2010). Child maltreatment and pediatric health outcomes: A longitudinal study of low-income children. *Journal of Pediatric Psychology, 35,* 511–522.

34. Gehlert, S., Sohmer, D., Sacks, T., Mininger, C., McClintock, M., & Olopade, O. (2008). Targeting health disparities: A model linking upstream determinants to downstream interventions: Knowing about the interaction of societal factors and disease can enable targeted interventions to reduce health disparities. *Health Affairs (Project Hope), 27,* 339–349.

35. Slade, A. (2012, August). *The leader's tipping point.* Slade & Associates. http://www.sladeresearch.com/2012/08/24/the-leaders-tipping-point/

36. Dube, S., Anda, R., Felitti, V., Edwards, V., & Williamson, D. (2002). Exposure to abuse, neglect, and household dysfunction among adults who witnessed intimate partner violence as children: implications for health and social services. *Violence and Victims, 17,* 3–17.

37. English, D., Graham, J., Litrownik, A., Everson, M., & Bangdiwala, S. (2005). Defining maltreatment chronicity: Are there differences in child outcomes?. *Child Abuse and Neglect, 29,* 575–595.

38. Jaffee, S., & Maikovich-Fong, A. (2011). Effects of chronic maltreatment and maltreatment timing on children's behavior and cognitive abilities. *Journal of Child Psychology and Psychiatry, 52,* 184–194.

39. Jonson-Reid, M., Kohl, P., & Drake, B. (2012). Child and adult outcomes of chronic child maltreatment *Pediatrics, 129,* 839–845.

40. McCrory, E., De Brito, S., & Viding, E. (2010). Research review: The neurobiology and genetics of maltreatment and adversity. *Journal of Child Psychology and Psychiatry, 51,* 1079–1095.

41. Ozbay, F., Fitterling, H., Charney, D., & Southwick, S. (2008). Social support and resilience to stress across the life span: A neurobiologic framework. *Current Psychiatry Reports, 10,* 304–310.

42. Taussig, H., & Culhane, S. (2010). Impact of a mentoring and skills group program on mental health outcomes for maltreated children in foster care. *Archives of Pediatrics and Adolescent Medicine, 164,* 739–746.

43. Black, P., Woodworth, M., Tremblay, M., & Carpenter, T. (2012). A review of trauma-informed treatment for adolescents. *Canadian Psychology/Psychologie Canadienne, 53,* 192.

44. Biglan, A. (2015). *The nurture effect: How science of human behavior can improve our lives and our world.* Oakland, CA: New Harbinger.

45. Barth, R., Landsverk, J., Chamberlain, P., Reid, J., Rolls, J., Hurlburt, M., . . . Kohl, P. (2005). Parent-training programs in child welfare services: Planning for a more evidence-based approach to serving biological parents. *Research on Social Work Practice, 15,* 353–371.

46. Barth, R., & Liggett-Creel, K. (2014). Common components of parenting programs for children birth to eight years of age involved with child welfare services. *Children and Youth Services Review, 40,* 6–12.

47. Kohl, P., Schurer, J., & Bellamy, J. (2009). The state of parent training: Program offerings and empirical support. *Families in Society, 90,* 248–254.

48. Lanier, P., Benz, J., Swinger, D., Mousette, P., Kohl, P., & Drake, B. (2011). Parent-child interaction therapy in a community setting: Examining outcomes, attrition, and treatment setting. *Research on Social Work Practice, 21,* 689–698.

49. Office of Planning, Research and Evaluation. (n.d.). *Early Head Start university partnership grants: Buffering children from toxic stress, 2011–2016.* http://www.acf.hhs.gov/programs/opre/research/project/early-head-start-university-partnership-grants-buffering-children-from

50. Pecora, P., Sanders, D., Wilson, D., English, D., Puckett, A., & Rudlang-Perman, K. (2014). Addressing common forms of child maltreatment: Evidence-informed interventions and gaps in current knowledge. *Child and Family Social Work, 19,* 321–332.

51. Cohen, J, Mannarino, A., Murray, L., & Igelman, R. (2006). Psychosocial interventions for maltreated and violence-exposed children. *Journal of Social Issues, 62,* 737–766.

52. Allen, B., Gharagozloo, L., & Johnson, J. (2012). Clinician knowledge and utilization of empirically supported treatments for maltreated children. *Child Maltreatment, 17,* 11–21.

53. Raghavan, R., Inoue, M., Ettner, S., Hamilton, B., & Landsverk, J. (2010). A preliminary analysis of the receipt of mental health services consistent with national standards among children in the child welfare system. *American Journal of Public Health, 100,* 742.

54. Leslie, L., Raghavan, R., Zhang, J., & Aarons, G. (2010). Rates of psychotropic medication use over time among youth in child welfare/child protective services. *Journal of Child and Adolescent Psychopharmacology, 20,* 135–143.

55. McMillen, J., Fedoravicius, N., Rowe, J., Zima, B., & Ware, N. (2007). A crisis of credibility: Professionals' concerns about the psychiatric care provided to clients of the child welfare system. *Administration and Policy in Mental Health and Mental Health Services Research, 34,* 203–212.

56. Correll, C., & Carlson, H. (2006). Endocrine and metabolic adverse effects of psychotropic medications in children and adolescents. *Journal of the American Academy of Child and Adolescent Psychiatry, 45,* 771–791.

57. Graham, J., Banaschewski, T., Buitelaar, J., Coghill, D., Danckaerts, M., Dittmann, R., . . . Hulpke-Wette, M. (2011). European guidelines on managing adverse effects of medication for ADHD. *European Child and Adolescent Psychiatry, 20,* 17–37.

58. Sharpe, K. (2014, February). Medication: The smart-pill oversell. *Nature, 506,* 146–148.

59. Becker, J., Greenwald, R., & Mitchell, C. (2011). Trauma-informed treatment for disenfranchised urban children and youth: An open trial. *Child and Adolescent Social Work Journal, 28,* 257–272.

60. Ai, A., Foster, L., Pecora, P., Delaney, N., & Rodriguez, W. (2013). Reshaping child welfare's response to trauma: Assessment, evidence-based intervention, and new research perspectives. *Research on Social Work Practice, 23,* 651–668.

61. Jee, S., Tonniges, T., & Szilagyi, M. (2008). Foster care issues in general pediatrics. *Current Opinion in Pediatrics, 20,* 724–728.

62. Sprang, G., Craig, C., Clark, J., Vergon, K., Tindall, M., Cohen, J., & Gurwitch, R. (2013). Factors affecting the completion of trauma-focused treatments: What can make a difference? *Traumatology, 19,* 28.

CHAPTER 10

1. Wikipedia. (n.d.). Rumpelstiltskin. https://en.wikipedia.org/wiki/Rumpelstiltskin

2. Animal Planet (Producer). (2002–2014 series). *Animal cops.* United States: Discovery Communications.

3. Reich, J. (2006). *Fixing families: Parents, power, and the child welfare system.* New York, NY: Routledge

4. Valentine, D. P., & Freeman, M. (2002). Film portrayals of social workers doing child welfare work. *Child and Adolescent Social Work Journal, 19,* 455–471.

5. Mr. Peabody & Sherman Wiki. (n.d.). Ms. Grunio. http://mr-peabody-sherman.wikia.com/wiki/Ms._Grunion

6. Jenney, A., Mishna, F., Alaggia, R., & Scott, K. (2014). Doing the right thing? (Re)considering risk assessment and safety planning in child protection work with domestic violence cases. *Children and Youth Services Review, 47,* 92–101.

7. Arluke, A. (2004). *Brute force: Animal police and the challenge of cruelty.* West Lafayette, IN: Purdue University Press.

8. Parent, M. (1998). *Turning stones. A caseworker's story.* New York, NY: Ballantine Books.

9. Dumbrill, G. C. (2006). Parental experience of child protection intervention: A qualitative study. *Child Abuse and Neglect, 30,* 27–37.

10. English, D. J., Brummel, S. C., Graham, J. C., Clark, T., & Coghlan, L. (2002). *Factors that influence the decision not to substantiate A CPS referral phase III: Client perceptions of investigation.* State of Washington, Department of Social and Health Services, Children's

Administration, Office of Children's Administration Research, Olympia, WA. http://citeseerx.ist.psu.edu/viewdoc/download?doi=10.1.1.588.6823&rep=rep1&type=pdf

11. Maiter, S., Palmer, S., & Manji, S. (2006). Strengthening social worker-client relationships in child protective services addressing power imbalances and "ruptured" relationships. *Qualitative Social Work, 5,* 161–186.

12. Mullins, J., Cheung., J., & Lietz, C. (2012). Family preservation services: Incorporating the voice of families into service implementation. *Child and Family Social Work, 17,* 265–274.

13. Palmer, S., Maiter, S., & Manji, S. (2006). Effective intervention in child protective services: Learning from parents. *Children and Youth Services Review, 28,* 812–824.

14. Merkel-Holguin, L., Hollinshead, D., Hahn, A., Casillas, K., & Fluke, J. (2015). The influence of differential response and other factors on parent perceptions of child protection involvement. *Child Abuse and Neglect, 39,* 18–31.

15. Gladstone, J., Dumbrill, G., Leslie, B., Koster, A., Young, M., & Ismaila, A. (2012). Looking at engagement and outcome from the perspectives of child protection workers and parents. *Children and Youth Services Review, 34,* 112–118.

16. Chapman, M., Gibbons, C., Barth, R., & McCrae, J. (2003). Parental views of in-home services: What predicts satisfaction with child welfare workers? *Child Welfare, 82,* 571–596.

17. Kemp, S., Marcenko, M., Hoagwood, K., & Vesneski, W. (2009). Engaging parents in child welfare services: Bridging family needs and child welfare mandates. *Child Welfare, 88,* 101–126.

18. Horejsi, C., Craig, B., & Pablo, J. (1992). *Reactions by Native American parents to child protection agencies: Cultural and community factors.* Washington, DC: Child Welfare League of America.

19. October, T., Hinds, P., Wang, J., Dizon, Z., Cheng, Y., & Roter, D. (2016). Parent satisfaction with communication is associated with physician's patient-centered communication patterns during family conferences. *Pediatric Critical Care Medicine, 17,* 490–497.

20. Fryer, G., Bross, D., Krugman, R., Denson, D., & Baird, D. (1990). Good news for CPS workers. *Public Welfare, 48,* 38–41.

21. Huebner, R. A., Jones, B. L., Miller, V. P., Custer, M., & Critchfield, B. (2006). Comprehensive family services and customer satisfaction outcomes. *Child Welfare, 85*(4), 691–714.

22. Winefield, H., & Barlow, J. (1995). Client and worker satisfaction in a child protection agency. *Child Abuse and Neglect, 19,* 897–905.

23. Meehan, T., Bergen, H., & Stedman, T. (2002). Monitoring consumer satisfaction with inpatient service delivery: The Inpatient Evaluation of Service Questionnaire. *Australian and New Zealand Journal of Psychiatry, 36,* 807–811.

24. Riley, S., Stromberg, A., & Clark, J. (2005). Assessing parental satisfaction with children's mental health services with the youth services survey for families. *Journal of Child and Family Studies, 14,* 87–99.

25. Norman, E. (2009). *No one would believe it: Experiences of a child abuse investigator.* Author.

26. Ayre, P. (2001). Child protection and the media: Lessons from the last three decades. *British Journal of Social Work, 31,* 887–901.

27. Westbrook, T., Ellis, J., & Ellett, A. (2006). Improving retention among public child welfare workers: What can we learn from the insights and experiences of committed survivors? *Administration in Social Work, 30,* 37–62.

28. Juhasz, I., & Skivenes, M. (2016). The population's confidence in the child protection system–A survey study of England, Finland, Norway and the United States (California). *Social Policy and Administration*. Epub. http://onlinelibrary.wiley.com/doi/10.1111/spol.12226/full

29. Curry, J., McCarragher, T., & Dellmann-Jenkins, M. (2005). Training, transfer, and turnover: Exploring the relationship among transfer of learning factors and retention in child welfare. *Child and Youth Services Review, 27*, 931–948.

30. Mandell, D., Stalker, C., de Zeeuw Wright, M., Frensch, K., & Harvey, C. (2013). Sinking, swimming and sailing: Experiences of job satisfaction and emotional exhaustion in child welfare employees. *Child and Family Social Work, 18*, 383–393.

31. Smith, B., & Donovan, S. (2003). Child welfare practice in organizational and institutional context. *Social Service Review, 77*, 541–563.

32. Shdaimah, C. (2009). "CPS is not a housing agency"; Housing is a CPS problem: Towards a definition and typology of housing problems in child welfare cases. *Children and Youth Services Review, 31*, 211–218.

33. St. Louis Housing Authority. (2016, February) *Section 8 waiting list status: Closed*. Affordable Housing Online. http://affordablehousingonline.com/housing-authority/Missouri/St-Louis-Housing-Authority/MO001/

34. Bride, B., Jones, J., & MacMaster, S. (2007). Correlates of secondary traumatic stress in child protective services workers. *Journal of Evidence-Based Social Work, 4*(3–4), 69–80.

35. Child Welfare Information Gateway. (n.d.). *Causes of disproportionality*. US DHHS. https://www.childwelfare.gov/topics/systemwide/cultural/disproportionality/causes/

36. Hill, R. (2006). Synthesis of research on disproportionality in child welfare: An update. Casey/CSPP Alliance For Racial Equity In the Child Welfare System.

37. Hines, A., Lemon, K., Wyatt, P., & Merdinger, J. (2004). Factors related to the disproportionate involvement of children of color in the child welfare system: A review and emerging themes. *Children and Youth Services Review, 26*, 507–527.

38. Drake, B., Jolley, J. M., Lanier, P., Fluke, J., Barth, R., & Jonson-Reid, M. (2011). Racial bias in child protection? A comparison of competing explanations using national data. *Pediatrics, 127*, 471–478.

39. Drake, B., & Rank, M. (2009). The racial divide among American children in poverty: Assessing the importance of neighborhoods. *Children and Youth Services Review, 31*, 1264–1271.

40. Sarche, M., & Spicer, P. (2008). Poverty and health disparities for American Indian and Alaska Native children. *Annals of the New York Academy of Sciences, 1136*, 126–136.

41. McRoy, R., & Runnels, R. (2014). African American children and families. In R. Fong, A. Dettlaff, J. James, & C. Rodriguez (Eds.), *Addressing racial disproportionality and disparities in human services: Multisystemic approaches* (pp. 41–69). New York, NY: Columbia University Press.

42. Maguire-Jack, K., & Klein, S. (2015). Parenting and proximity to social services: Lessons from Los Angeles County in the community context of child neglect. *Child Abuse and Neglect, 45*, 35–45.

43. Freisthler, B., Merritt, D., & LaScala, E. (2006). Understanding the ecology of child maltreatment: A review of the literature and directions for future research. *Child Maltreatment, 11*, 263–280.

44. Harris, M., & Hackett, W. (2008). Decision points in child welfare: An action research model to address disproportionality. *Children and Youth Services Review, 30,* 199–215.

45. Jonson-Reid, M., Drake, B., & Zhou, P. (2013). Neglect subtypes, race, and poverty individual, family, and service characteristics. *Child Maltreatment, 18,* 30–41.

46. Bartholet, E., Wulczyn, F., Barth, R., & Lederman, C. (2011, June). *Race and child welfare.* Chapin Hall Issue in Brief. Chicago: Chapin Hall. http://www.chapinhall.org/sites/default/files/publications/07_13_11_Race_Child_Welfare_IB.pdf

47. Pelton, L. (2015). The continuing role of material factors in child maltreatment and placement. *Child Abuse and Neglect, 41,* 30–39.

48. Putnam-Hornstein, E., Needell, B., King, B., & Johnson-Motoyama, M. (2013). Racial and ethnic disparities: A population-based examination of risk factors for involvement with child protective services. *Child Abuse and Neglect, 37,* 33–46.

49. Fox, K. (2003). Collecting data on the abuse and neglect of American Indian children. *Child Welfare, 82,* 707–726.

50. Zhai, F., & Gao, Q. (2009). Child maltreatment among Asian Americans characteristics and explanatory framework. *Child Maltreatment, 14,* 207–224.

51. Arias, E. (2016). *Changes in life expectancy by race and Hispanic origin in the United States, 2013–2014.* NCHS Data Brief, no. 244, 1–8. https://www.cdc.gov/nchs/data/databriefs/db244.pdf

52. Camacho-Rivera, M., Kawachi, I., Bennett, G., & Subramanian, S. (2015). Revisiting the Hispanic health paradox: The relative contributions of nativity, country of origin, and race/ethnicity to childhood asthma. *Journal of Immigrant and Minority Health, 17,* 826–833.

53. Johnson-Motoyama, M., Putnam-Hornstein, E., Dettlaff, A., Zhao, K., Finno-Velasquez, M., & Needell, B. (2015). Disparities in reported and substantiated infant maltreatment by maternal Hispanic origin and nativity: A birth cohort study. *Maternal and Child Health Journal, 19,* 958–968.

54. Widom, C., Czaja, S., & DuMont, K. (2015). Intergenerational transmission of child abuse and neglect: Real or detection bias? *Science, 347,* 1480–1485.

55. Chaffin, M., & Bard, D. (2006). Impact of intervention surveillance bias on analyses of child welfare report outcomes. *Child maltreatment, 11,* 301–312.

56. Connell, C., Bergeron, N., Katz, K., Saunders, L., & Tebes, J. (2007). Re-referral to child protective services: The influence of child, family, and case characteristics on risk status. *Child Abuse and Neglect, 31,* 573–588.

57. Drake, B., Jonson-Reid, M. & Kim, H. (2017). Surveillance bias in maltreatment: A tempest in a teapot. International *Journal of Environmental Research and Public Health.*

58. Child Welfare Information Gateway. (2016, February). *State statutes.* https://www.childwelfare.gov/topics/systemwide/laws-policies/state/?CWIGFunctionsaction=statestatutes:main&CWIGFunctionspk=1

59. Child Welfare Information Gateway. (2016). *Foster care statistics 2014.* Washington, DC: US Department of Health and Human Services, Children's Bureau.

60. Ards, S., Myers, S., Malkis Erin, A., & Zhou, L. (2003). Racial disproportionality in reported and substantiated child abuse and neglect: An examination of systematic bias. *Children and Youth Services Review, 25,* 5–6.

61. Dettlaff, A., Rivaux, S., Baumann, D., Fluke, J., Rycraft, J., & James, J. (2011). Disentangling substantiation: The influence of race, income, and risk on the substantiation decision in child welfare. *Children and Youth Services Review, 33,* 1630–1637.

62. Rivaux, S., James, J., Wittenstrom, K., Baumann, D., Sheets, J., Henry, J., & Jeffries, V. (2008). The intersection of race, poverty, and risk: Understanding the decision to provide services to clients and to remove children. *Child Welfare, 87,* 151–168.

63. Bartholet, E. (2009). The racial disproportionality movement in child welfare: False facts and dangerous directions. *Arizona Law Review, 51,* 871–932.

64. Roberts, D. (2012). Prison, foster care, and the systemic punishment of black mothers. *UCLA Law Review, 59,* 1474–1501.

65. Sribnick, E. (2013, July). *The legacy of racism in child welfare.* New York, NY: Institute for Children, Poverty & Homelessness. http://www.icphusa.org/index.asp?page=26&blog=64&focus=

66. Zuravin, S., & DePanfilis, D. (1997). Factors affecting foster care placement of children receiving child protective services. *Social Work Research, 21,* 34–42.

67. Lorthridge, J., McCroskey, J., Pecora, P., Chambers, R., & Fatemi, M. (2012). Strategies for improving child welfare services for families of color: First findings of a community-based initiative in Los Angeles. *Children and Youth Services Review, 34,* 281–288.

68. Russell, J., Miller, N., & Nash, M. (2014). Judicial issues in child maltreatment. In J. Korbin & H. Krugman (Eds.), *Handbook of child maltreatment* (pp. 503–515). Dordrecht: Springer Netherlands.

69. Krieger, N. (2003). Does racism harm health? Did child abuse exist before 1962? On explicit questions, critical science, and current controversies: An ecosocial perspective. *American Journal of Public Health, 93,* 194–199.

70. Cook, J. (1995). A history of placing-out: The orphan trains. *Child Welfare, 74,* 181.

71. Graham, L. (2009). Reparations, self-determination and the seventh generation. In M. Fletcher, W. Singel, & K. Fort (Eds.), *Facing the future: The Indian Child Welfare Act at 30.* East Lansing: Michigan State University Press.

72. Cooper, T. (2013). Racial bias in American foster care: The national debate. *Marquette Law Review, 97,* 2013–2077.

73. Carlton-LaNey, I. (1999). African American social work pioneers' response to need. *Social Work, 44,* 311–321.

74. Stevens, C. (2003). Unrecognized roots of service-learning in African American social thought and action, 1890–1930. *Michigan Journal of Community Service Learning, 9,* 25–34.

75. Massey, D., & Denton, N. (1993). *American apartheid: Segregation and the making of the underclass.* Cambridge, MA: Harvard University Press.

76. Duster, T. (1988). Social implications of the "new" black urban underclass. *The Black Scholar, 19,* 2–9.

77. King, M. L., Jr. (1967, August). *Southern Christian Leadership Conference presidential address.* http://www.hartford-hwp.com/archives/45a/628.html

78. Sullivan, L. (2011, October). Native foster care: Lost children, shattered families. *All Things Considered.* National Public Radio. http://www.npr.org/2011/10/25/141672992/native-foster-care-lost-children-shattered-families

79. Scarcella, C., Bess, R., Zielewski, E., Warner, L. & Geen, B. (2004). The cost of protecting vulnerable children IV. *How child welfare fared in during the recession.* NY, NY: The Urban Institute.

80. Sellick, C. (2011). Privatising foster care: The UK experience within an international context. *Social Policy and Administration, 45,* 788–805.

81. Sellick, C. (2012). Towards a mixed economy of foster care provision. *Social Work and Social Sciences Review, 13,* 25–40.

82. Casey Family Programs. (n.d.). *Review of performance-based contracting in child welfare.* http://www.cdss.ca.gov/ccr/res/pdf/performance/2.%20CaseyFamilyPBCreview.pdf

83. McCullough, C., & Lee, E. (2007). *Program and fiscal design elements of child welfare privatization initiatives.* Topical paper # 2. The Urban Institute for the Office of the Assistant Secretary for Planning and Evaluation, US Department of Health and Human Services.

84. O'Hanlon, K. (2012). *Privatization fails: Nebraska tries again to reform child welfare.* Washington, DC: Center for Public Integrity.http://www.publicintegrity.org/2012/08/21/10706/privatization-fails-nebraska-tries-again-reform-child-welfare.

85. Therolf, G. (2013, December). Private foster care system, intended to save children, endangers some. *Los Angeles Times.* http://www.latimes.com/local/la-me-foster-care-dto-htmlstory.html

86. Joseph, B. (2015, February). The brief life and private death of Alexandria Hill. *Mother Jones.* http://www.motherjones.com/politics/2015/01/privatized-foster-care-mentor

87. Shusterman, G., Fluke, J., Hollinshead, D., & Yuan, Y. (2005). Alternative responses to child maltreatment: Findings from NCANDS. *Protecting Children, 20,* 32–42.

88. Piper, K. (2016). Differential response in child protection: How much is too much? *APSAC Advisor, 28,* 23–28.

89. Drake, B. (2013). Differential response: What to make of the existing research? A response to Hughes et al. *Research on Social Work Practice, 23,* 539–544.

90. Hudson, M. (2016). Minnesota's experience with differential response. *APSAC Advisor, 28,* 17–22.

91. Loman, L., & Siegel, G. (2015). Effects of approach and services under differential response on long term child safety and welfare. *Child Abuse and Neglect, 39,* 86–97.

92. Winokur, M., Ellis, R., Drury, I., & Rogers, J. (2015). Answering the big questions about differential response in Colorado: Safety and cost outcomes from a randomized controlled trial. *Child Abuse and Neglect, 39,* 98–108.

93. Lepore, J. (2016, February). Baby Doe: A political history of tragedy. *New Yorker.* http://www.newyorker.com/magazine/2016/02/01/baby-doe

94. Melton, G. (2005). Mandated reporting: A policy without reason. *Child Abuse and Neglect, 29,* 9–18.

95. Wald, M. (2014). Beyond maltreatment: Developing support for children in multiproblem families. In J. Korbin & H. Krugman (Eds.), *Handbook of child maltreatment* (pp. 251–280). Dordrecht: Springer Netherlands.

96. Center for Public Policy Priorities. (2012). *Child protective services in Texas: Buying what we want.* http://library.cppp.org/files/4/2012_01_CP_BudgetCPS.pdf

97. Talbott, J. (2004). Deinstitutionalization: Avoiding the disasters of the past. *Psychiatric Services, 55,* 1112–1115.

98. Barth, R., Wulczyn, F., & Crea, T. (2004). From anticipation to evidence: Research on the Adoption and Safe Families Act. *Virginia Journal of Social Policy and Law, 12,* 371–399.

99. Argys, L., & Duncan, B. (2013). Economic incentives and foster child adoption. *Demography, 50,* 933–954.

100. Lindsey, D. (2004). *The welfare of children.* New York, NY: Oxford University Press.

101. Drake, B., & Jonson-Reid, M. (2015). Competing values and evidence: How do we evaluate mandated reporting and CPS response? In B. Mathews & D. Bross (Eds.), *Mandated reporting laws and identification of severe child abuse and neglect.* Dordrecht: Springer.

102. Dedel, K. (2010). *The problem of child abuse and neglect in the home* (guide #55). New York, NY: Center for Problem Oriented Policing. http://www.popcenter.org/problems/child_abuse/3

103. Cross, T., Finkelhor, D., & Ormrod, R. (2005). Police involvement in child protective services investigations: Literature review and secondary data analysis. *Child Maltreatment, 10,* 224–244.

104. MacEachern, A., Jindal-Snape, D., & Jackson, S. (2011). Child abuse investigation: Police officers and secondary traumatic stress. *International Journal of Occupational Safety and Ergonomics, 17,* 329–339.

105. Pecora, P., Whittaker, J., Maluccio, A., & Barth, R., DePanfilis, D., & Plotnick, R. (2009). *The child welfare challenge: Policy, practice, and research.* Piscataway, NJ: Aldine/Transaction.

CHAPTER 11

1. US DHHS. (2016). *Building community building hope: Prevention resource guide.* US Children's Bureau. https://www.childwelfare.gov/pubPDFs/guide.pdf

2. Bandura, A., & Walters, R. (1977). *Social learning theory.* New York, NY: General Learning Press.

3. Sanders, M., & Mazzucchelli, T. (2013). The promotion of self-regulation through parenting interventions. *Clinical Child and Family Psychology Review, 16,* 1–17.

4. McDonell, J., Ben-Arieh, A., & Melton, G. (2015). Strong communities for children: Results of a multi-year community-based initiative to protect children from harm. *Child Abuse and Neglect, 41,* 79–96.

5. Martorell, G., & Bugental, D. (2006). Maternal variations in stress reactivity: Implications for harsh parenting practices with very young children. *Journal of Family Psychology, 20,* 641.

6. Crnic, K., Gaze, C., Hoffman, C. (2005). Cumulative parenting stress across the preschool period: relations to maternal parenting and child behaviour at age 5. *Infant and Child Development, 14,* 117–132.

7. Mackler, J., Kelleher, R., Shanahan, L., Calkins, S., Keane, S., & O'Brien, M. (2015). Parenting stress, parental reactions, and externalizing behavior from ages 4 to 10. *Journal of Marriage and Family, 77,* 388–406.

8. Renner, L., & Boel-Studt, S. (2013). The relation between intimate partner violence, parenting stress, and child behavior problems. *Journal of Family Violence, 28,* 201–212.

9. Sheidow, A., Henry, D., Tolan, P., & Strachan, M. (2014). The role of stress exposure and family functioning in internalizing outcomes of urban families. *Journal of Child and Family Studies, 23,* 1351–1365.

10. Mayo Clinic Staff (2015, August). *Stress management.* http://www.mayoclinic.org/healthy-lifestyle/stress-management/in-depth/exercise-and-stress/art-20044469

11. Segal, J., Smith, M., Segal, R., & Robinson, L. (2016, June). Stress symptoms, signs, and causes. *Helpguide.org.* http://www.helpguide.org/articles/stress/stress-symptoms-causes-and-effects.htm

12. Moore, K., Kinghorn, A., & Bandy, T. (2011, April). *Parental relationship quality and child outcomes across subgroups.* Child trends research brief. (#2011-13). Washington, DC: Child Trends. http://www.childtrends.org/wp-content/uploads/2011/04/Child_Trends-2011_04_04_RB_MaritalHappiness.pdf

13. Ginsburg, K. (2007). The importance of play in promoting healthy child development and maintaining strong parent-child bonds. *Pediatrics, 119,* 182–191.

14. Feiler, B. (2013, October). Overscheduled children: How big a problem? *New York Times.* http://www.nytimes.com/2013/10/13/fashion/over-scheduled-children-how-big-a-problem.html

15. McGuire, M. (2014, March). *100 + books parents say they LOVE to read aloud with their kids.* Scholastic.com. http://www.scholastic.com/parents/blogs/scholastic-parents-raise-reader/100-books-parents-say-they-love-to-read-aloud-their-kids

16. McCubbin, H., & Patterson, J. (1983). The family stress process: The double ABCX model of adjustment and adaptation. *Marriage and Family Review, 6*(1–2), 7–37.

17. Byrne, S., Rodrigo, M., & Martín, J. (2012). Influence of form and timing of social support on parental outcomes of a child-maltreatment prevention program. *Children and Youth Services Review, 34,* 2495–2503.

18. Fattore, T., Mason, J., & Watson, E. (2009). When children are asked about their well-being: Towards a framework for guiding policy. *Child Indicators Research, 2,* 57–77.

19. Knox, M., Burkhart, K., & Hunter, K. (2010). ACT against violence parents raising safe kids program: Effects on maltreatment-related parenting behaviors and beliefs. *Journal of Family Issues, 32,* 55–74.

20. Briggs, F., & Hawking, R. (n.d.). Children's perceptions of personal safety. *Child Matters.* http://www.childmatters.org.nz/file/Diploma-Readings/Block-2/Sexual-Abuse/3.2-chn-perceptions-of-personal-safety.pdf

21. Ceballo, R., & McLoyd, V. (2002). Social support and parenting in poor, dangerous neighborhoods. *Child Development, 73,* 1310–1321.

22. Riina, E., Lippert, A., & Brooks-Gunn, J. (2016). Residential instability, family support, and parent–child relationships among ethnically diverse urban families. *Journal of Marriage and Family, 78,* 855–870.

23. Thompson, R. (2015). Social support and child protection: Lessons learned and learning. *Child Abuse and Neglect, 41,* 19–29.

24. Smith, E., Faulk, M., & Sizer, M. (2016). Exploring the meso-system: The roles of community, family, and peers in adolescent delinquency and positive youth development. *Youth and Society, 48,* 318–343.

25. Geiger, J., Hayes, M., & Lietz, C. (2013). Should I stay or should I go? A mixed methods study examining the factors influencing foster parents' decisions to continue or discontinue providing foster care. *Children and Youth Services Review, 35,* 1356–1365.

26. Weisz, V., & Thai, N. (2003). The court-appointed special advocate (CASA) program: Bringing information to child abuse and neglect cases. *Child Maltreatment, 8,* 204–210.

27. Adhia, A., Potter, S., Stapleton, J., Zuckerman, B., Phan, N., & Bair-Merritt, M. (2017). Encouraging bystanders to promote positive parenting and prevent child maltreatment in retail settings: Results of an exploratory qualitative study. *Journal of Aggression, Maltreatment and Trauma, 26,* 1–21.

28. Palusci, V., & Haney, M. (2010). Strategies to prevent child maltreatment and integration into practice. *APSAC Advisor, 22,* 8–17.

29. Block, R., & Palusci, V. (2006). Child abuse pediatrics: A new pediatric subspecialty. *Journal of Pediatrics, 148,* 711–712.

30. Child Welfare Information Gateway. (2016, February). *State statutes.* https://www.childwelfare.gov/topics/systemwide/laws-policies/state/?CWIGFunctionsaction=statestatutes:main&CWIGFunctionspk=1

31. Barth, R., Landsverk, J., Chamberlain, P., Reid, J., Rolls, J., Hurlburt, M., . . . Kohl, P. (2005). Parent-training programs in child welfare services: Planning for a more evidence-based approach to serving biological parents. *Research on Social Work Practice, 15,* 353–371.

32. Chaffin, M., Bard, D., Bigfoot, D., & Maher, E. (2012). Is a structured, manualized, evidence-based treatment protocol culturally competent and equivalently effective among American Indian parents in child welfare?. *Child Maltreatment, 17,* 242–252.

33. Kramer, T., Sigel, B., Conners-Burrow, N., Savary, P., & Tempel, A. (2013). A statewide introduction of trauma-informed care in a child welfare system. *Children and Youth Services Review, 35,* 19–24.

34. Kerns, S., Pullmann, M., Negrete, A., Uomoto, J., Berliner, L., Shogren, D., . . . Putnam, B. (2016). Development and implementation of a child welfare workforce strategy to build a trauma-informed system of support for foster care. *Child Maltreatment, 21,* 135–146.

35. Rastegar, D. (2013). Making effective referrals to specialty care. In R. Saitz (Ed.), *Addressing unhealthy alcohol use in primary care* (pp. 63–71). New York, NY: Springer.

36. Thiedke, C. (2007). What do we really know about patient satisfaction? *Family Practice Management, 14,* 33.

37. Gershoff, E., Aber, J., & Raver, C. (2005). Child poverty in the United States: An evidence-based conceptual framework for programs and policies. In R. Lerner, F. Jacobs, & D. Wertlieb (Eds.), *Applied developmental science: An advanced textbook* (pp. 269–324). Thousand Oaks, CA: Sage.

38. Drake, B., & Rank, M. (2009). The racial divide among American children in poverty: Assessing the importance of neighborhoods. *Children and Youth Services Review, 31,* 1264–1270.

39. Fowler, P., Henry, D., Schoeny, M., Landsverk, J., Chavira, D., & Taylor, J. (2013). Inadequate housing among families under investigation for child abuse and neglect: Prevalence from a national probability sample. *American Journal of Community Psychology, 52,* 106–114.

40. Klevens, J., Barnett, S., Florence, C., & Moore, D. (2015). Exploring policies for the reduction of child physical abuse and neglect. *Child Abuse and Neglect, 40,* 1–11.

41. Slack, K., Holl, J., Lee, B., & McDaniel, M. (2003). Child protective intervention in the context of welfare reform: The effects of work and welfare on maltreatment reports. *Journal of Policy Analysis and Management, 22,* 517–536.

42. Huang, J., Sherraden, M., Kim, Y., & Clancy, M. (2014). Effects of child development accounts on early social-emotional development: An experimental test. *JAMA Pediatrics, 168,* 265–271.

43. Schreiner, M., & Sherraden, M. (2007). *Can the poor save? Saving and asset building in individual development accounts.* Piscataway, NJ: Transaction.

44. Chase-Lansdale, P., & Brooks-Gunn, J. (2014). Two-generation programs in the twenty-first century. *The Future of Children, 24,* 13–39.

45. LaForett, D., & Mendez, J. (2010). Parent involvement, parental depression, and program satisfaction among low-income parents participating in a two-generation early childhood education program. *Early Education and Development, 21,* 517–535.

46. Sabia, J., & Nielsen, R. (2015). Minimum wages, poverty, and material hardship: New evidence from the SIPP. *Review of Economics of the Household, 13,* 95–134.

47. Sawhill, I., & Karpilow, Q. (2014, January). *Raising the minimum wage and redesigning the EITC.* Washington, DC: Brookings Institution.

48. Corrigan, P. (2012). Where is the evidence supporting public service announcements to eliminate mental illness stigma? *Psychiatric Services, 63,* 79–82.

49. Walther, J., DeAndrea, D., Kim, J., & Anthony, J. (2010). The influence of online comments on perceptions of antimarijuana public service announcements on YouTube. *Human Communication Research, 36,* 469–492.

50. Prinz, R., Sanders, M., Shapiro, C., Whitaker, D., & Lutzker, J. (2009). Population-based prevention of child maltreatment: The US Triple P system population trial. *Prevention Science, 10,* 1–12.

51. Poole, M., Seal, D., & Taylor, C. (2014). A systematic review of universal campaigns targeting child physical abuse prevention. *Health Education Research, 29,* 388–432.

52. Wald, M. (2014). Beyond maltreatment: Developing support for children in multiproblem families. In J. Korbin & H. Krugman (Eds.), *Handbook of child maltreatment* (pp. 251–280). Dordrecht: Springer Netherlands.

53. Olds, D., Eckenrode, J., Henderson, C. Kitzman, H., Powers, J., Cole, R., . . . Luckey, D. (1997). Long-term effects of home visitation on maternal life course and child abuse and neglect: Fifteen-year follow-up of a randomized trial. *JAMA, 278,* 637–643.

54. Peacock, S., Konrad, S., Watson, E., Nickel, D., & Muhajarine, N. (2013). Effectiveness of home visiting programs on child outcomes: A systematic review. *BMC Public Health, 13,* 1–14.

55. Reynolds, A., Rolnick, A., & Temple, J. (2015). *Health and education in early childhood.* New York, NY: Cambridge University Press.

56. Sweet, M., & Applebaum, M. (2004). Is home visiting an effective strategy? A meta analytic review of home visiting programs for families with young children. *Child Development, 75,* 1435–1456.

57. Fifolt, M., Lanzi, R. G., Johns, E., Strichik, T., & Preskitt, J. (2016). Retention and attrition in a home visiting programme: Looking back and moving forward. *Early Child Development and Care,* 1–13. Advance online publication. http://www.tandfonline.com/doi/abs/10.1080/03004430.2016.1189420

58. Holland, M., Christensen, J., Shone, L., Kearney, M., & Kitzman, H. (2014). Women's reasons for attrition from a nurse home visiting program. *Journal of Obstetric, Gynecologic, and Neonatal Nursing, 43,* 61–70.

59. Paradis, H., Sandler, M., Manly, J., & Valentine, L. (2013). Building healthy children: Evidence-based home visitation integrated with pediatric medical homes. *Pediatrics, 132,* S174–S179.

60. Dubowitz, H., Lane, W., Semiatin, J., & Magder, L. (2012). The SEEK model of pediatric primary care: Can child maltreatment be prevented in a low-risk population? *Academic Pediatrics, 12,* 259–268.

61. Breitenstein, S., Gross, D., & Christophersen, R. (2014). Digital delivery methods of parenting training interventions: A systematic review. *Worldviews on Evidence-Based Nursing, 11,* 168–176.

62. Feil, E., Baggett, K., Davis, B., Sheeber, L., Landry, S., Carta, J., & Buzhardt, J. (2008). Expanding the reach of preventive interventions development of an Internet-based training for parents of infants. *Child Maltreatment, 13,* 334–346.

63. Nieuwboer, C., Fukkink, R., & Hermanns, J. (2013). Online programs as tools to improve parenting: A meta-analytic review. *Children and Youth Services Review, 35,* 1823–1829.

64. Ginsburg, H., & Rosenthal, M. (2006). The ups and downs of the Swedish welfare state: General trends, benefits and caregiving. *New Politics, 11,* 41. http://newpol.org/content/ups-and-downs-swedish-welfare-state-general-trends-benefits-and-caregiving

65. Pösö, T., Skivenes, M., & Hestbæk, A. D. (2014). Child protection systems within the Danish, Finnish and Norwegian welfare states: Time for a child centric approach? *European Journal of Social Work, 17,* 475–490.

66. Fang, X., Brown, D., Florence, C., & Mercy, J. (2012). The economic burden of child maltreatment in the United States and implications for prevention. *Child Abuse and Neglect, 36,* 156–165.

67. Chamberlain, P., Feldman, S., Wulczyn, F., Saldana, L., & Forgatch, M. (2016). Implementation and evaluation of linked parenting models in a large urban child welfare system. *Child Abuse and Neglect, 53,* 27–39.

68. Hebert, S., Bor, W., Swenson, C., & Boyle, C. (2014). Improving collaboration: A qualitative assessment of inter-agency collaboration between a pilot Multisystemic Therapy Child Abuse and Neglect (MST-CAN) program and a child protection team. *Australasian Psychiatry, 22,* 370–373.

69. Pelton, L. (2015). The continuing role of material factors in child maltreatment and placement. *Child Abuse and Neglect, 41,* 30–39.

70. Loman, L., & Siegel, G. (2012). Effects of anti-poverty services under the differential response approach to child welfare. *Children and Youth Services Review, 34,* 1659–1666.

71. Chamberlain, L., & Kaczorowski, J. (2014). "You get what you pay for": Resources for training and practice in community pediatrics matter. *Pediatrics, 134,* 173–175.

72. Spivey, M., Schnitzer, P., Kruse, R., Slusher, P., & Jaffe, D. (2009). Association of injury visits in children and child maltreatment reports. *Journal of Emergency Medicine, 36,* 207–214.

73. O'Donnell, M., Nassar, N., Leonard, H., Jacoby, P., Mathews, R., Patterson, Y., & Stanley, F. (2009). Rates and types of hospitalisations for children who have subsequent contact with the child protection system: A population based case-control study. *Journal of Epidemiology and Community Health.* http://jech.bmj.com/content/early/2010/06/04/jech.2009.093393.short

74. Putnam-Hornstein, E., & Needell, B. (2011). Predictors of child protective service contact between birth and age five: An examination of California's 2002 birth cohort. *Children and Youth Services Review, 33,* 1337–1344.

75. Putnam-Hornstein, E., Wood, J., Fluke, J., Yoshioka-Maxwell, A., & Berger, R. (2013). Preventing severe and fatal child maltreatment: Making the case for the expanded use and integration of data. *Child Welfare, 92,* 59.

76. Putnam-Hornstein, E., Needell, B., & Rhodes, A. (2013). Understanding risk and protective factors for child maltreatment: The value of integrated, population-based data. *Child Abuse and Neglect, 37,* 116–119.

77. Shaw, T., Barth, R., Mattingly, J., Ayer, D., & Berry, S. (2013). Child welfare birth match: Timely use of child welfare administrative data to protect newborns. *Journal of Public Child Welfare, 7,* 217–234.

78. Vaithianathan, R., Maloney, T., Putnam-Hornstein, E., & Jiang, N. (2013). Children in the public benefit system at risk of maltreatment: Identification via predictive modeling. *American Journal of Preventive Medicine, 45,* 354–359.

79. Garrett, P. (2005). Social work's "electronic turn": Notes on the deployment of information and communication technologies in social work with children and families. *Critical Social Policy, 25,* 529–553.

80. Hertzman, C., Meagher, N., & McGrail, K. (2013). Privacy by design at Population Data BC: A case study describing the technical, administrative, and physical controls for privacy-sensitive secondary use of personal information for research in the public interest. *Journal of the American Medical Informatics Association, 20,* 25–28.

81. Ko, S., Ford, J., Kassam-Adams, N., Berkowitz, S., Wilson, C., Wong, M., . . . Layne, C. (2008). Creating trauma-informed systems: Child welfare, education, first responders, health care, juvenile justice. *Professional Psychology: Research and Practice, 39,* 396.

82. Ford, J., Kerig, P., Desai, N., & Feierman, J. (2016). Psychosocial interventions for traumatized youth in the juvenile justice system: Research, evidence base, and clinical/legal challenges. *Journal of Juvenile Justice, 5,* 31–49.

83. Kerns, S., Cevasco, M., Comtois, K. A., Dorsey, S., King, K., McMahon, R., . . . Davis, C. (2015). An interdisciplinary university-based initiative for graduate training in evidence-based treatments for children's mental health. *Journal of Emotional and Behavioral Disorders, 24,* 3–15.

84. Barth, R., Kolivoski, K., Lindsey, M., Lee, B., & Collins, K. (2014). Translating the common elements approach: Social work's experiences in education, practice, and research. *Journal of Clinical Child and Adolescent Psychology, 43,* 301–311.

85. Chaffin, M., Hecht, D., Bard, D., Silovsky, J. F., & Beasley, W. (2012). A statewide trial of the SafeCare home-based services model with parents in Child Protective Services. *Pediatrics, 129,* 509–515.

86. Kohl, P., Feely, M., Dunnigan, A., Lewis, E., Auslander, W., Guo, S., Jonson-Reid, M., & Doré, P. (in press). Short-term effects of Pathways Triple P on parent and child behavior with a child welfare sample.

87. Chamberlain, P., Feldman, S., Wulczyn, F., Saldana, L., & Forgatch, M. (2016). Implementation and evaluation of linked parenting models in a large urban child welfare system. *Child Abuse and Neglect, 53,* 27–39.

88. Webster-Stratton, C. (2014). Incredible Years® parent and child programs for maltreating families. In S. Timmer & A. Urquiza (Eds.), *Evidence-based approaches for the treatment of maltreated children* (pp. 81–104). Dordrecht: Springer Netherlands.

89. Barth, R., & Liggett-Creel, K. (2014). Common components of parenting programs for children birth to eight years of age involved with child welfare services. *Children and Youth Services Review, 40,* 6–12.

90. Kohl, P., Jonson-Reid, M., & Drake, B. (2011). Maternal mental illness and the safety and stability of maltreated children. *Child Abuse and Neglect, 35,* 309–318.

91. Walsh, C., MacMillan, H., & Jamieson, E. (2003). The relationship between parental substance abuse and child maltreatment: Findings from the Ontario Health Supplement. *Child Abuse and Neglect, 27,* 1409–1425.

92. West, S. L., & O'Neal, K. K. (2004). Project DARE outcome effectiveness revisited. *American Journal of Public Health, 94,* 1027–1029.

93. Petrosino, A., Turpin-Petrosino, C., Hollis-Peel, M., & Lavenberg, J. (2013). "Scared Straight" and other juvenile awareness programs for preventing juvenile delinquency. *Cochrane Library.* http://onlinelibrary.wiley.com/doi/10.1002/14651858.CD002796.pub2/pdf

94. National Institutes of Health. (2016, February). *Estimates of funding of various research condition and disease categories.* http://report.nih.gov/categorical_spending.aspx

95. Bloomberg. (2013, October). *Major League Baseball team valuation: Chicago Cubs concessions.* http://www.bloomberg.com/infographics/2013-10-23/mlb-team-values.html

96. Leeming, D., & Page, J. (1999). *Myths, legends, and folktales of America: An anthology.* New York: Oxford University Press.

97. Rooks, N. (2012, September). The myth of bootstrapping. *Time.* http://ideas.time.com/2012/09/07/the-myth-of-bootstrapping/

98. Aesop. (2015). The ant and the grasshopper. *Aesop's Fables.* East of the web. http://www.eastoftheweb.com/short-stories/UBooks/AntGra.shtml

99. Gruendel, J. (2015, November). *Designing for outcomes through a two-generation lens-good science and good common sense.* Institute for Child Success. http://www.instituteforchildsuccess.org

100. Schickedanz, A., Dreyer, B., & Halfon, N. (2015). Childhood poverty: Understanding and preventing the adverse impacts of a most-prevalent risk to pediatric health and well-being. *Pediatric Clinics of North America, 62,* 1111–1135.

101. McMullen, J. (1991). Privacy, family autonomy, and the maltreated child. *Marquette Law Review, 75,* 569–598.

102. Brennan, S., & Noggle, R. (1997). The moral status of children: Children's rights, parents' rights, and family justice. *Social Theory and Practice, 23,* 1–26.

103. McFall, M. (2009). *Licensing parents: Family, state and child maltreatment.* Lanham, MD: Lexington Books.

104. Reading, R., Bissell, S., Goldhagen, J., Harwin, J., Masson, J., Moynihan, S., . . . Webb, E. (2009). Promotion of children's rights and prevention of child maltreatment. *Lancet, 373,* 332–343.

105. Funke, C. (2005). *Inkheart.* New York, US: Scholastic.

INDEX

Page numbers followed by *f* indicate figures; page numbers followed by *t* indicate tables; page numbers followed by *b* indicate boxes